D0743282

Institutional Buildings

Architectural Record Books

Affordable Houses
Apartments, Townhouses and Condominiums, 2/e
The Architectural Record Book of Vacation Houses, 2/e
Buildings for Commerce and Industry
Buildings for the Arts
Engineering for Architecture
Great Houses for View Sites, Beach Sites, Sites in
   the Woods, Meadow Sites, Small Sites, Sloping Sites,
   Steep Sites and Flat Sites
Hospitals and Health Care Facilities, 2/e
Houses Architects Design for Themselves
Houses of the West
Institutional Buildings
Interior Spaces Designed by Architects
Office Building Design, 2/e
Places for People: Hotels, Motels, Restaurants, Bars,
   Clubs, Community Recreation Facilities, Camps, Parks,
   Plazas, Playgrounds
Public, Municipal and Community Buildings
Religious Buildings
Recycling Buildings: Renovations, Remodelings,
   Restorations and Reuse
Techniques of Successful Practice, 2/e
A Treasury of Contemporary Houses

Architectural Record Series Books

Ayers: Specifications for Architecture, Engineering
   and Construction
Feldman: Building Design for Maintainability
Heery: Time, Cost and Architecture
Heimsath: Behavioral Architecture
Hopf: Designer's Guide to OSHA
Portman and Barnett: The Architect As Developer

Institutional Buildings

Architecture of
the Controlled Environment

by Louis G. Redstone, FAIA

An Architectural Record Book
McGraw-Hill Book Company

New York   Hamburg   Montreal   Singapore
St. Louis   Johannesburg   New Delhi   Sydney
San Francisco   London   Panama   Tokyo
Auckland   Madrid   Paris   Toronto
Bogotá   Mexico   São Paulo

Acknowledgment
In editing this book, I want to acknowledge the valuable assistance of Leo G. Shea, FAIA, for his help in the evaluation and the selection of the material.

"Introductory Guidelines for Planning a Modern Courthouse" and "The Client-Architect Relationship in Courthouse Design" reprinted by permission of the author from *Courthouse Design: A Handbook for Judges and Court Administrators* by Allan Greenberg.

"Commentary: Symbolism in Architecture" by Allan Greenberg, reprinted by permission of the author.

"What Do the Real Clients, The Aging, Think about the Current Facilities?" by Margaret Bemiss, reprinted by permission of the author.

The editors for this book were Jeremy Robinson and Patricia Markert
The designer was Patricia Barnes Mintz
The production supervisors were Elizabeth Dineen and Teresa Leaden
The book was set in Avant Garde Gothic and Optima by Jemet, Inc. and The Clarinda Company, and printed and bound by Halliday Lithograph Corporation.

Library of Congress Cataloging in Publication Data
  Main entry under title:
  Institutional buildings.

    Articles first published in Architectural record.
    "An Architectural record book."
    Includes index.
    1. Public buildings—United States. 2. Public institutions—United States—Buildings. I. Redstone, Louis G. II. Architectural record.
NA4208.I57   725'.50973   79-20204
ISBN 0-07-002343-3

1234567890   HDHD   89876543210

TABLE OF CONTENTS

INTRODUCTION

Although the sections of this book carry titles on apparently different subjects, they are in fact very closely related. Inadequate and neglectful child care, the lack of timely treatment of mental problems, and society's seeming inability to cope with the factors that motivate criminal behavior all point to its main theme: the need for institutional buildings in which programming and planning for the individual becomes one of the key factors.

The planning team plays a significant role in creating designs for these important facilities. Deep insight and much basic research are required from all members of a team which may include sociologists, psychiatrists, planners, administrators, community representatives, and the residents themselves, as well as architects, to achieve an understanding approach to the inmates as individuals.

In a survey conducted in November 1975 on the departments of correction of all fifty states by the National Clearinghouse for Criminal Justice Planning and Architecture, University of Illinois at Urbana, it was found that, with few exceptions, the number of adults committed to state institutions is on the rise. In a special publication, "To Build or Not to Build," the National Clearinghouse included these statements:

> There are 3,319 jails in the United States which are either at county level or located in Municipalities of 25,000 or greater population. Eighty-six percent of these institutions provide no facilities for exercise or other recreation for their inmates. Nearly 90 percent have no educational facilities. Only half provide medical facilities; one of four has no visiting facility; and there are 47 institutions (about 1.4 percent) which are without an operating flush toilet. These 3,319 county and urban institutions contain nearly 100,000 cells. One in four of these cells has been in use for longer than 50 years, including more than 5,000 cells that are over 100 years old.[1]
>
> Fully 50 percent of the nation's maximum security prisons (56 of 113) were opened prior to 1900 and the age of such institutions is generally correlated to the overall condition.[2]
>
> Chief Justice Warren E. Burger referred to contemporary prisons as "non-correctional correctional institutions." Concerned penologists go even further and call them schools of crime. It is no secret that most of the 430,000 or so persons now behind bars in these United States live under inhuman, destructive conditions, that our prisons and jails are old, run-down and overcrowded and that, as U.S. Bureau of Prisons Director Norman Carlson and others in the field agree, their architectural forms are based on antiquated penological concepts.[3]

The above statistics, from 1971, do not adequately portray the present day conditions in the criminal justice system. Since 1975 the number of correctional facilities has not kept pace with the increased number of sentenced criminals. Throughout the country, there is a recognition of the vital need to provide new and updated facilities. In the state of Michigan alone, as of April 1979, Governor William G. Milliken stated he would propose as many as five new state prisons in the next ten years to relieve the overcrowding, which is expected to increase. He based this, in part, on the stricter attitude taken toward criminals by the public and the courts.

The initial decision to be made in planning correctional institutions is the location and type of facility. Important elements to be considered include proximity to the area from which the inmates come, access via public transportation, the presence of community services (i.e., hospitals, social services, and special educational facilities), and the ultimate presence of job opportunities.

Where an ample site is available, a campus type complex of low buildings is preferred. In urban downtown or other limited sites, high-rise buildings may be used to advantage. Cities like Chicago, San Diego, and New York have already completed such facilities. Whether campus type or high-rise, the exterior appearance should blend in with the character of the surrounding area (type of exterior facing materials and size and pattern of windows, tied in with security requirements), with landscaping being a particularly effective help in blending such appearances.

Interior planning is beginning to stress new concepts of privacy, with secure single room occupancy, screening of toilet facilities, and visual "contact" with outdoors where proper, as well as proper visiting facilities and separation of different categories of offenders for physical protection. However, to achieve effective results, hand-in-hand with the improvement in physical facilities there needs to be an all embracing program of retraining, of counseling, of health care, of recreation and the nurturing of family ties.

Since the majority of inmates are expected to return to the community, their time spent in the correctional institution needs to be utilized to establish positive goals. In addition to teaching trades and skills, one of the most effective "tools" in reaching and motivating inmates is a creative recreation program which includes live theater and music presentations, the visual and plastic arts, writing, and other related forms of expression generated by visiting artists as well as by the inmates themselves. These programs play a very beneficial role in channeling the interests of the residents and directing their energies to bring out any dormant potential.

The positive effectiveness of such programs is evidenced in a recent exhibit by inmates for a Washington conference organized by the Creative Use of Leisure Time Under Restrictive Environments (CULTURE) group. Peter Bermingham, curator of the National Collection of Fine Arts, commented: "This exhibition of work by inmates...tries to focus on the achievement of those whose creative energy and spirit have been tapped, developed and challenged in ways most of them have never experienced before. The exhibit is, in a real sense, a celebration...of their achievement and the heroic dedication of those men and women who have guided their efforts. It is, of course, a challenge too, an attractive and exciting alternative..."[4] Correctional institutions will be in the realm of research and new development for the foreseeable future.

Another type of institutional building, the courthouse, plays as important a role today as it did in the nineteenth and early twentieth centuries. Two categories of structures are involved: new buildings and reusable historic ones. In both instances, planning concepts need to be adapted to the new social needs of the community.

Basic elements to be considered in planning include:

1. A functional internal traffic system based on separation of the public, juries, and prisoners including separate access and elevators for each court function, in addition to traffic systems for other municipal or county service functions.
2. Provision for expansion and flexibility for future change.
3. Design for acoustical privacy, which requires special attention in planning heating and ventilation systems.
4. Effective security control.

The objectives enumerated above may be more difficult to achieve in the reuse of old courthouse buildings than in new construction, since requirements and services have changed markedly since their original design. Great ingenuity on the part of the architect is often required to utilize to the utmost the existing structural fiber and at the same time comply with new and stringent building, safety, and health codes. The decision to reuse these grand old courthouse facilities or to build new ones ultimately has to be based on an elevation of their relative functional and economic feasibility, since the older structure can often be better adapted to a governmental use other than the original one.

The mental health facilities presented in this book also show changes in programming and in design approach, with architects evolving and developing spaces to encompass new therapeutic methods and administrative approaches. The facilities illustrated include rehabilitation centers, schools for the mentally retarded, psychiatric hospitals for children, narcotic addiction rehabilitation centers, and research facilities.

Although all the chapters in this book present different types of institutional buildings, "Buildings for the Elderly" only partially belongs to the institutional category. The residents would like to consider these buildings "home" and negate the stigma of being institutionalized. The growing proportion of the people over 65 in the United States points to the necessity for continuous adaptation to changing social needs. In the planning of these facilities, the architect must thoroughly understand the social and physical needs of the senior citizen. It is also important that the exterior design of the building blend with the character of the surrounding area.

An important type of facility which is rapidly growing in number is the child care center, which aids working mothers. According to a Special Labor Force Report published by the U.S. Department of Labor (Bureau of Labor Statistics) dated August 1975, there were 14 million working mothers in March 1975. In the families they headed, there were 27.6 million children. Of these, 6.5 million were under the age of 6 years, and 12.1 million were between 6 years and 17 years of age. (A tabulation of day care centers showed that there were 17,529 facilities in 35 states.)[5] Based on these figures one could project a figure of approximately 25,000 centers in the United States.

It can readily be seen from the large number of young children in these centers that the quality of physical and emotional care they will receive will have a major influence on the upcoming generations of our country and their ability to cope with its social and economic conditions.

This book presents a limited number of case studies in each of five categories of institutional buildings. While these are representative of the current trends, we can expect that the eighties will reflect the many social and political changes which are currently in the process. Our test, then, is how successfully the buildings we design today meet requirements of tomorrow.

Louis G. Redstone, FAIA

[1]National Criminal Justice Information and Statistics Service, 1970 National Jail Census, Statistics Report SC-1, Washington, D.C. (Law Enforcement Assistance Administration, U.S. Department of Justice [LEAA]).
[2]National Advisory Commission on Criminal Justice Standards and Goals, Corrections, Washington, D.C., 1973, p. 343, Table 11.1.
[3]Bess Balchen, "Prisons: The Changing Outside View of the Inside," AIA Journal, September, 1971.
[4]"Culture from Inside" by Margo Koines, Nov.-Dec. 1978 issue of American Journal of Correction. Quotation of Peter Bermingham, page 4.
[5]Publications from U.S. National Center for Social Statistics. "Children Served by Public Welfare Agencies and Voluntary Child Welfare Agencies and Institutions," H.E. 17.645.975, 1975.

CHAPTER ONE
Correctional Facilities

CORRECTIONAL FACILITIES

During the past decade in the United States, correctional facilities have come under the hot lights of public scrutiny and have been a subject of controversy and debate. There are not enough of them, they are too expensive to build and run, they are too brutal, they are too humane, they don't work, and so the arguments go. Small wonder, for at the very heart of the idea of correctional facilities—or jails and prisons, as they used to be called—lie basic and perplexing issues that are troubling not just because they are unresolved, but also because they involve the collision of heartfelt beliefs about morality and ethics, and even about social guilt and expiation. Incarceration, which can be seen as a benign alternative to the meting out of direct and brutal physical punishment, responds, of course, to society's need to remove from its midst people whom it sees as threatening in one way or another. But, on the other hand, many societies—including our own—feel the urge to make that removal somehow "humane," even for those who have performed the most inhumane acts.

Are these two things—confinement and humanity—in any way compatible? Other questions involve not the function but the ultimate goal of correctional facilities. Are they there to punish—to penalize a person for having done something in the first place, to keep him from doing it again, and to encourage others not to imitate him? Or are they places for rehabilitation and, as the name implies, correction? Added to all of this is the fact that many inmates in correctional facilities have been there before and will probably return again, because—in the opinion of some—the crimes they were sentenced for are not to them anything in comparison with the crimes they feel they have suffered at the hand of the society that imprisons them. According to this view, "correction" can best take place not within the prison walls but outside in the world at large. None of these many and contrasting views can be dismissed, but few of them have managed to become welded together into any kind of national consensus about what the functions and ultimate goals—much less the form—of a good correctional facility will be. Thus it can come as a surprise to virtually no one that, as public opinion seems to say, prisons don't work. How could they, since there is no general agreement about what they are meant to do?

But in recent years there have been several important developments that have at least begun to spur the debate forward. Perhaps the most significant is the intervention of the Federal courts in demanding facilities that are humane as well as secure. Paul Silver, of Gruzen & Partners, three of whose correctional facilities are shown on the following pages, says that "in effect, this development has forced action on the part of reluctant legislatures who would have been content to leave bad enough alone. Their action, while often begrudging, has in some instances created interesting challenges for architects. The questions of the degree of humanity and the degree of security create a conflict of the kind that is ordinarily resolved and clarified before design begins. Here, however, the architect finds himself caught in the thick of the battle, having to help direct the process in a rather unique way." But Silver is quick to point out that there are no pat answers: "If the architect is to produce an environment that is both humane and secure, what does 'humane' mean in this context? It is often seen as a static imitation of a middle-class life style, with furniture and windows that recall real houses in a fairly superficial way. But it all too often ends with the sad fact that the resulting environment is merely new in tone, lacking the traditional symbols of incarceration but creating new and subtle ones of its own."

Another development related to the attempt somehow to make prisons "humane," has produced smaller correctional facilities, as opposed to the foreboding gray institutions of the past, and in many cases these are not isolated but located within the hearts of large towns and cities. Fred Powers, of Hellmuth, Obata & Kassabaum, whose projects are also shown, points out that "the present trend is to locate facilities in areas close to families, to professional resources, and to employment opportunities so that there can be follow-up leads into employment once prisoners are released." Some communities have been known to object to this happening, while others have regarded the correctional facility as a source of employment, an industry, and therefore a worthwhile community asset.

The collection of buildings shown on the following pages represents the work of several architects in solving specific prison design problems. All reflect some or all of the trends already described, though none can be regarded as prototypical, since a prototypical solution has to be for a prototypical problem, and, as we have seen, that is yet to be defined. "I am concerned," Paul Silver says, "that all our tremendous efforts will achieve little if we do not understand the limits of our current accomplishments in the hope of striving for something truly significant. It seems to me that we must begin by acknowledging that true 'normativeness' may not be possible in an environment for incarceration, and that the best we can hope for is the reduction of the stress that comes with the loss of freedom."

WASHTENAW COUNTY CORRECTIONS/LAW ENFORCEMENT CENTER, ANN ARBOR, MICHIGAN

This facility is designed for a predominantly pre-trial population, but with some facilities for sentenced offenders. Housing 239 men and women, it is located on a 39-acre site bounded on one side by houses in the $100,000 range and on the other by a major apartment complex. The architects therefore were very sensitive to height limitations, to creating a scale throughout that was compatible with the neighbors, and to providing the ample court-required outdoor exercise spaces with internal courtyards (see drawing, right) rather than a more spread-out campus scheme that a site of this size might have suggested.

The County Law Enforcement Center is located close to the road, convenient to public parking and visually related to other County buildings on the site. A service yard serves as a buffer between this public area and the security areas. Adjoining the service yard is a building element containing admissions, processing and booking functions, and such central support facilities as library, classrooms, offices, the gymnasium, staff dining room, and clinics. Inmate housing units, enclosing outdoor exercise courtyards, are located on a series of terraces running down the sloping site. The outer wall of the housing units functions as the security perimeter, minimizing fences or walls.

Housing units are divided into living units

Balthazar Korab photos except as noted

Barbara Elliott Martin

of 16 single-occupancy rooms grouped around a split-level living room—and meals, library service are delivered to these shared spaces. Two housing units—or clusters of 32 inmates—share a common day room opening to an outdoor court.

WASHTENAW COUNTY CORRECTIONS/LAW ENFORCEMENT CENTER, Ann Arbor, Michigan. Architects: *Hellmuth, Obata & Kassabaum; Colvin-Robinson Associates, Inc., associated architects.* Engineers: *Jack D. Gillum & Associates, Ltd (structural); Ayres & Hayakawa (mechanical/electrical).* Civil engineer/landscape architect/interior design: *Hellmuth, Obata & Kassabaum.* General contractor: *Spence Brothers.*

5

RAMSEY COUNTY DETENTION CENTER, ST. PAUL, MINNESOTA

This facility is designed to house 150 inmates in a cliff-side facility overlooking the Mississippi River. It is intended only for short-term detention—average stays are 1½ days for misdemeanants and 10 days for felons. This short-term imprisonment played an important part in the design concept: it suggested that the facility should be subdivided, under a unit-management concept, into 16-room housing units, each with a day room and dining space. Each unit is 4,000 square feet in area. There is adequate space for games and exercise equipment in each unit, but there is no large indoor or outdoor recreation area.

Says Paul Silver of Gruzen and partners: "Here, more than in any other facility we have done, the restrictedness of the living area raises important concerns. A unit of 16 rooms produces a relatively small total group living area. Doubling the unit size to 32 rooms would have produced twice the available free area, and possibly altered the 'compressiveness' of the environment; yet this would have made security more difficult and probably required mixing inmates detained for minor and more serious crimes—which is not desirable programmatically. The question remains: is 4,000 square feet enough space to house 16 people for two weeks (or perhaps more time for some) without negative depressive effects that could lead to extreme behavior? We really do not know."

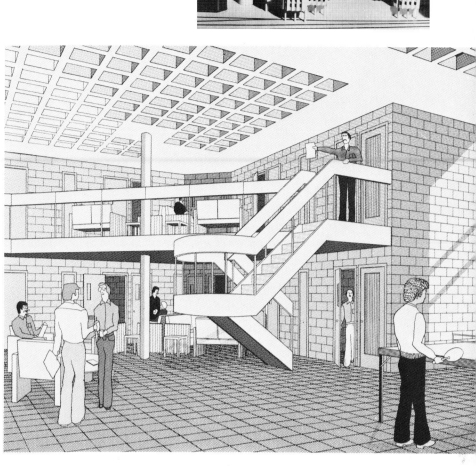

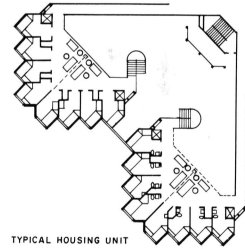

TYPICAL HOUSING UNIT

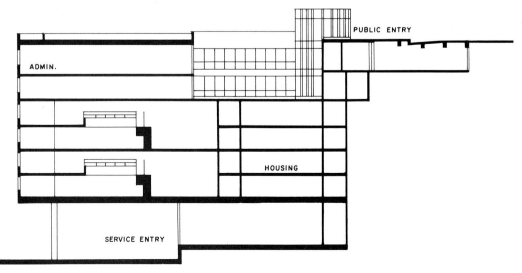

PUBLIC ENTRY

ADMIN.

HOUSING

SERVICE ENTRY

The park on top of the facility (drawing above) is a public facility—an amenity that helped reduce neighborhood reluctance in accepting the facility.

RAMSEY COUNTY ADULT DETENTION CENTER, St. Paul, Minnesota. Owner: *Ramsey County*. Architects: *The Wold Association—Fred J. Shank, principal in charge; Clarke D. Wold, project coordinator; Raymond A. Keller, project architect*. Associated architects: *Gruzen & Partners—Peter Samton, director of design; Paul Silver, director justice facilities; Virendra Girdhar, principal designer*. Consulting engineers: *Kirkham Michael Associates*. Food service consultant: *Van Hemerd Associates*. General contractor: *Steenberg Construction Co.*

MARYLAND RECEPTION, DIAGNOSTIC AND CLASSIFICATION CENTER, BALTIMORE

This urban facility, designed for a population usually held for 30 to 60 days, deals with some of the concerns voiced by Paul Silver of the Gruzen firm on the previous page.

Like the Minnesota facility, this center is based on a unit-management concept—but here the unit is 32 inmates. And in addition to one large indoor recreation area, there are three outdoor spaces—best seen in the photo above right—made secure by building elements themselves. The largest space is in a central courtyard on the roof of the administrative and diagnostic floors, surrounded and secured by the living spaces. The two smaller spaces are on the rooftop, secured by building walls which also extend to enclose

mechanical spaces. This design technique for acquiring outdoor space also met the architects' desire to create a building which would have minimum impact on the character of the residential neighborhood. Indeed, when complete, the new facility will be in scale and in character with new high-rise apartments planned for the area. The residential character of the center is also enhanced by the use of large windows (which of course work to minimize the sense of enclosure and confinement inside), and by the design of the lobby and public spaces. These street-side facilities are designed as important public spaces and will be furnished in a non-institutional way. In short—"perhaps to the limit of our current

Louis Checkman

ability to provide a sense of freedom within while maintaining security," says Silver—the building reduces to a minimum the traditional symbols of incarceration.

MARYLAND RECEPTION, DIAGNOSTIC AND CLASSIFICATION CENTER, Baltimore, Maryland. Owner: *Maryland Department of General Services.* Architects: *McLeod Ferrara & Ensign—William L. Ensign, principal in charge; Stewart E. Duval, project coordinator.* Associated architects: *Gruzen & Partners—Peter Samton, director of design; Paul Silver, director, justice facilities; Virendra Girdhar, principal designer.* Engineers: *Greene & Seaquist Inc. (structural); Syska & Hennessy Inc. (mechanical/electrical).* General contractor: *Baltimore Contractors.*

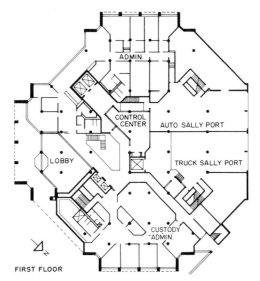

FIRST FLOOR

FOLEY SQUARE COURTHOUSE ANNEX: ATTORNEYS' OFFICE AND METROPOLITAN CORRECTIONAL CENTER NEW YORK CITY

As a large correctional center located in a metropolitan area with high crime, this project represents a major effort to create a humane prison environment. The architects concentrated on reducing negative stresses associated with incarceration by creating a "normative" environment, according to architect Paul Silver, that gives a freedom of movement to the prisoner within an obviously limited area. To achieve this, the design included providing large open interior spaces, with extensive number of windows, decentralized dining areas, acoustical control to minimize noise, and a visually inconspicuous security system. Every detail was studied, including specifying non-traditional hardware.

FOLEY SQUARE COURTHOUSE ANNEX: THE OFFICE BUILDING FOR THE U.S. ATTORNEYS AND THE METROPOLITAN CORRECTIONAL CENTER, New York, New York. Owner: *General Services Administration, U.S. Department of Justice.* Architect: *Gruzen & Partners—Jordan Gruzen and Peter Samton, partners-in-charge of planning and design; Lloyd Fleischman, project director; Paul Silver, director of justice facilities; Gordon Vance, project manager; Robert Genchek, principal designer.* Engineers: *Strobel Associates (structural); Cosentini Associates (mechanical).* Landscape architects: *M. Paul Friedberg & Associates.* Food service consultants: *Romano & Associates.* General contractor: *Castagna & Sons.*

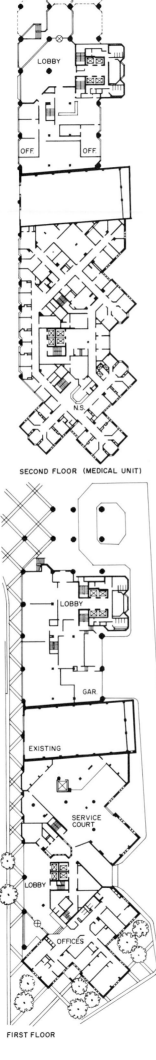

SECOND FLOOR (MEDICAL UNIT)

FIRST FLOOR

LEXINGTON ASSESSMENT AND RECEPTION FACILITY, LEXINGTON, OKLAHOMA

As one of the developments at this regional correction center (which serves many counties in central Oklahoma), the housing units were designed as a prototype for the state's correctional system. This facility houses 240 inmates who are serving both short- and long-term sentences.

In appearance, the project is residential in scale and character. Each housing unit is comprised of two modules, linked to a separate education/vocational building which also contains the unit manager's office. Each unit houses 80 persons, but each prisoner has a private cell. The rooms are clustered in groups of 20 around a split-level day room. A central control room for each module provides electronic monitoring of all doors and entrances.

One housing unit is set off from the other two for persons requiring special supervision, and can be isolated if necessary. Between this housing and the other units are common facilities of gymnasium, library, chapel, and dining hall.

LEXINGTON ASSESSMENT AND RECEPTION FACILITY, PHASE II, Lexington, Oklahoma. Architects: *Benham-Blair & Affiliates, Inc. and Hellmuth, Obata & Kassabaum.* Engineers: *Benham-Blair & Affiliates, Inc. (structural/mechanical); Hayakawa Associates (electrical).* General contractor: *Harmon Construction Company.*

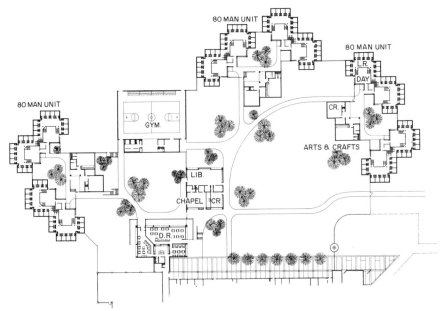

80 MAN UNIT

80 MAN UNIT

80 MAN UNIT

L.R.

DAY

CR.

GYM.

ARTS & CRAFTS

LIB.

CHAPEL CR

D.R.

MENDOCINO COUNTY DETENTION CENTER AND JUSTICE COURT UKIAH, CALIFORNIA

This facility for sentenced misdemeanants is located on a highly unusual site—near a prominent residential area. The design, therefore, is highly responsive to the community.

Four buildings form a pleasant mini-campus for both male and female inmates in a primarily minimum-security system (although there is an area designated for medium security). The men are housed in two residential buildings and the women are located in a building which also provides housing for men awaiting trial and administrative offices, infirmary and visiting rooms. The fourth building in the complex is for recreation and dining.

As a minimum-security complex, the cells are located along the perimeter, which is lined with windows. These cells surround an open area which leads to a central day room (along with laundry and counseling facilities).

In an effort to blend the buildings with the site and increase its acceptance by the neighborhood community, the design was kept simple, with appropriate scale and massing of the buildings, a wood exterior and covered walkways.

MENDOCINO COUNTY DETENTION CENTER AND JUSTICE COURT, Ukiah, California. Architect: *Kaplan-McLaughlin*. Engineers: *Anderson & Culley (structural); JYA Design Associates (mechanical); The Engineering Enterprise (electrical)*. General contractor: *Todd Construction Company*.

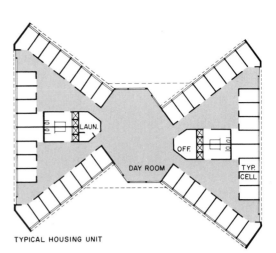

TYPICAL HOUSING UNIT

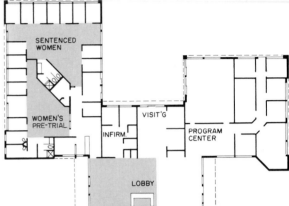

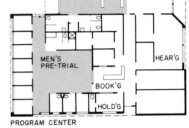

PROGRAM CENTER

COMMUNITY CENTER

FEDERAL CORRECTIONAL FACILITY BUTNER, NORTH CAROLINA

This medium- to high-security Federal correctional institution was originally conceived as a service facility to house mentally disturbed and otherwise abnormal inmates from other Federal prisons in the East. The goal was to design a complex that was more "humane" than prisons normally are—with less visible security systems, fewer inmates, and an over-all look that was not institutional or oppressive. To those ends, the traditional gun tower was eliminated, and only an irregularly octagonal double fence defines the outer perimeter. Three clusters of housing units designed for mentally ill inmates are located together on one part of the site (see model photo opposite), and most of the rest of the buildings help enclose an outdoor space that is thought of as a kind of village green. With this "cottage-like" arrangement of buildings, though, adequate care was taken to make for adequate visual control of inmates by a minimum number of staff. The photo above shows the chapel and auditorium building in the center of the green.

FEDERAL CORRECTIONAL INSTITUTION, Butner, North Carolina. Owner: *United States Department of Justice, Bureau of Prisons.* Architects: *Middleton, McMillan, Architects, Inc.—project designer: Ronald W. Touchstone.* Engineers: *Frank B. Hicks Associates* (structural); *Mechanical Engineers, Inc.* (mechanical); *John Bolen Engineers* (electrical). General contractor: *G. C. Tandy Construction Co.*

Gordon Schenck photos

Gordon Schenck photos

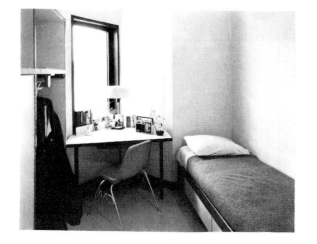

The top photo above shows a common area in one of the housing buildings. In the background are doors, made of wood, to individual inmates' rooms. In the foreground are doorways leading to showers and to toilets. The photo on the left is of an inmate's room—where, again, the attempt was to achieve as normal a look as possible. The windows are bent out in a saw-tooth pattern to relieve the rectilinearity of the inside and also to break up the long facade outside. The photo immediately above shows the main entrance to the facility through which everyone entering or leaving passes, controlled by the booth on the left.

Corlis Reems photo

Hawthorne Cedar Knolls Residential Treatment Center, Hawthorne, New York

■ This building is an experimental unit in a building program to augment and modify existing facilities in line with advanced techniques for treatment of delinquent boys and girls. Essential to the treatment—and determinants of the design—are a non-institutional environment and an absence of challenge from security measures. This first of the new buildings (existing buildings were taken over from a former private school) houses 32 boys in three groups of 12 each. Each group lives in its own wing of the building, has its own housemother and is buffered from the other groups by supporting facilities (offices for psychiatrists and residential rooms for counselors). There are no bars on windows and no uniformed guards. To increase the non-institutional character of the place, primarily conveyed by the almost entirely domestic scale of the building, the bedrooms vary in size and shape and corridors are relatively short and have varying ceiling heights. Bay windows and window-seats in the bedrooms further contribute to the residential environment. The largest element in the complex is the dining-living area which adjoins and opens onto the activities room. Even here, however, a residential feeling is provided in the open-hearth fireplace around which gatherings of all three groups can take place.

HAWTHORNE CEDAR KNOLLS RESIDENTIAL TREATMENT CENTER, Hawthorne, New York. Architects: *Kramer, Kramer & Gordon.* Engineers: *Lev Zetlin Associates,* structural; *Herbert Klein,* mechanical. Landscape design: *Peter Roland.* Contractor: *E. W. Howell Inc.*

The pleasantly scaled, simply landscaped court is more than a part of the circulation: its use for outdoor community gatherings in good weather is an important part of the Hawthorne treatment. In bad weather the groups gather around the fireplace in the living-dining room. Materials used on the buildings were chosen for durability (damage resistance is essential), ease of maintenance and appropriateness to the desired residential character of the unit. Brick cavity walls, exposed on both sides, continue the character of existing buildings as do the slate shingle roofs. Weathering steel fascias add warmth to the exterior. Floors are concrete slab, covered with either brick or vinyl. The master plan calls for eventual replacement of the present small-group cottages with large-group (36 boys or girls) units, and provision of a new high school.

STATE CORRECTIONAL CENTER,
EAGLE RIVER, ALASKA

Kiku Obata and Steven Dunham photos

Prison environments have almost never been designed as positive elements of an over-all program directed toward the eventual return of the offender to his community, and indeed, prison programs have not been based in a belief that such reintegration is possible. But slowly, over a good many years, the idea of prison reform has taken hold and now programs and the kind of prison buildings to make them fully implementable are beginning to be provided at both the state and Federal levels.

The new approach to prison treatment focuses on individualized programs of rehabilitation which will enable the offender to recognize and work out, with the help of counsellors, the problems which brought him to the correctional institution. Without minimizing the importance of medical and psychological/psychiatric treatment where needed, this new approach sets the individual on the path of self-responsibility as the first step to his return to the social context of the community. This is no longer a new philosophy of penology, but its implementation is new. Even newer is the recognition that a large part of the program's effectiveness is in the character of the physical environment within which the program takes place. What has happened to bring about this realization is that the dehumanized environment of the old-fashioned kind of prison simply did not lend itself to the methods of the new program, and that if the new program were to succeed, the participants—both inmates and counsellors—needed the physical set-up which would give reality to the principles of privacy and human dignity on which the programs are premised.

Programs of this kind and new buildings designed to make them possible are appropriate for minimum and minimum/medium security institutions. (The problems of other kinds of prisons with different degrees of imprisonment will undoubtedly be influenced by the experience with these lesser-security buildings, particularly as to size and number of inmates.) Increasingly, the preferred location is in or very near a city so that community resources—educational, for instance—can be utilized in the program.

The new kind of environment looks more like a college campus, or a resort complex than a prison, and this may initially cause misunderstanding and criticism. Architects have instinctively felt that environment affects behavior; the proof of their belief may lie in this new kind of prison design.

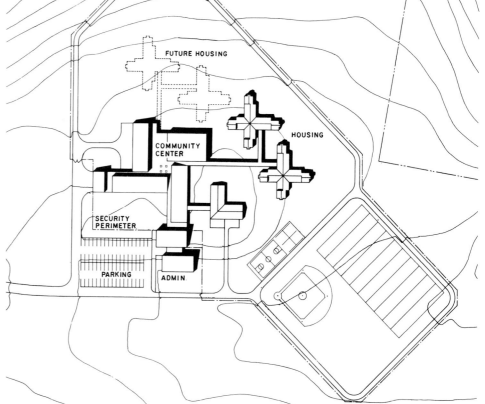

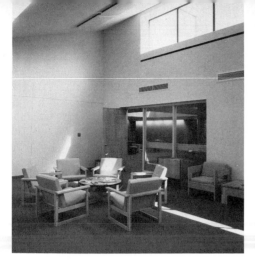

Outstanding among new correctional institutions, the South Central Correctional Institute at Eagle River, Alaska, represents, in its radically different architectural concept, the new approach not only to prison design but to prison programs. The living environment that it provides is as nearly normal as possible, permitting small freedoms within the larger, necessary restrictions of the institution as a whole but providing, along with the counselling system, strong incentives to development by the offender of individual responsibility.

The site—virgin land with a muskeg ground cover and many small-diameter trees—is 13 miles north of Anchorage. The buildings are small and residential in scale and character, and the materials and forms used are non-institutional: wood and plywood siding, pitched and shed roofs, large windows (of security glass), single-story structures (except in the housing units which are split-level). Many of the trees remain, even within the perimeter fence, and the over-all effect is of a small private school or college campus. Covered walks connect the housing units and administration building. Inside the buildings, color is used to enhance the open, light character of the rooms, and goodlooking modern furnishings are used throughout. All sleeping rooms are single, with a living room for each 10-person unit (a number which the staff can handle and counsel), and a quiet room with adjacent counsellor's office. Each housing unit has rooms for 40 persons and the staff responsible for custody, counselling, education, work and recreation of the unit's inmate residents. Since each inmate must choose to participate in the system's community reintegration program and some do not immediately do so, a maximum security Special Handling Unit, located between housing and administration, houses them until they either complete their terms or are willing to accept the requirements of the program. The choice is left to the newcomer, located to see and hear the program in action.

STATE CORRECTIONAL CENTER, Eagle River, Alaska. Architects: *Crittenden, Cassetta & Cannon/Hellmuth Obata Kassabaum—Gyo Obata, Daniel Gale, Kenneth Cannon, William Valentine, Patrick Leamy,* project team. Engineers: *Anderson, Bjornstad, Kane and Pregnoff/Matheu /Beebe* (structural); *Alaska Testing Laboratory* (foundation); *Ayres & Hayakawa and Crews, MacInnes & Hoffman* (mechanical/electrical). Consultants: *Surveys Inc.* (cost); *Flambert & Flambert* (food service). Contractor: *Bachner-Northwest.*

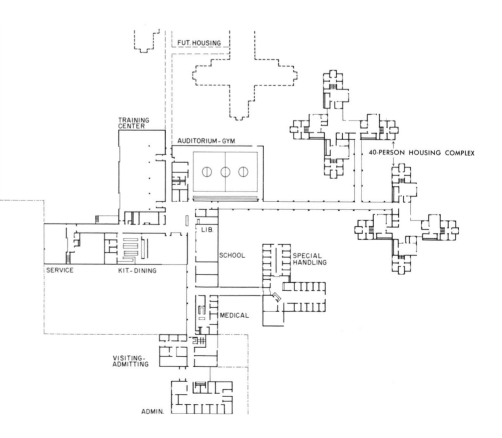

Alaska's problems, like its size and small population, are not the same as those of other states and major U.S. cities: 59 per cent of its convictions are for some form of public nuisance, but violent crimes also figure in its statistics. At Eagle River, most types of crimes are represented; here each man can be treated for two years (preferably the last two). The architectural concept of the housing unit is of prime importance in the rehabilitation program, giving inmate and counsellor maximum exposure to each other. Counsellor's office adjoins the quiet room. Staff and inmates eat together in cheerful dining room.

FEDERAL YOUTH CENTER, PLEASANTON, CALIFORNIA

The Federal Youth Center at Pleasanton, California, is the first of several regional youth correctional institutions built by the Federal Bureau of Prisons to plans which reflect the reforms in prison programs at this national level. The non-institutional look expresses the program emphasis on community reintegration for the offender and its over-all character indicates the age group to which those who are sent there belong: all are between 18 and 25, and their offenses run the gamut of human frailty. Their youth and their first-time status, however, give them better than average potential for rehabilitation and reintegration.

This is a minimum/medium security institution, controlled by perimeter fencing and an electronic detecting system, and television monitors inside, but without the usual conspicuous guard towers. The environment which results from the rehabilitation program and its implications permits, within certain restrictions, more normal living conditions than the old type of prison. This "village" planned around a man-made lake on an almost featureless 87-acre site 30 miles from San Francisco, consists of two 120-person housing units and the necessary core facilities: admission and administration, education and training, dining and recreation. The heart of the "village" and of the program is the 30-person housing subunit, where direct contact between counsellor and inmate takes place on a continuing basis, with the counsellor and the program the main deterrents to security problems. Sub-units may be combined to function as a unit for a specific rehabilitation program. Vandalism to date has been minimal, inmates showing an exceptional regard for the buildings and grounds. The materials used are atypical for prisons: wood frame with redwood plywood, built-up roofing and asphalt shingles on the core facilities; reinforced concrete block and precast concrete floor and roof decks. Laminated security glass is used throughout, affording vistas to courts, to lake, and to distant foothills.

FEDERAL YOUTH CENTER, Pleasanton, California. Architect: *Frank L. Hope & Associates—Edward J. Gee, project architect; Austris J. Vitols, project designer.* Engineers: *Frank L. Hope & Associates* (structural); *Lowney-Kaldveer Associates* (foundation); *Marion, Cerbatos & Tomasi, Inc.* (mechanical/electrical). Landscape architects: *Michael Painter & Associates.* Consultants: *Perini Corp. and URS/Cahill Construction Co.* (construction manager); *The Koch Co.* (cost). Contractors: *Overaa Construction Co.* (foundation); *Johnson & Mape* (shell and finish).

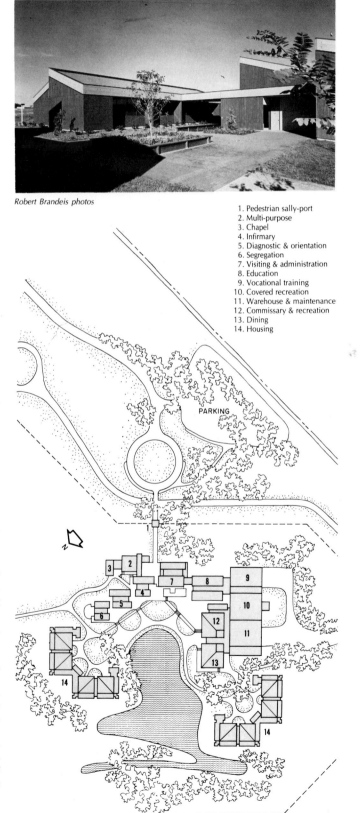

Robert Brandeis photos

1. Pedestrian sally-port
2. Multi-purpose
3. Chapel
4. Infirmary
5. Diagnostic & orientation
6. Segregation
7. Visiting & administration
8. Education
9. Vocational training
10. Covered recreation
11. Warehouse & maintenance
12. Commissary & recreation
13. Dining
14. Housing

Dining facilities at Pleasanton are informal in character, in keeping with the overall program, and particularly with the "menu-selection" manner of meal service. The appearance is, in fact, that of a high school or college cafeteria, particularly appropriate here, since the "residents" are all between the ages of 18 and 25. Color, with the earth colors predominating, is used throughout the common areas either in super graphics on walls or in the furnishings. The exposed wood ceiling in the dining area accentuates the "outside world" environment which is a constant reminder of the rehabilitation program's goal.

Each feature of the complex is effectively a part of the institution's program, and contributes either subtly or openly to the individual inmate's eventual rehabilitation. The lake, for instance, on which all buildings focus, is man-made, created to heighten the humanizing experience of the place. The site—an old army camp used during World War II, and unused since—is almost completely flat but has a view of the distant foothills. The views from the buildings, whether distant or near, are always of something worth looking at, in contrast to the kind of outlook possible from the old-fashioned prison.

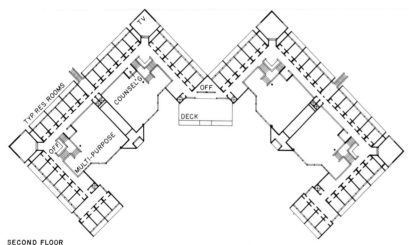

SECOND FLOOR

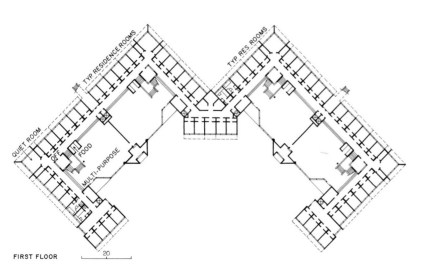

FIRST FLOOR

The housing units are designed to promote the sense of community which is so important a part of the reform program, and at the same time to preserve a sense of privacy for the individual. Accordingly there are single rooms for each inmate, arranged on two levels off the day or "living" room. Offices for correctional officers, who are also counsellors are located in each housing unit, and interior surveillance is by television cameras rather than by guards. Two housing units have been built, each consisting of four 30-room sub-units. Additional sub-units can be added. Although the over-all character of the units is residential, it is more in the character of a college dormitory than a private house. Nevertheless, as much as possible, the feeling of individuality and of community is provided in the furnishings, wall-to-wall carpeting, color and in the shape and proportion of the big room itself, with its floor-to-ceiling glass wall (which, in some units, permits a view toward the lake) and the glass-enclosed sally-port (doorway). The "tower" element beside the stairway has a canteen on the first floor and a counselling room on the second.

THE COURTS AT CLINTON

Joshua Freiwald photos

"There are about 350 courts on this gentle hill-side, varying in size from 9- by 9-feet to 25- by 50-feet. Many have gardens which, in the summer season, come into color. The varied greens of vegetables and oranges and reds of marigolds dominate. Boundaries between the courts are most often low 'fences' constructed of earth-filled, number-ten cans stacked on top of each other. There are also low wood fences, and courts in which the boundary definition is provided by intercourt pathways alone. The terraces of the courts area are buttressed by stacked rock; these, too, provide boundaries. Court entrances are sometimes gated, sometimes merely a gap in the fence. Sprinkled among the courts are light-frame guard stands, roughly the height of lifeguard chairs. These are covered by peaked sunshades. No other roofs or covers are allowed on the courts, so that observation from the wall towers and the guard posts is not obstructed.

"A typical court contains a variety of furniture and appliances. The decor is ersatz: one or two chairs—often wooden fan-back garden chairs; a table; a stove; several hutches or cabinets; some have 'refrigerators.' The floor is most often left earthen although in some courts it has been paved. . . .

"Freestanding kitchen sinks are distributed in the courts area. They are the water supply and clean-up spots and are shared, as in campgrounds. Cooking, eating, talking, game-playing, garden watering, and so forth make up the major activities of the summertime yard. Food may be bought at the commissary and prepared here, although this is limited to canned goods or imperishables. . . .

"The courts are open between 3:10 p.m. and 4:30 p.m. on weekdays; on weekends and holidays, they are open from 8:00 a.m. to 4:30 p.m. Bad weather or prison-wide disciplinary action may also close the courts temporarily. On weekends, these activities may be preempted by movies or religious services. . . .

Stability and continuity: the basis for an ordered social organization

"Every court has a manager and an assistant manager. Officially, the manager is the 'owner' of the court, and he is responsible for infractions that may occur on it. In practice, it seems that this dominance is mellowed by the informal group processes of the members. Nevertheless, the manager has disproportionate power with regard to accepting new members, evicting current members, and shaping the activities of the court. Seniority is a major factor in becoming a manager. Courts are 'inherited' in that they pass from one manager to the next on the basis of the pecking order of the court.

"There are several ways for an inmate or a group of inmates to get a court if one is desired. Perhaps the most common one is through friendship with an inmate who is already on a court. . . . A potential member may be scrutinized by the manager and other members of the court. . . . Preference goes to individuals who either fit in with the dominant activities of a particular court or whose connections on the

Warden Lavalle has been around corrections a long time . . . forty years. For twenty-five of those years he has been at Clinton. His rules are clear. This simplifies life at the institution for everybody —staff and inmates alike. . . .

The town of Dannemora and the prison are closely linked. The main street faces the wall. There are guards at Clinton who repesent the fourth generation of their families working at the prison. . . .

Individual courts take many shapes. This is important. Some years ago, the administration tried to regularize the layouts of the courts by imposing a rectilinear grid and setting up picnic tables. . . . Neither the grid nor the tables lasted very long. . . .

inside or on the outside enhance the welfare of the fellow court members. Thus men who have access to valued information, goods, or services are desirable members. . . . New memberships (and ejections from a court) must be approved by the yard sergeant. In most cases, this is routine although, in some cases, the new member is disallowed by the sergeant.

"A second avenue to court membership is somewhat more formal. Rather than approaching a particular court, an inmate or several inmates put their names on a waiting list. If a court becomes available by dint of the departure of all of its members, or disciplinary action against them or some other reason, the new list of names is given the court. . . . Managers whose courts have not maintained a membership size that is up to capacity may often be warned by the sergeant that they should expand their membership or risk having the court handed over to a new group. . . .

To different groups, the courts have different meanings

"To some members of the staff, the courts were seen as valuable insofar as they helped to relieve the pent-up frustrations and anxieties of prison life. The staff saw the courts as limited free zones in which inmates were allowed the maximum of autonomy within the routine of the prison. Others saw the courts as a valuable control device that offered leverage in staff-inmate dealings. Nearly all felt that the courts were an objective statement of humanitarian instincts. To some inmate-users, the courts were seen to provide a release from the humdrum and drabness of daily life. They afforded a degree of privacy, creature comforts and protection from unwanted encounters. . . . Likewise the courts serve to break up the nameless mass of fellow inmates into groups that reflect similar interests, background, or tastes. The hierarchy of the courts afford a ready-made structure for establishing power relations among inmates, thus reducing conflict.

"Other inmates saw the courts as 'irrelevant.' To these, the pains of prison life are so great that the courts make little difference. And what, they ask, is cooking in a hobo jungle going to teach you about getting along outside?

"A third inmate group is hostile to the courts. To these, the courts serve to fractionalize and distract the inmate population—to divert them from courses of cooperative action which may better their common circumstances.

"In the broader view, the role of the courts in Clinton prison appears to be pluralist in character. Formal sanction for small inmate groups, the legitimizing of inmate territories, and the structuring of indigenous authority through the manager system has over the years created an institution which serves to diffuse inmate leadership, minimize formal control, and bring socialization to prison life. . . . The most important feature of the courts is that they constitute an experiment in the shift from control through the suppression of inmate social organization to control through the manipu-

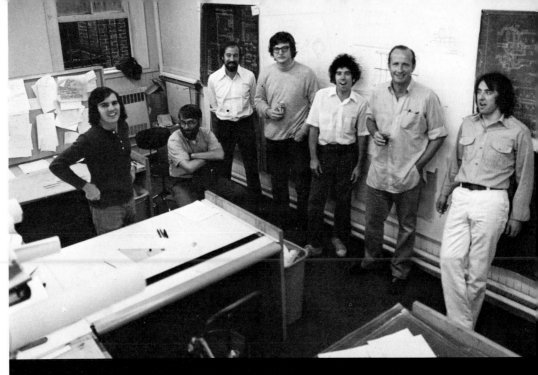

Project staff from *Kaplan and McLaughlin* (left to right): Roy Latka, John Kibre, Lee Brechner, Ron Roizen, Bill Berg, Herbert McLaughlin, Ken Rupard. Not shown: Herbert Reimer and Ian Brown of *Morris Ketchum, Jr. and Associates.*

lation and legitimization of inmate groups. Insofar as the courts achieve valuable ends for both parties with a minimum of friction, the experiment is interesting and full of possibilities.

The court system is fragile and its future unclear

"Several groups of staff and prisoners reported that the courts were 'not as nice as they used to be.' The reason given for this decline was the influx of 'city men' or prisoners boarded at Clinton for New York City's jails. These men may have sentences as short as 90 days, and to them, the benefits of the courts are less salient. In fact, the decline in sentence lengths generally, it was argued, is hurting the courts system. As one inmate remarked: 'If they get cold, they burn one of the chairs because they aren't here long enough to care about not having that chair around.' . . . And new strains are being felt in the courts—the pressure for alliance among the court members of different courts and the push for larger collectives. Whether or not the diminished reward value and the new strains will in time reduce the courts to nothing more than an area with many fences and oil drums remains to be seen. This is a time of crisis for state penal institutions, and the courts system has doubtless been strained although it continues, for the present at least, to be a stabilizing influence."

Design implications of the courts for an altered correctional setting

Corrections is turning away from facilities like Clinton and declaring a preference for smaller, community-based institutions where the goal of inmate rehabilitation may have a better chance for success. What features of the Clinton courts can be transplanted to these new institutions is a matter for prudent conjecture. Several design principles seem clearly indicated:

■ Irregularity: Attempts at symmetry, rectilinearity, and obvious order—such as architects are accustomed to—have been met with resistance in the Clinton courts. A court environment must be casual, irregular, adaptable and malleable in the hands of the inmates.

■ Flexibility: Flexibility within individual spaces may be difficult to achieve but every effort should be made to encourage it. Standard architectural devices such as cabinets, space dividers, etc. will probably not be useful. The inmates will have to evolve their own systems and designs.

■ Terrain: This is a general concept which can cover much of what is hoped to be achieved in design, including a sense of irregularity, of openness to the exterior, of the changeability of the land which is occupied by the courts. It implies a slope which has been found to be vital at Clinton in terms of promoting a sense of irregularity and allowing visibility. It also implies in all probability that indoor courts might have earth as their basic material. Nothing else is so easily modified or adapted by the inmate.

■ Size: The over-all size of an indoor court should probably be limited to 100-150 men for reason of noise and security. Smaller total sizes might create problems of choice of court-mates.

■ Movement: Design should encourage free and varied movement. Naturally there will be constraints due to security. The plan should be so arranged that the jailor will be able to observe movement and control it while at the same time not interrupting. The spaces through which the prisoner walks should be as varied as possible. He should have his choice of routes from one place to another.

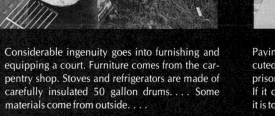

Considerable ingenuity goes into furnishing and equipping a court. Furniture comes from the carpentry shop. Stoves and refrigerators are made of carefully insulated 50 gallon drums. . . . Some materials come from outside. . . .

Paving patterns are varied and often carefully executed. . . . Some contraband—mostly from the prison commissary—finds its way into the courts. If it causes no problems, and usually it doesn't, it is tolerated. . . .

CORRECTIONAL ARCHITECTURE:

Reflecting a New Emphasis
on Specialization and Rehabilitation

In a recently completed state prison, correctional officials authorized the construction of a large swimming pool in a corner of the exercise compound. Knowing that disclosure of the pool's presence would subject them to angry charges of "coddling" criminals, authorities carefully buried the pool under a heavy mantle of earth. The pool is a commitment to the future, to be dug up—like a time capsule—when the climate of public opinion permits.

Much of what is happening now in the field of corrections is distilled in this incident. Officials favoring maximum security and those advocating reform continue their familiar debate—but even a buried swimming pool suggests that the reformers are gaining ground.

The following study examines this change in social attitudes and the legal reforms which ultimately affect the design of prisons. The increasing specialization of programming and the new interest in locating prisons in the midst of the community reflect a growing emphasis on rehabilitation.

Marvin Rand

We look to correctional officials for miracles but we are asking them to make bricks without straw. Americans spend more on household pets than on police; more on tobacco than on the whole process of criminal justice.

The result of public apathy and indifference is long neglect. More than a hundred prisons now in use were in operation before Grant took Richmond. At least four, still functioning today, date to the time of the Louisiana Purchase. In Trenton, New Jersey, one prison, built in 1798, is—at last report—still in use. This degree of neglect is probably found in no other building type.

The prison prototype we have constructed affects its users with extraordinary force. It grew out of the public's demand for protection and vengeance. From the beginning, its chief concern has been custody. Its tall turrets, its security wall, its barred windows form a striking image of repression. In a piece for the American Correction Association, architect Sid Folse has written: "The antiquated cell blocks in almost all states run to a general pattern, and at their worst, they are grim, forbidding places. Tiers of inmates are stacked like crates in warehouses, four or five high. There are harsh shadows, ominous vistas down long corridors, a few overhanging light bulbs; windows are few—or absent. What paint exists is in the dingy color range of creams and tobacco browns which offer nothing but monotony. . . . The clang of locks

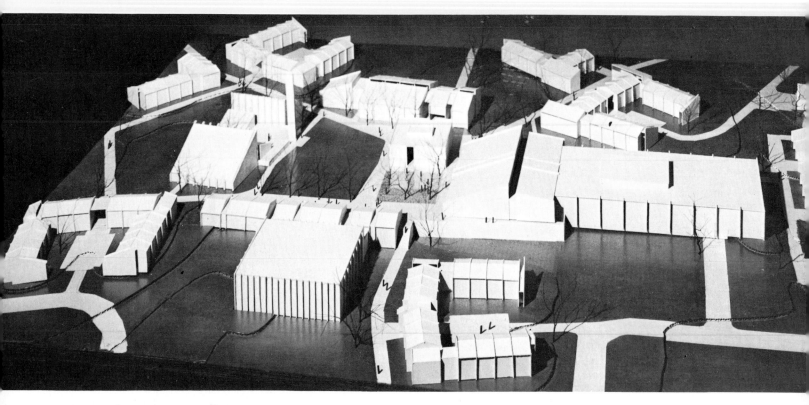

Up from authoritarianism: a shift toward humanized, campus-like plans

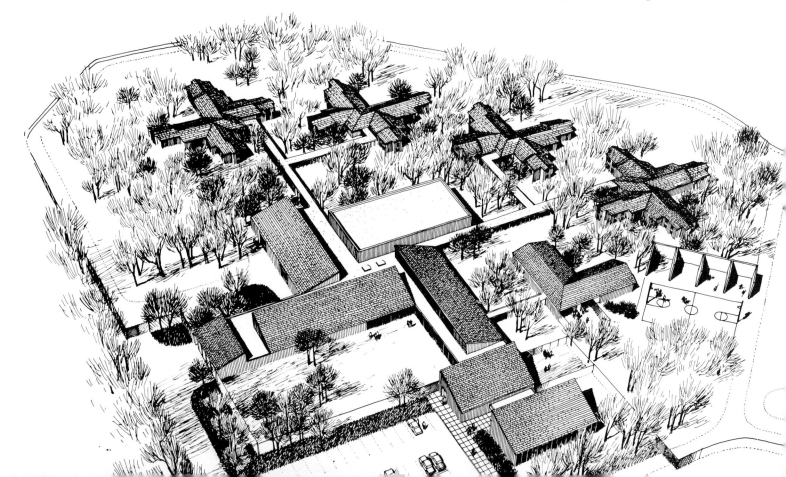

and doors, of steel striking steel, has been one of the accepted horrors of incarceration since ancient times. . . . At the base of toilets and urinals, in some institutions, uric acid acting over many decades has eaten inches deep into cement, has corroded metal and left a permanent reek." When these conditions are aggravated by serious overcrowding, is it surprising that strange prison subcultures develop or that the reflex to violence is automatic? Is it surprising that wardens and overworked staffs concentrate almost exclusively on maintaining order and control? Is it even possible, in institutions like these, to talk of rehabilitation? The word simply has no meaning. But this is the prison that confines most inmates today.

Other signs of neglect are not wanting. Two years ago, at the fortress-like Kansas State Penitentiary at Lansing, 226 inmates, 19 in one night, slashed their Achilles tendons in protest and despair at what they considered a repressive administration.

"They couldn't be repaired in the prison hospital" said medical director Dr. R. S. McKee "because most of our instruments had disappeared."

Neglect also has a vicious side. The Arkansas prison farms—Tucker and Cummins—offer a glimpse of our prison system at its worst. Responding to sinister rumors of cruelty and abuse, then Governor Winthrop Rockefeller ordered an investigation of the camps in 1966. The investigators found that discipline had eroded to

The plan for the Illinois State Penitentiary in Vienna reflects a growing concern for humanized prison environments. Acknowledging that the practice of warehousing criminals has contributed to criminality, correctional officials are urging designs that place some value on human dignity and emphasize rehabilitation. Small scale housing units allow segregation of inmates by type, easier surveillance, and more congenial, hopeful surrounding.

Architects: Curtis & Davis with Samuel E. Sanner & Associates.

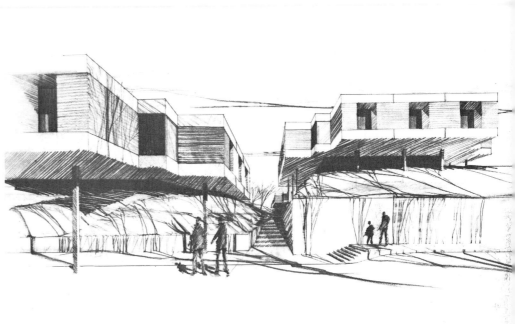

Frank Lotz Miller

At The Liberty Institute in Hickman County, Tennessee (rendering and site plan, right) 600 young inmates are housed in private rooms that together with common facilities, form a self-contained rural community. Typical housing unit (above) is planned for twenty-two inmates and includes a landscaped court. These units are grouped informally to soften the institutional character and promote a low-rise campus atmosphere.

Architects: Curtis & Davis with Howard Nielson Lyne Batey & O'Brien.

Using an "incentive system" in which the inmate is given more freedom as he proves he can live by the rules, this State Correctional Center in south-central Alaska (left) is a cluster of 40-man living units with centralized common facilities. Pitched roofs and plywood siding give the units a typically residential character. The grouping of buildings, heightens the sense of community. (See page 23.)

Architects: Hellmuth, Obata & Kassabaum with Crittenden, Cassetta, Wirum & Cannon.

the point that it was left largely in the hands of "trustee inmates." Forced homosexuality was openly tolerated. Many shallow graves containing broken, mutilated bodies gave credence to claims that prisoners were commonly tortured, beaten and killed. Extortion by "correctional officials" of money and sexual favors from the families of prisoners was also alleged.

Concerned and able correctional authorities shudder with anger at revelations like these. They know that such conditions are by no means typical but that the callous public indifference that gave rise to such excesses persists.

But by far the most discouraging expression of this neglect is the apparent inability of the correctional system to correct. While excellent at custody and even better at punishment, the system's record for rehabilitation has been minimal. In 1968, Myrl Alexander, then Director of the Federal Bureau of Prisons, said it this simply: ". . . As a means to change criminal be-

havior, imprisonment is still a failure." Dr. Karl Menninger, in *The Crime of Punishment* is more emphatic: "Our prison system is a shambles—beastly, unworkable and expensive . . . Its sole effect: to degrade and humiliate, to rob people of their human dignity." Two statements: one passionate, one matter-of-fact, but both pragmatic and both leading to the same essential truth—our system for correction is not working. The evidence indicates that, instead of curtailing crime, prisons manu-

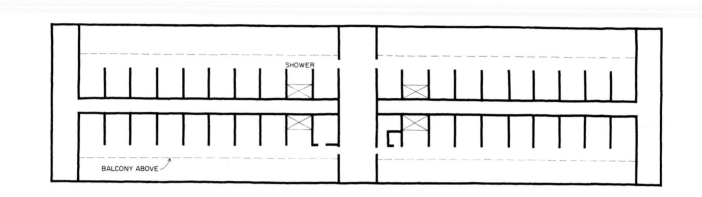

The cellblock redesigned for habitability and control

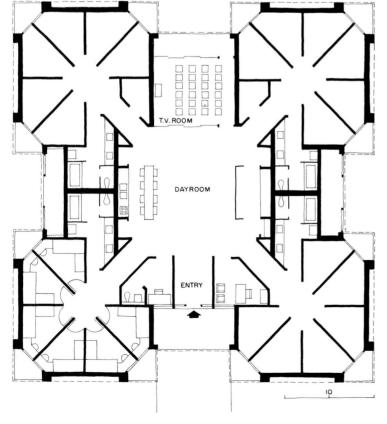

Site plan and cell arrangement for the South Carolina Women's Institution at Columbia. Cells are grouped in four units of six each. Each cell has a small window and the cells are oriented so that inmates can converse comfortably. A T.V. room and washrooms serve as buffers between the living units and open to a large central recreation space.

Architects: Geiger-McElveen-Kennedy in association with Curtis & Davis.

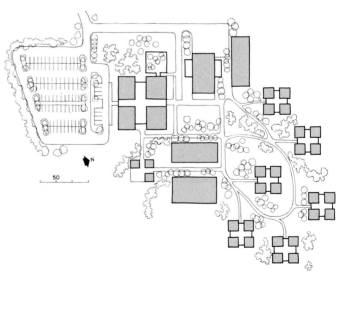

facture criminals. Many describe our prisons as "post graduate courses in criminality."

This failure to correct manifests itself most alarmingly in high rates of recidivism. Statistics on recidivism tend to be slippery. They must be treated with caution since much depends on when the "books" are closed. Such figures also lump those who revert to a life of crime together with those who are returned to prison for some minor violation of their paroles. But these cautions notwithstanding, nearly every authority agrees that the overwhelming majority of felonies committed each day are perpetrated by men already known to the criminal justice system through prior convictions. Former Attorney General Ramsey Clark puts this figure at 80 per cent; other writers set it slightly lower. All agree that the figure is much too high.

And so the study of prison design begins with a history of failure. But . . .

If signs of neglect still predominate, signs of hope are present too:

1) There is reform in the law affecting the definition of confinement

The parts of our criminal justice system—police, courts, corrections—are so interdependent that reform cannot proceed easily in one area if it lags in the others. The legal framework for reform was greatly strengthened in 1963 by passage of the Model Sentencing Act. In its first article

At left, a traditional high security, double- or triple-tiered cellblock. Cells are arranged in long rows and face a blank exterior wall. Showers and washrooms are often located outside the cell.

At right, a plan prepared for the South Carolina Department Corrections uses space more economically and provides what is obviously a more humanizing setting. Cells form the outside wall and face in on a dayroom. Long corridor perspectives are broken by two changes of level.

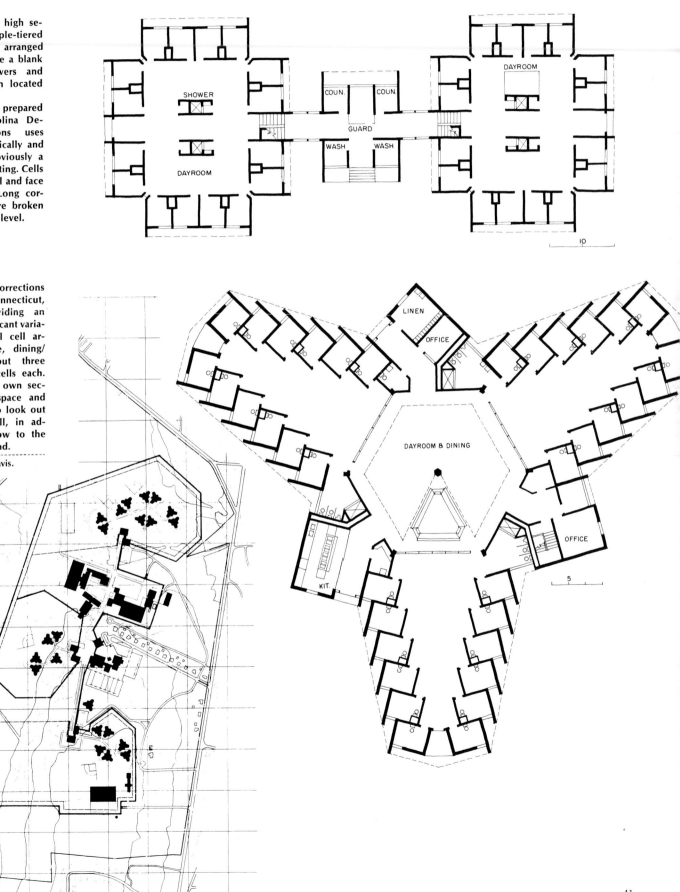

At the Cheshire Corrections Community in Connecticut, designers are providing an architecturally significant variation on the normal cell arrangement. A large, dining/dayroom spaces out three clusters of twelve cells each. Each cluster has its own secondary recreation space and cells are arranged to look out into both. Each cell, in addition, has a window to the surrounding farmland.
Architects: Curtis & Davis.

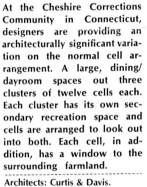

the Act stated that ". . . persons convicted of crime shall be dealt with in accordance with their individual characteristics, circumstances, needs and potentialities as revealed by case studies . . ." Judges were granted important options in sentencing offenders instead of offenses.

The Prisoner Rehabilitation Act of 1965 set the groundwork for community treatment centers and half-way houses by extending the definition of confinement to include certain kinds of facilities outside prison walls. The Crime Control Act in 1968 established the Law Enforcement Assistance Administration (L.E.A.A.) to review the needs of corrections in all the states, to provide guidance and discretionary funding for state and local programs. And by serving L.E.A.A. as consultants, architects have been—and continue to be—involved in upgrading prison standards.

2) There is reform in the conditions of confinement

Leadership in matters of prison reform must—and has—come from Washington. Since its establishment in 1930, The Federal Bureau of Prisons has enjoyed enlightened—if underfunded—leadership. Some of the Federal institutions are too old, many are overcrowded or just too large for effective management. Since World War II, the Bureau has closed two of its decaying facilities—the men's penitentiary at Alcatraz and the Federal reformatory at Chillicothe, Ohio. To replace them, the Bureau built a

George Cserna

The cells shown here are typical of most in newer institutions. While security requirements still predominate, surfaces are still hard and finishes durable, care has been taken to upgrade the basic level of habitability. There is an emphasis on single-cell occupancy. Fixtures are selected with at least some concern for appearance and use. Louvered windows with bars integral (or sometimes grilles) have mostly replaced traditional barred openings. In short, cell design is beginning to reflect the growing interest in rehabilitation instead of mere custody.

Cells: privacy and minimum comforts

Frank Lotz Miller

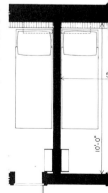

Standards for cells vary considerably. Typical cell, lower left, at Wisconsin Correctional Institution (Curtis & Davis) resembles a minimally-furnished college dormitory. Cells at Leesburg, N.J., upper left, (Gruzen & Partners) and at Westchester Women's Jail, above and right, (LaPierre, Litchfield & Partners) are slightly more spartan. All three belong to the upper end of the spectrum.

Federal penitentiary at Marion, Illinois and the Kennedy Youth Center at Morgantown, West Virginia. Both are model facilities. At the latter, opened in 1969, youngsters of both sexes study and work in an environment without fences or other symbols of custody. They are motivated by an elaborate system of privileges and pay. By constructive behavior, a student can progress from "trainee" to "apprentice" to "honor student." With each promotion he acquires a greater personal freedom, more comfortable surroundings and, eventually, furlough and release. The deterrent to escape is removal to a less congenial institution.

In discussing their results, staff members are cautiously optimistic. They point out that theirs is a carefully selected prison population with violent offenders and repeaters screened out.

■ **Future Federal facilities**
A new Behavioral Research Center for Butner, North Carolina is a specialized 300-400 bed facility to diagnose and treat a wide variety of acutely disturbed offenders including youths. In addition to its rehabilitative function, the facility includes a center for training correctional staff in dealing with deviant behavior. (See page 16.)

Funds have been appropriated for two urban detention centers (New York and Chicago), regional correctional complexes (Northeast and West) and metropolitan correction centers in five cities (San Francisco, Philadelphia, San Diego, Houston and El Paso.

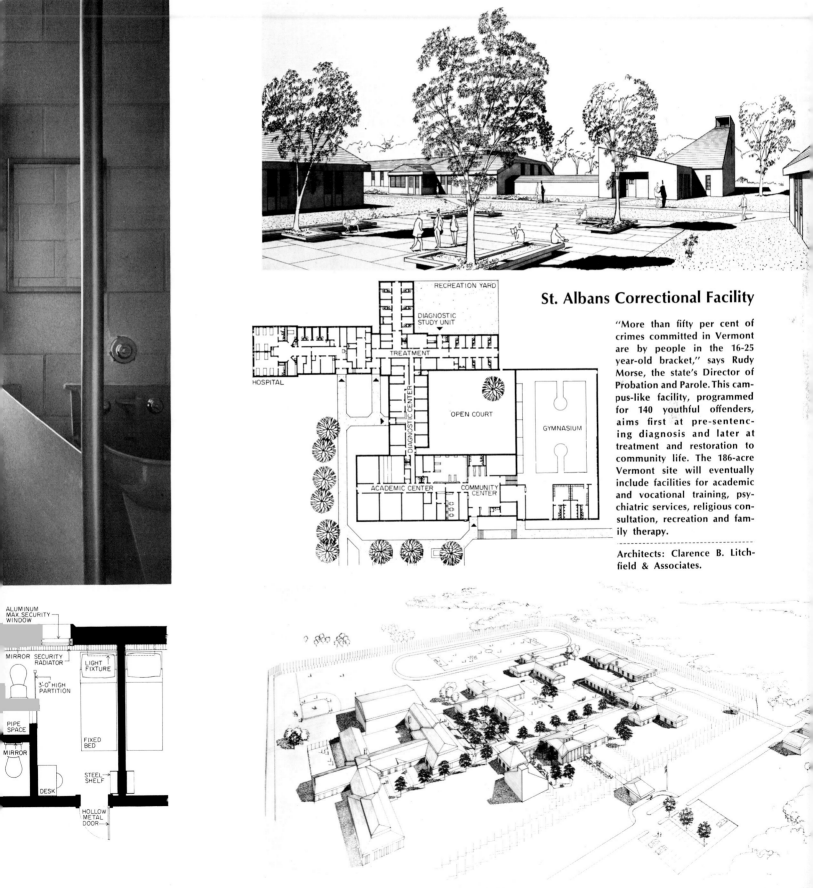

St. Albans Correctional Facility

"More than fifty per cent of crimes committed in Vermont are by people in the 16-25 year-old bracket," says Rudy Morse, the state's Director of Probation and Parole. This campus-like facility, programmed for 140 youthful offenders, aims first at pre-sentencing diagnosis and later at treatment and restoration to community life. The 186-acre Vermont site will eventually include facilities for academic and vocational training, psychiatric services, religious consultation, recreation and family therapy.

Architects: Clarence B. Litchfield & Associates.

■ State, city and county corrections

Independent of the Federal system, but looking to it for guidance and funding, are correctional systems for each of the fifty states. These tend to be crazy-quilt networks that include state penitentiaries for long-term offenders and county or city jails, run by a sheriff, for misdemeanants or those awaiting trial. Police know little about a man they apprehend. His potential for violence—even his identity—may not be known for many days. For this reason, most jails must be maximum security installations. Often suffering from unclear jurisdictions and lack of cooperation, and seldom having any capability for rehabilitation, these facilities can be the bane of penologists. When they are consolidated with other criminal justice functions—as in the Spokane Public Safety Building (below) or the Orange County Jail (page 47) they are most apt to be effective. Duplication of functions can be curtailed, important records made more immediate, and prisoner transportation all but eliminated.

At the state level, the most difficult problems exist. Overcrowding and decrepitude are their worst. First offenders have long been locked up with hardened criminals. Educational opportunities are minimal, work meaningless and rehabilitation all but impossible. But even here, improvements have been noticeable.

Spokane Public Safety Building

This handsome structure in Spokane, Washington, was one of the first in the country to combine the full range of city and county criminal justice functions. By sharply reducing the usual duplication of these functions, the architects have been able to provide space for educational and rehabilitative programs that previously were nonexistent. The facility includes sheriff's office, police quarters, courts, prosecuting attorney's office and separate jails for men, women and youthful offenders. The new structure is linked to the existing courthouse building which stands as a city landmark. It is smaller in scale than its older neighbor but clearly retains its own identity.

Architects: Walker & McGough.

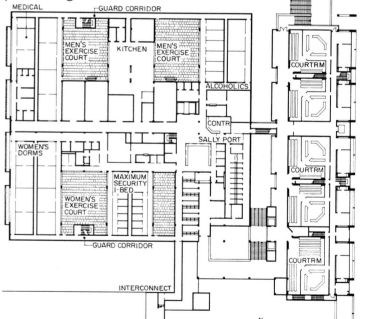

Gordon Peery photos

New spaces, new planning requirements

In California, with a prison population of 28,000, excellent diagnostic facilities have been developed at Vacaville and Chino. Before being sentenced, prisoners are given educational, medical, social, vocational and psychological evaluations. From the results, judges can sentence men to appropriate institutions that offer differential modes of treatment. Specialized treatment centers for juveniles, for instance, are located throughout the state. If the spiral of crime has a soft underbelly anywhere, surely it is at this juvenile level. Young offenders are only recently beginning to receive the benefit of special funding and research.

In other states there are other signs. At Oregon State Penitentiary, a $600,000 vocational building is now rising. In Kansas, the Boy's Industrial School has had marked success in reducing juvenile crime. A number of states have re-evaluated correctional work programs and are now training inmates in marketable skills—data processing and electronics among them.

In early 1971, at Temple University's Department of Architectural Design and Construction, chairman Carl Massara supervised his students in a prison design project for downtown Philadelphia. Among the fresh ideas that emerged: a city prison that places a small shopping center on the street and provides an opportunity for prisoners to sell goods made behind prison walls. Not only would such an outlet assist prisoners in rehabilitating themselves, it

Leesburg Medium Security Prison

When complete, this prison in southern New Jersey will house 504 male inmates classified as medium-security risks. The six living units each contain eighty four single cells distributed over two levels and arranged around a large court to form a security perimeter. Each unit, in addition, has its own interior courtyard. The central, glasswalled dining hall is linked to administrative and educational spaces, an infirmary and chapel. The whole plan is loosely arranged to minimize the sense of confinement while maximizing the variety of visual experience. Informal outdoor walkways allow prisoners to experience the changing seasons.

Architects: Gruzen and Partners.

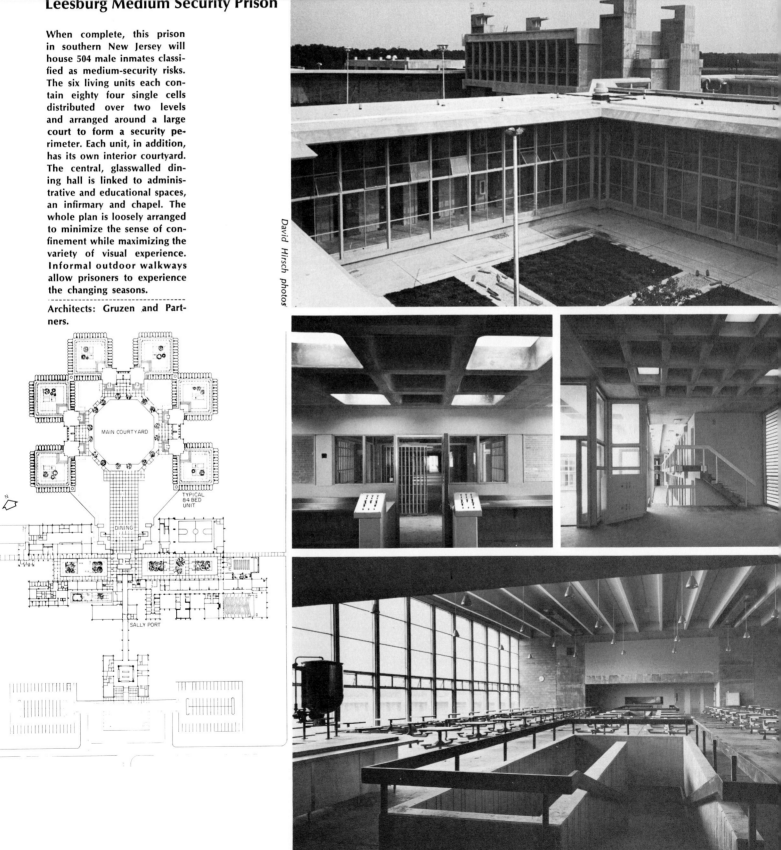

David Hirsch photos

would contribute to the economy of a community in need of retail stores.

▪ The search for alternatives

Few people concerned with criminal justice in America doubt that our prisons and jails contain many men, women and children who would offer no serious threat to society if released immediately to selected community treatment facilities. These include narcotics offenders and alcoholics who need highly specialized treatment

centers—not jails. These include "one-time offenders" and "nuisance offenders" in jail for non-support, vagrancy and similar minor offenses. In the past, this also included men who refused induction into the armed services.

By conservative estimate, violent and dangerous criminals represent only 15 per cent of the population now confined. These must be kept out of circulation—indefinitely if necessary. Many of the rest, at little public risk, could be released into

community treatment centers under the supervision of an augmented parole and probation force. Such probationary arrangements are far less expensive than confinement and would allow correctional resources to be concentrated on whose who need them most.

Working at the University of Illinois at Urbana architects Frederic Moyer, Fred Powers, and Michael Plautz, with sociologist Dr. Edith Flynn, have used a grant from L.E.A.A. to study community-based alterna-

Gordon Peery photos

Washington Institute for Women

Located fifteen minutes from Purdy, Washington, this new facility for adult women aims almost exclusively at rehabilitation and is designed to express this goal. Common-use buildings define the central court-yard while housing units form two additional court-yards to the north and west. Most residents carry keys to their own rooms and are al-

lowed an unusual degree of freedom. By sensitive detailing and treatment of scale and massing, the architects have succeeded in creating a pleasant atmosphere, devoid of all symbols of security, neglect and indifference.

Architects: Walker/McGough/Foltz/Lyerla in joint venture with John M. Morse.

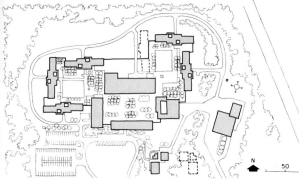

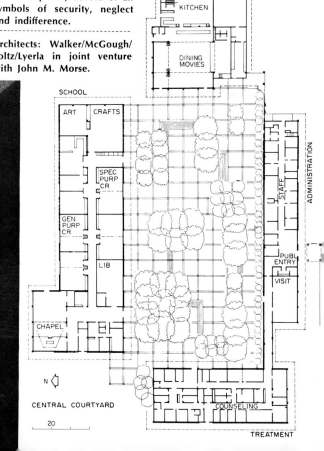

tives to incarceration. Information on the study, published in 1971 and titled *Guidelines for the Planning and Design of Regional and Community Correctional Centers for Adults*, is available from the National Clearinghouse for Criminal Justice Planning and Architecture.

■ Work release and furloughs

Work release programs are not new. Wisconsin pioneered the idea in 1913 and more than half the states have now developed such programs. Generally, they permit inmates in the last months before release to work in the community during the day and return to custody at night. These arrangements have forcefully demonstrated their ability to ease an inmate's reintegration into society. Roughly 500 inmates are currently on work release in the Federal system. Fewer than one in twenty fails to live up to its terms. These are returned immediately to prison where they serve out additional terms.

Among the states, work release has been generally successful. South Carolina's work release centers have provided a model. William Leeke, the State's Director of Corrections, has acquired several vacant facilities on dollar-a-year leases for use as halfway houses. Carefully-screened applicants are placed in these centers prior to release. During their stay, they earn salaries, pay taxes, and help support their families. If successful, they are released into the community with a job, a record of employment, and some accumulated savings.

Such centers usually cause understand-

Orange County Jail

Part of a new civic center for Santa Ana, California, this three-building complex is designed to house 1,335 prisoners (1,200 men and 135 women) in maximum security. The inside cell block denies prisoners access to the exterior wall and permits the use of a continuous, perforated concrete grille in place of barred windows. The split level arrangement of tiers allows visual surveillance from a guard corridor at an intermediate level. Closed circuit television augments this surveillance capability by monitoring all remote spaces. The project also includes separate dining facilities for both men and women, an infirmary, a chapel, and several special treatment spaces. All security spaces incorporate electro-mechanical locking devices operated from a protected central control.

Architects: Albert C. Martin and Associates; general contractor: F. E. Young Construction, Inc.

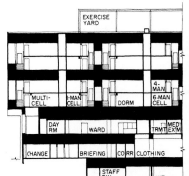

able anxieties in the communities where they are located. Inmates on work release do escape and sometimes commit fresh crimes. But of those who escape, many return voluntarily, most others are quickly caught. Since all inmates on work release are to be paroled or released outright in a matter of months, the worst than can happen is that a crime will be committed six months sooner. Many experts argue we should accept this risk if the long-term possibility of crime is significantly reduced.

Prison furlough programs are newer. Like work release, they aim in part at testing an inmate's stability and readiness to return to society. They are granted only for short periods and to comparatively few prisoners. Oregon has such a program and results are hopeful. Twenty inmates went home briefly one Thanksgiving and fifty-one at Christmas. All returned.

3) And thus there is reform in the principles of prison design

Custody but new concerns
Certain long standing conventions in the design of correctional institutions are being challenged in the prisons shown on these pages.

The search for close-in sites continues
For reasons of economy, politics, and penal philosophy, prison sites used to be sought in isolated, rural locations—typically in the northwest corner of the state, out there where the road ends. This resulted in many

R. Di Maggio below

Youth Reception and Correction Center

A large complex by contemporary standards, this Yardville, New Jersey, facility for youthful offenders combines a 400-bed short-term diagnostic center with a longer term, high security institution for 500 inmates. A small special unit of 60 beds (for psychologically disturbed youngsters) is also included. Housing is distributed in a giant, two-story arc around a central, landscaped court; the building perimeter itself forming a security barrier. Interlocking circular structures house communal functions for education, treatment, dining and administration.

Architects: Alfred Clauss and Kramer, Hirsch & Carchidi.

Cortlandt Hubbard photos

difficulties. A high grade correctional staff was difficult to assemble and keep. Distant travel was a hardship for prisoner's families. More often than not, they could not afford the trip. Today, legislatures and correctional departments look for "close-in" sites near courts, near cities and universities where communities can have a part in reliabilition by offering jobs to inmates on work release and by providing education.

■ **In most cases architects have worked to**

avoid stiff formality
They have broken down the stultifying symmetry and scale of earlier models to create a community or campus-like environment. Bars, grates, towers and locks, while still present, tend to blend into the architectural character rather than dominate it.

■ **New facilities tend to place greater reliance on electronic surveillance**
While concurring in its obvious economies,

architect John Grosfeld (La Pierre, Litchfield, Weidner & Grosfeld) warns that closed-circuit T.V. has important drawbacks. "Picture resolution is not always of satisfactory quality. Furthermore, prisoners tend to resent electronic monitoring and express that resentment by vandalizing the equipment."

■ **The prison administrators' preference for single-occupancy cells is beginning to replace the traditional prison dormitory.**

Omaha-Council Bluffs Correctional Facility

TYPICAL MODULE

This design for a regional correctional facility in Omaha departs significantly from typical jail solutions. The designers have planned a structure that is non-institutional, non-authoritarian and asymmetrically massed around a large open court. Though security has not been compromised, the whole design has an unexpectedly open and permeable quality.

Housing units are one-man cells ranged in groups of 12 around open recreational space—a system that permits both control and segregation of prisoners in the most flexible way. Infirmary, diagnostic center, educational space and visiting areas are located on the ground floor.

Architects: Kaplan & McLaughlin in joint venture with Kirkham, Michael and Associates.

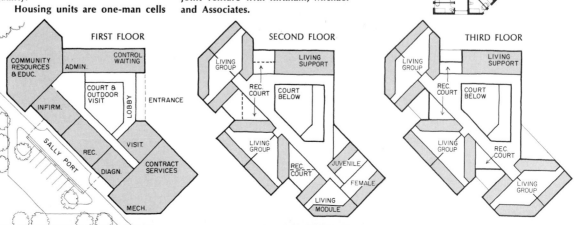

Cells are being grouped in 12- to 18-man clusters and rearranged in ways that have clear social and architectural implications.

The controlled setting

While the temptation is always present to build large facilities, there is a general recognition that the behemoths of the past —San Quentin, Sing Sing, Atlanta, Leavenworth—offered no prospect for rehabilitation. Most new facilities have 600 capacity.

Increasing specialization

Both at the Federal and state levels, they have tended to become more specialized also. The Illinois Security Hospital (page 51) and the St. Albans Correctional Facility (page 43) are clearly programmed, designed and staffed to treat two particular classifications of offenders. As diagnosis and treatment techniques improve, this kind of specialization seems likely to increase.

These humanizing influences reflect a more balanced view of corrections—a view that places rehabilitation on at least a par with custody and punishment as social objectives.

Rehabilitation programs have been written before. Most remained paper programs. Rehabilitation spaces have been created before. Under pressure of overcrowding, they have often been absorbed into custodial space.

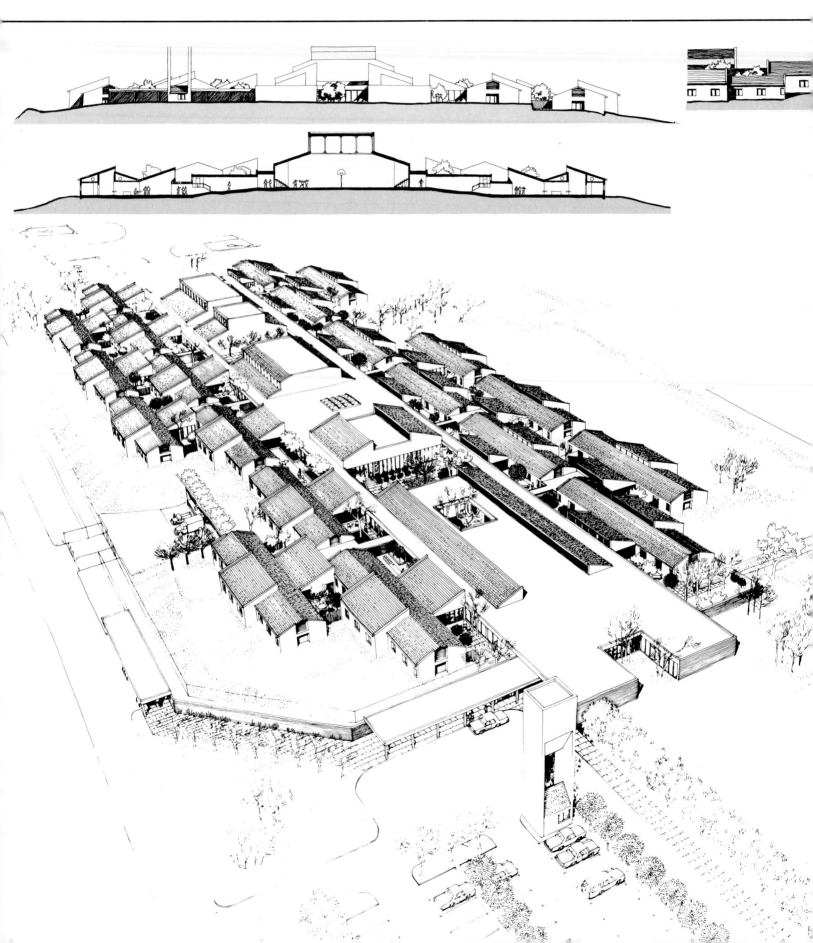

Whether this newest generation of correctional facilities will succeed in correcting is still uncertain. Many signs point to hope. Architect Herbert McLaughlin (Kaplan & McLaughlin) has expressed this forthright view: "The design of a jail must work to the purpose of humanity. It must provide both the jailer and the inmate with a sense of themselves as non-threatened, worthy individuals. . . . We are learning from the newly emerging discipline of socio-physical design how environments give behavioral cues. These lessons must be applied to jails. An atmosphere which provides privacy, choice, informality and control is not only possible, it is mandatory."

In a letter to Dr. Karl Menninger, Daniel Gale, A.I.A., speaks to the point: 'I think it is becoming clear that inmates have to live in small, treatable groups, be supervised by counselors, not jailers, be given the opportunity to keep busy in fruitful pursuits, express themselves as individuals, be further educated and, perhaps most important to my mind, be permitted to develop a sense of responsibility. . . . The architect must help the division of corrections, assuming he is fortunate enough to have a capable and concerned one, sell, sell, sell, to the public, the legislature, the division of public works, and in some cases the correctional staff itself and the funding

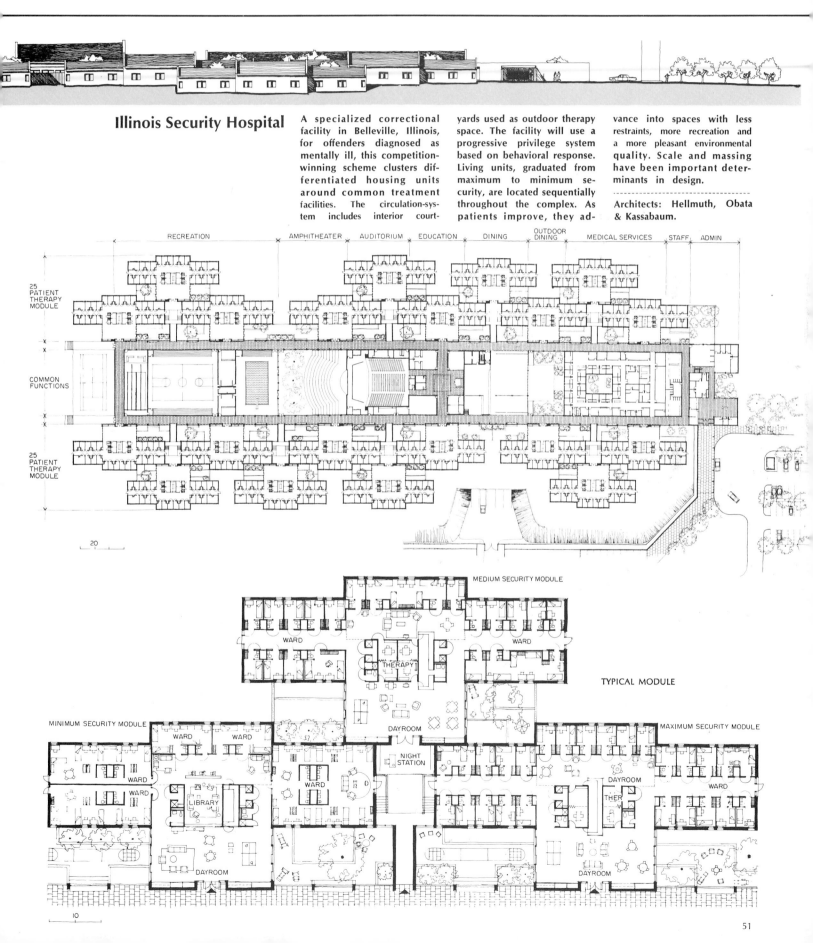

Illinois Security Hospital

A specialized correctional facility in Belleville, Illinois, for offenders diagnosed as mentally ill, this competition-winning scheme clusters differentiated housing units around common treatment facilities. The circulation-system includes interior courtyards used as outdoor therapy space. The facility will use a progressive privilege system based on behavioral response. Living units, graduated from maximum to minimum security, are located sequentially throughout the complex. As patients improve, they advance into spaces with less restraints, more recreation and a more pleasant environmental quality. Scale and massing have been important determinants in design.

Architects: Hellmuth, Obata & Kassabaum.

agency. . . . Our role, then, can only be to master plan a system, or parts of a system, to give facilities their proper weight in the total plan, then execute those facilities with as broad an understanding as possible. . . . Fantastic things are possible."

Western Correctional Center

Believed to be the first high-rise plan for a state prison in the country, this facility for Burke County, North Carolina, is included because of its urban implications and the obvious building and land economies it suggests. Common use elements, inside a security perimeter, are located in the base. Classification, treatment and custody units form the tower.

Architects: Charles Morrison Grier & Associates with Curtis & Davis.

ROOF EXERCISE
MAXIMUM SECURITY
INFIRMARY

CUSTODY HOUSING

CLASSIFICATION
SCHOOL-LIBRARY
MECH. EQUIPMENT KITCHEN
ADMINISTRATION GYM.

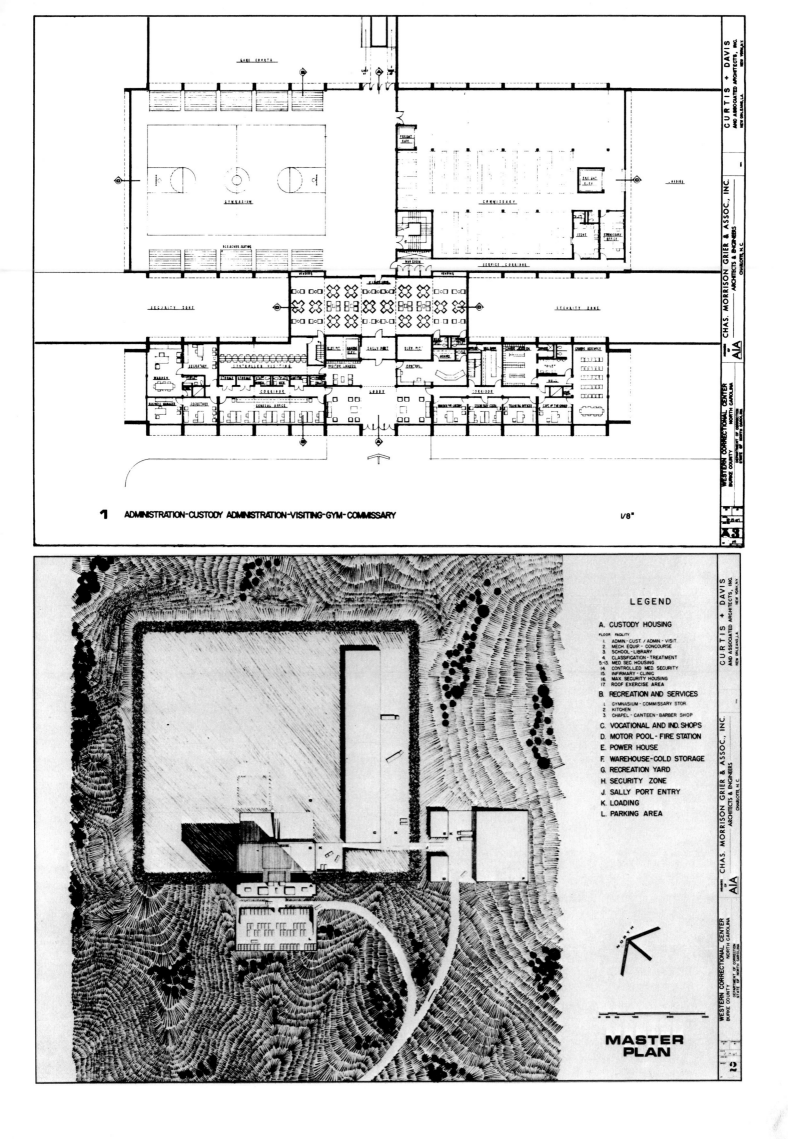

1 ADMINISTRATION-CUSTODY ADMINISTRATION-VISITING-GYM-COMMISSARY   1/8"

LEGEND

A. CUSTODY HOUSING

FLOOR FACILITY
1. ADMIN - CUST / ADMIN - VISIT.
2. MECH EQUIP - CONCOURSE
3. SCHOOL - LIBRARY
4. CLASSIFICATION - TREATMENT
5-13. MED. SEC. HOUSING
14. CONTROLLED MED. SECURITY
15. INFIRMARY - CLINIC
16. MAX. SECURITY HOUSING
17. ROOF EXERCISE AREA

B. RECREATION AND SERVICES

1. GYMNASIUM - COMMISSARY STOR.
2. KITCHEN
3. CHAPEL - CANTEEN - BARBER SHOP

C. VOCATIONAL AND IND. SHOPS

D. MOTOR POOL - FIRE STATION

E. POWER HOUSE

F. WAREHOUSE - COLD STORAGE

G. RECREATION YARD

H. SECURITY ZONE

J. SALLY PORT ENTRY

K. LOADING

L. PARKING AREA

NORTH

MASTER PLAN

CHAPTER TWO

Courthouses, Police Stations

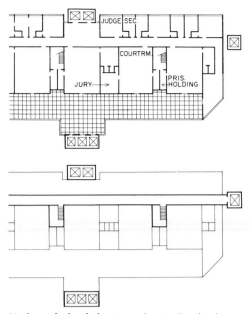

Introductory guidelines for planning a modern courthouse

Horizontal circulation (see above). On the lower level are corridors for the public and for the court staff, each with its own elevators. Courtrooms and jury rooms are between the corridors, judges' chambers across the private one. Prisoners are brought in by a third corridor on the upper level.
Vertical circulation (below). Small private lobbies serving pairs of courtrooms are reached by elevators for court staff and for prisoners.

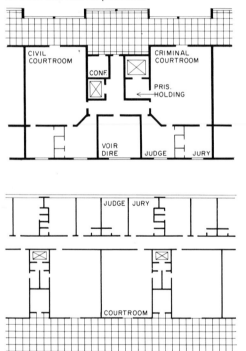

Jury deliberation rooms (above). These can be placed on the outside wall of the building when a horizontal circulation system is used—if there is no objection to the jury walking across the private corridor to reach them.
Future expansion (below). Two diagrams show the schematic possibilities for adding onto a courthouse building without disrupting its operations.

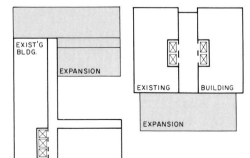

The physical organization of the modern courthouse has been completely transformed by the enlarged scale of its operations and the growth of its administrative staff. The problem is not simply one of providing additional courtrooms and office space to cope with an increased case load; it is that the original architectural and functional arrangement of most older courthouses cannot support the court as it now functions, and becomes a hindrance to efficient operations, security and public safety. What is required is a new set of planning guidelines on which the design of new courthouses can be based.

Administrative and judicial functions require very different kinds of space

The first guideline provides for the separation of the administrative and social-service departments from the courtrooms and their associated functions. The latter include judges' chambers, hearing rooms, jury assembly and deliberation rooms, conference rooms and law library. The court's administrative and social-service departments require flexible office space in which the layout of partitions can be altered to respond to administrative or procedural changes. The courtrooms and their associated spaces, on the other hand, are unlikely to change during the life span of the building.

The architectural and engineering characteristics of flexible and permanent space are, of course, quite different, suggesting their separation onto different floors in a multi-story building, or into zones in a one-story courthouse. Normal office partitioning cannot be used for court functions because it is difficult to obtain acoustical privacy. Where acoustical privacy is required, special precautions must be taken which tend to eliminate flexibility. The walls must penetrate the suspended ceiling and be sealed against the structural slab. Pipes and ducts are specially insulated, and the movement of air must be planned to inhibit the transfer of sound. This means that the air-conditioning system has to be tailored to suit a particular layout of rooms, and a change in partition layout requires revamping the whole system. Since permanent spaces serve for the life of the building and since changes are difficult and costly, the information given to the architect about these spaces must be comprehensive and minutely detailed.

Multiple circulation systems are needed in courthouses

Separate systems of corridors, lobbies and elevators must provide access to the courtrooms for the public, for prisoners and for judges, jurors and staff. In most courthouses built be-

---

NEW HAVEN COUNTY COURTHOUSE, New Haven, Connecticut. Architects: *William F. Pedersen & Associates, Inc.*—project architects: *William F. Pedersen, Fred B. Bookhart, Jr., David M. Chin and John W. Persse.* Engineers: *Macchi & Hoffman* (structural), *Technical Design Associates* (mechanical/electrical). Consultant: *Allan Greenberg,* (Connecticut Judicial Department). General contractor: *Dwight Building Company.*

fore 1950, public spaces are used by judges, jurors, attorneys, staff and sometimes even prisoners to reach the courtrooms or judges' chambers. Today, considerations of convenience, efficiency and security require that segregated circulation areas be provided.

The horizontal system provides lobbies and corridors to connect *all* the courtrooms on each floor with public, staff, juror and prisoner elevators (see diagram at the left). The public has its own bank of elevators and its own lobby. A private corridor at the rear of the courtrooms is used by judges, staff, and jurors for access to judges' chambers, offices, courtrooms and, if necessary, voir dire (preliminary questioning) rooms. The connections between the private corridor and public lobby must be monitored by a receptionist in order to control access and maintain security. Prisoners use a special corridor, located on a mezzanine level directly above the private corridor, to reach the courtrooms. A staircase connects this corridor to a prisoner holding room adjacent to each courtroom, and a special prison elevator provides vertical circulation from the cell block to the courtroom floors.

The vertical circulation system provides two separate private elevators to serve a series of courtrooms stacked one above the other. One elevator is used to transport prisoners from the cell block to a prisoner holding room adjacent to the courtroom. The other is for the use of judges, jurors and staff. It opens into a private lobby which provides access to the judge's chamber, the rear of the courtroom and, if necessary, a voir dire room. A connection to the public lobby is available for attorneys and members of the public who have appointments to see a judge.

The resulting pattern is of pairs of courtrooms, stacked one above the other on successive floors of the building, grouped around a private staff elevator and lobby. This arrangement has a formative impact on the planning of the rest of the building, since the space on any non-courtroom floor will be interrupted by these private elevators. In the jury assembly room, they must be clearly marked in order to avoid jurors arriving at the wrong courtroom.

The vertical system is best suited to judicial systems in which judges travel on circuit. In this case, a set of resident chambers must be provided for the judges who live in the judicial district. This is in addition to those behind each courtroom for the use of the sitting judges, most of whom will travel to the courthouse from another judicial district. The resident judges' chambers are best located away from the courtrooms, on another floor of the building, preferably near the law library.

The vertical system provides good access between the courtroom floors, the law library, the pool of judges' secretaries, and the various departments of the court. The judges' secretaries serve both sitting and resident judges, but are best located near the resident judges' chambers away from the busy courtrooms. Each department must be planned in proximity to the private elevator core serving the court-

Gerald Allen   Joseph Molitor

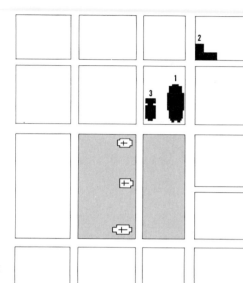

Musical chairs on the New Haven Green

In 1965 the Connecticut Judicial Department was faced with the problem of obsolete facilities and a major shortage of courtrooms and office space in New Haven. The three courts, the higher and lower trial courts and juvenile court, were located, in the City Hall Annex, the Old County Courthouse (1), and a late nineteenth century house. A three-phase solution was developed by the State Judicial Department and Public Works Department. The *first phase* was to plan and construct a new 165,000 square foot building for the higher trial court on a site (2) across the street from the Old County Courthouse. *Phase two* was to move the lower trial court out of the City Hall Annex into the Old County Courthouse. This robust building of 1913, by William Allen and Richard Williams, is based on the design of St. Georges Hall, Liverpool, by Harvey Lonsdale Elmes. A major renovation of the building was planned. The *third phase* of the plan called for the acquisition of the New Haven library building (3) by the state, and its conversion into a juvenile courthouse. A study indicated that the building, an excellent Cass Gilbert structure of 1908, could be adapted to the needs of the Juvenile Court with only minor modifications to its splendid interior spaces. This phase of the plan waited for completion of the new city library which is part of a government center complex, designed by Paul Rudolph. This game of musical chairs has resulted in the preservation of two important buildings on this historic New Haven Green, and also saved the taxpayers some hard-earned dollars.

rooms which are used to hear its cases so as to provide for the convenient movement of personnel and documents.

The horizontal system is appropriate when judges are assigned their own courtrooms on a permanent basis. Its main drawback is that jury deliberation rooms are interior, windowless spaces. If there is no objection to the jury walking out of the courtroom, across the private corridor, to jury deliberation rooms on the exterior side of the building, this problem can be circumvented. (See diagram.)

The height of the building is also an important factor in choosing between the horizontal or vertical circulation system. Because of the cost of extra elevators, the vertical circulation system is not suitable to a building of less than six floors.

The circulation system is an important factor in selecting appropriate locations for the various functions and departments in the building. The optimum location depends on interdepartmental communications, public convenience and security, as well as on factors like the volume of visitors and the frequency and nature of the transactions that take place. All this information must be systematically recorded and classified on the basis of priority. One of the most important considerations is that circulation routes in the courthouse should be self-evident.

Architects and court administrators often overlook the fact that the majority of people, especially jurors and witnesses, are in the building for the first time. In many new courthouses, the public experiences considerable difficulty locating both the people and the services they need. When members of the public constantly stop to ask for directions it is a sure sign of a poorly planned building. The majority of visitors usually have destinations in administrative or social service departments. If these are all concentrated on the lower floors of the building, public access is considerably simplified. Some departments may even want a separate entrance directly off the sidewalk.

Centralization has the additional advantage of limiting traffic on courtroom floors to people directly concerned with court proceedings, thereby improving security. The courtrooms should occupy the midsection of the building. The library, judges' chambers, jury assembly room and other areas which require some privacy can be assigned the upper floors. This arrangement results in a division of the building into three zones—office areas, courtrooms and private areas.

Interdepartmental proximity requirements are also an important factor in selecting locations for the various departments and functions. Certain departments require direct access to the private circulation system serving the courtroom for the movement of both court records and personnel. These include the offices of the clerk and the prosecuting attorney, and other departments depending on local circumstances. The segregation of jurors from the public is necessary for efficient control over

their movements and to preclude any contact with plaintiffs, defendants, their friends, witnesses, attorneys or other interested parties. For obvious reasons, the connections between the segregated circulation routes and public lobbies must be minimized and carefully controlled. In addition to these "process" factors, the shape and size of the site, the character of the surrounding environment and the zoning restrictions can impose severe limitations on the building's shape, height and floor area, restricting the number of options available for locating departments.

Ways to provide for future expansion in new courthouses

Although future developments are not always predictable, many changes in the court can be anticipated with sufficient certainty to warrant provisions being made to accommodate them in the new building. These may include the creation of new departments, the merging of older ones or, at a smaller scale, the adoption of microfilm for storing records. The initial phase of expansion (10-15 years) is best included in the new building. A difficult question to resolve is whether to provide this space on one or two floors that remain unused until needed, or to distribute it in smaller units on each floor of the building. In the office areas, it is advisable to provide an additional safeguard by making generous initial space allocations. The movable partitions can be rearranged to accommodate additional personnel and equipment as the work load increases. Provision for eventual expansion by new building also requires careful thought. The circulation system and elevator locations must be planned at the beginning in order to achieve a good and economical connection to a future addition to the courthouse.

Public convenience should be a major design consideration

The public is composed of a large number of people who infrequently visit the courthouse as witnesses, litigants and spectators. The circulation routes and spaces used by each group must be studied, and additional information on user expectations obtained by questionnaires and interviews, and by consultation with the staff who deal with the public in each department. The following guidelines are useful to the consideration of public convenience and satisfaction:

- Functions serving large numbers of people should be grouped on the lower floors of the courthouse. In addition to elevators, an open stair or escalator should be used to provide direct communication between these floors.
- An information booth should be located at the main entrance to the courthouse, and at other locations, such as the jury assembly room and witness lounge, where large numbers of people gather.
- A clearly legible, color-coded system of directories and signs should be prominently displayed. The location of offices, courtrooms, witness lounges, jury assembly rooms, toilets, information stations, vending machines, snack bars and telephones must be indicated.
- Spaces for a wide variety of activities such as reading, working, conversation, games and watching television should be provided in jury assembly rooms and witness lounges.

A voice amplification system should be provided in all large courtrooms to assure that the public and press can hear the proceedings. Comfortable seats and coat racks are also necessary in the spectator area.

At this point, a cautionary note must be sounded, for it is all too easy to become preoccupied with technology, operations research and long-range trends and projections, and to overlook the physical and psychological well-being of the staff and public in the courthouse building. This human factor, with which the fourth planning guideline is finally concerned, is difficult to articulate with precision, but it must be considered. The problem is more than simply choosing comfortable chairs and providing sufficient toilets. A basic question must be asked: "What kind of human environment is best for the particular transactions that take place?" Factors like the absence of noise and distraction, adequate and comfortable lighting, convenient places to sit while waiting, and windows in areas where they will be most appreciated must be considered in order to assure that each space is comfortable and pleasant, and well suited to its particular function. The architect and the building committee, moreover, must take specific steps to gather information on user needs by in-depth interviews with courthouse staff, who should be asked to study the plans and models and suggest improvements.

The new New Haven County Courthouse is a monumentally simple building. Its limestone facade, built close to the sidewalk, continues the line of one of New Haven's major streets (photo opposite page). The main entrance is at the corner of the building (photo right), and it leads into a large ground-floor lobby with public elevators and a reception desk (plan below). General offices are on this floor. The courtroom floors above are arranged according to the vertical circulation scheme described on the previous page—with small private lobbies (and private elevators) generally serving pairs of courtrooms. The private elevators also reach the jury assembly room on the top floor. A law library is on the next to the top floor, and is shown in the photo below right.

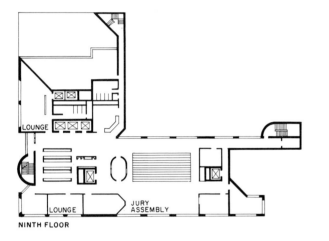

NINTH FLOOR

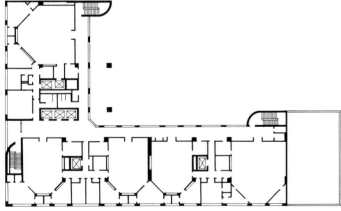

FOURTH FLOOR

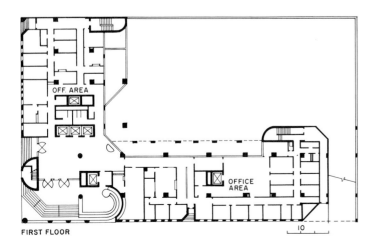

FIRST FLOOR

The client-architect relationship in courthouse design

A recent visit to new courthouses in various parts of the country indicates that users' dissatisfaction with new court facilities was generally directed at the architect, even though the contractor or public works department may have been at fault. Further, there were similar frustrations on the part of some of the architects. They complained of uncooperative judiciary and public works departments, and lack of information and guidelines on which to base a design. This suggests that there may be a basic flaw in the architect-client relationship during the crucial programming and planning phases of courthouse projects.

Since this relationship is a function of the architect-client contract document, it would be well to examine the AIA standard form of architect-client contract, and raise two fundamental questions. First: "What is the proper relationship between client and architect?" Second: "Who is the real client?"

The first question relates to the definition of the respective responsibilities of the architect and client. The AIA contract states that, "The Architect prepares, for *approval by the Owner,* the schematic design studies consisting of drawings and other documents illustrating the scale and relationship of project components to *meet the Owner's requirements.*" The preamble notes that the architect "develops his best solution from the *Owner's criteria,*" and that the Owner "*must clearly describe his requirements . . . and give prompt and thorough attention to all sketches, drawings, and documents submitted to him by his architect.*"

The architect, furthermore, is "*entitled to rely on the accuracy and completeness of the services, information, surveys, reports, etc., furnished by the Owner, and cannot be held responsible for the errors contained therein.*" This depicts the traditional client-architect relationship in which the architect simply designs to a program issued by the client.

For today's complexities
traditional roles need help
Inherent difficulties were succinctly formulated by Lord Richard Llewelyn Davies in the *RIBA Journal,* January 1961:

"Modern society is too complex for the architect to have an automatic understanding of what is wanted in a building; the client does not (always) know this either. . . . For many modern buildings there is no single client. Many people are concerned with the function-

ing of a hospital or a college (or a courthouse). Each may understand the workings of some part of it, but no one understands it completely as a whole. Again, the long life of buildings when compared with the rate of change of human organization, means that people often adjust their pattern of life or work to fit an old building. If they are asked to specify their needs for a new one they think in terms of an old and familiar environment, they cannot break out to see what they really want. Therefore, the client's brief is nearly always wrong, and a bad brief inevitably results in disastrous architecture."

This approach generally inhibits the range of alternatives considered and results in a new facility in which the general arrangement approximates the old structure. Other problems arise from the fact that most clients are unable to fully grasp the three dimensional implications of architectural drawings, and consequently it is difficult for them to review plans and request changes or adjustments. Further, the architect frequently lacks the requisite judicial experience to detect errors and shortcomings in the program.

A full-service alternative
to the classic relationship
An alternative architect-client relationship is available for court systems that are not prepared to accept the responsibility of developing a building program or to review and approve plans. The architect can be retained to research, document, analyze, and synthesize the administrative and operational organization of the court, and to develop the program for the new courthouse. This is specifically provided for in the AIA Owner-Architect contract agreement as "Additional Services." This role for the architect has been defined by Michael Wong in *Space Management and the Courts: A Summary,* published by the U.S. Department of Justice, as a "comprehensive and systematic approach for deriving feasible solutions to administrative, operational, personnel, and spatial problems" to provide "alternative solutions, accounting for current and anticipated developments of a legislative, political, economic, and social nature." The architect now functions as both a programmer and a tutor, for the problem is no longer simply to design a building, but involves reexamination of the structure of the justice system.

This architect-client relationship raises extremely serious problems. First, many if not

most architects lack experience in the field of operations research per se, and have even less knowledge of the complexity of the court's operations and the problems facing it. Second, it is unlikely that the judges and staff would accept this situation of delegated authority, whatever the architect's qualifications might be. Further, the tutorial proposition assumes that the courts have a completely fluid structure that is readily open to change, and that the pressures of day-to-day operations and bureaucratic inertia can be ignored. Third, in order for the architect to succeed in this role, it is essential that there be a substantial body of research that can be used to evaluate the advantages or shortcomings of any proposal. This does not yet exist, unfortunately, in the field of courthouse design. From the clients' point of view, projects in which the architect programs and reorganizes the facility, therefore, tend to be utopian, difficult to translate into reality, and arbitrary in their internal arrangement.

A joint programming effort
should be developed
It is obvious that both the traditional architect-client relationship and the architect's forced role as judiciary systems consultant have serious drawbacks. Both client and architect have important knowledge and experience to contribute to the project, and a compromise in which the responsibility for developing the program is shared, offers advantages.

The notion of client-architect collaboration, while essential, is not in itself a sufficient answer. Guidelines to determine the respective input of client and architect to their joint task of preparing a program and set of plans for a building project must be established. A strategy to assign this responsibility is suggested in *A Managers' Guide to Operations Research,* by Russell L. Ackoff and Patrick Rivette (John Wiley and Sons, 1967). Basically, when operations research specialists work on an executive problem, the knowledge of its content, provided primarily by management and operating personnel, is supplemented by study of the operations themselves. The researchers can then abstract the form of the problem and describe it in a mathematical model, upon which appropriate mathematical techniques can be brought to bear for a solution. It is in the formalization of implementation procedures that the solution is given meaning. Hence managers, operating personnel, and researchers must work together in joint venture if meaningful solutions to real problems are to be obtained.

This suggests four distinct operations — description, observation, abstraction, and implementation — that are relevant to the analogous architect-court task of programming and planning a building.

Description involves collecting information about the administration, operation, and organization of the court and is clearly a client input. It must include all current or long-range plans to improve the administration of justice.

Observation is the study of the Court's operation. It is the architect's task and it implies a responsibility to refer back to the client for more data wherever the description is inadequate or does not correspond to observation.

Abstraction is the process of synthesizing the information derived from the two previous phases into a set of principles on which to base the design of the new courthouse. This is primarily the architect's function but it is essential that the conclusions be jointly reviewed with the client.

Implementation involves the development of schematic design proposals which are then tested against data derived from description, observation, and abstraction until a satisfactory set of plans is developed. This again is primarily the architect's task, but the client has a crucial role to play in evaluating the various solutions and suggesting improvements.

Proposed changes in
the architect-client contract

It is obvious that the relevant clauses of the standard architect-client contract discussed earlier can be more specific in the courthouse-programming situation. In particular, the sentence: "The Architect prepares, for approval by the Owner, the schematic design studies consisting of drawings and other documents illustrating the scale and relationship of project components to meet the Owner's requirements," must be broadened to encompass the more complex requirements of a *collaborative architect-client relationship.* The following is a suggested alternative in four clauses to replace this sentence:

1. The client will provide the architect with a comprehensive description of the organization and administration of the court and its related agencies, its projected growth, and any current and longer-range plans for administrative improvements or changes.

2. The architect, in conjunction with any consultants he deems necessary, will observe operation of the court and its related agencies, and request any additional information necessary for the development of a program.

3. The architect, and any consultants he deems necessary, will abstract the information collected under clauses 1) and 2) into a program. This will outline a set of parameters on which to base the design of the proposed building, a schedule of room sizes and a description of departmental and interdepartmental relationships. This will be accompanied by a written justification supporting the various conclusions. This document will be reviewed by the client and adjusted until it is acceptable to both parties, who will signify their approval in writing.

4. The architect will then implement this program by developing sets of schematic plans for review by the client. Both parties will again signify approval of the chosen solution.

If this collaborative architect-client relationship is to succeed, the client must voice all doubts, review all documents, and study alternate systems of spatial arrangement submitted until an optimum plan is developed. The architect must elicit information from the client until all aspects of the program are specified in sufficient detail, and suggest and explore new avenues of approach in courthouse design. Perspective drawings, scale models, and mock-ups must be used to help illustrate the concepts, ideas and layouts to the judges and court personnel, who may have difficulty reading architectural drawings. The success of the project will be a direct function of the zeal and cooperation of client and architect.

If courts are not prepared
who then is the client?

Having established that the success of a courthouse design is largely dependent on close collaboration between the judiciary and the architect, the second question, *"Who in fact is the client?"* can be addressed. It has been assumed up to now that the occupant of the building, the judiciary, is the client, and in an ideal situation this would certainly be the case. However, in the case of public buildings a third party is involved. In most cities, counties, and states, the courthouse and all other public buildings, are assigned by statute to the custody of the commissioner of public works, who is responsible for all routine maintenance and new construction. Therefore, if the legislative body appropriates funds for the design and construction of a new or renovated courthouse, it is the public works commissioner who enters into contracts with the architect and builder. The right to review and approve plans, to negotiate with the architect, and to control the release of funds thus lies in the public works department, and not with the judiciary. The latter is then left without any *contractual basis* for collaboration with the architect on the design of its own courthouse.

The weak negotiating position of the user traps the architect, judiciary, and public works department into an extremely difficult and cumbersome working relationship. Consultation with the judges and court personnel by the architect and public works department is apt to be perfunctory. The public works department usually has little knowledge of or interest in the court's operation, and presses for a simple and economical building that can be constructed with a minimum of delay. The combination of the pressures that result from the public works department's discretionary control over the payment of architects' fees, and the important role of political considerations in the selection of architects, tends to create a situation in which the architect may have little or no incentive to seek out the user's complaints or suggestions. Except when the architect is unusually dedicated, there is likely to be little input from the court system where it is not a party to the contract. In this respect the judiciary, being a separate branch of government, is worse off than agencies in the executive branch, of which the public works department is also a part.

Three-way communication
is essential to the process

There is an obvious need to formalize channels of communication among the architect, judicial system, and public works department. When the court is at odds with the public works department over some aspect of the design of the new building, the architect can be rendered inoperative by conflicting sets of instructions. In such case, the judiciary must realize that the problem does not lie with the architect, and must develop an appropriate strategy vis-a-vis the public works department. If it is the architect who is unresponsive or uncooperative, the complaint should be directed to the public works department as the "client," who can then issue the appropriate instructions to the architect. Courts, too, sometimes fail to recognize their obligation to cooperate fully. Situations of this sort require considerable tact and diplomacy on the part of all participants in the process.

It is imperative that the judiciary be involved in the project from the earliest legislative maneuvers. A mere consulting role usually means that the judiciary participates too little and too late. If possible, a clause stating that the plans must meet with the approval of the chief justice or chief court administrator should be inserted into the bonding bill or enabling act. If this is not possible, wording that stresses the importance of consulting the judiciary may be used, i.e., ". . . plans to be developed by the architect in consultation with the court. . . ." The ideal situation, of course, is one in which the legislature assigns the funds directly to the judiciary. The building project can then be administered by the public works department, but all expenditures and plans will require the approval of the chief judge or chief court administrator.

It is now evident that the answers to our two initial questions (What is the proper client-architect relationship? Who is the client?) raise difficult problems. Close collaboration between the architect and judiciary is imperative to ensure the development of a functional and appropriate new courthouse. Yet, the judiciary is generally not a party to the contract between the public works department and the architect, and consequently has no standing in the matter. The resolution of this problem will require patience, tenacity, a readiness to cooperate, and a full understanding of all the factors involved. The responsibility to press for a solution must rest with the judiciary. That is the party with the most at stake.

Mecklenburg County Courthouse

Gordon H. Schenck, Jr.

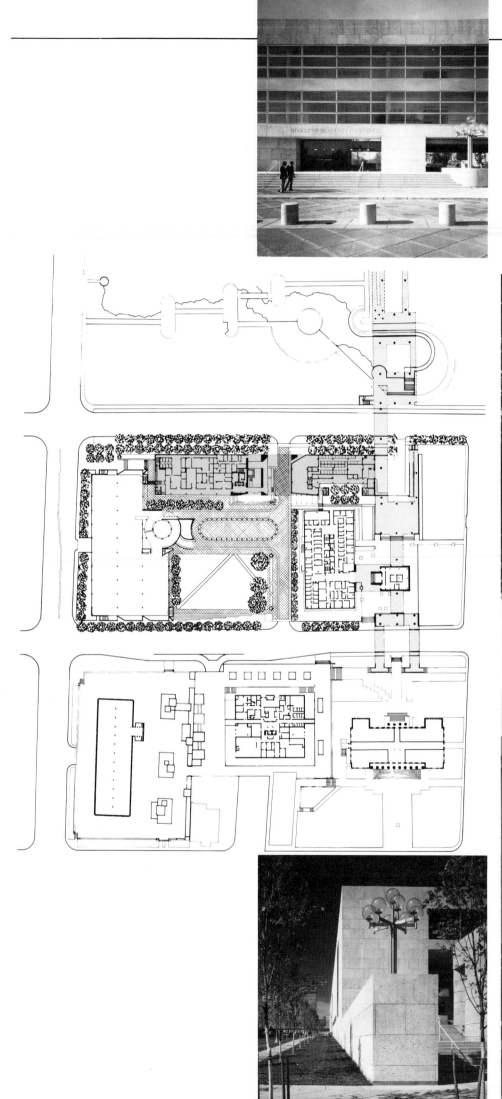

The architectural firm of Wolf Associates in Charlotte has gained an enviable reputation for being one of the South's—and, for that matter, one of the country's—most meticulous purveyors of architectural design. Their buildings are finely honed, elegant to a fare-thee-well, and powerful—so powerful, indeed, that they ineluctably cause even casual observers to sit up and take notice, and to offer strong criticisms as well as heartfelt congratulations. A case in point is one of Wolf Associates' most recently completed buildings, the new Mecklenburg County Courthouse in Charlotte, shown here

and on the previous and the following two pages. The building is located in the heart of a city and county government center and also in the midst of a wide open urban mesa that was the result of the inevitably cataclysmic first act of what used a decade ago to be called urban renewal. Wolf Associates' task was not just to design a building, but also to make some over-all sense of the existing architectural elements on the site—a county office building (most to the right of the three shaded buildings in the plan on the opposite page), a major public park (at the top of the plan), and an elevated pedestrian walkway crossing a public street. A new 450-car garage, designed by another firm, had also to be provided for (most to the left of the three shaded buildings), and the hope was also to create some focal point for the whole complex in the form of a new public plaza—evocative, the architects suggest, of old courthouse squares of the past. The courthouse itself, lying between the new parking garage and the county office building and pedestrian walkway, is a long, sleek building clad in Cordova shell limestone and, on the plaza side, a glass and aluminum curtain wall. It functions not just as a courthouse, but also as a circulation spine that links the garage to the walkway and to the county office building. On its street side (shown in the small photograph at the bottom of the opposite page and in the photograph on the page before that) the building sports a facade that is large in scale, the limestone being punctured with openings that provide viewers from inside with selective prospects of the park across the way. The largest of all these openings is the streetside entrance—not just to the building, but through it, to the new public plaza that has been created beyond (below). . . .

305 COURTROOM

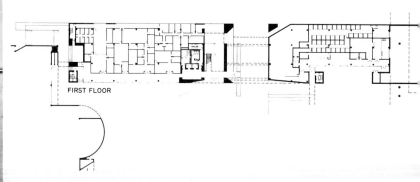

FIRST FLOOR

300 JURY ROOM

Inside, the courthouse uses a dual-corridor system to separate public and private circulation; the public corridors overlook the plaza through the glass curtain wall (right). On the opposite side of the building, private corridors provide access to the rear of each courtroom.

As a piece of architecture, the building is obviously Modernist in persuasion, in that it uses the handsome and apparently machine-made materials in which Modern architecture traditionally clads itself. Less obviously, perhaps, it is Modernist in that it takes a literal view of function, and an abstract view of symbol. Thus the function of circulation—not some arguably higher judicial ''function''—mainly determines the shape of the building, and the recollection of courthouse squares from the past is attempted by abstractly evoking their form—as opposed to something perhaps more palpable, their look.

MECKLENBURG COUNTY COURTHOUSE, Charlotte, North Carolina. Architects: *Wolf Associates.* Engineers: *King-Hudson Associates* (structural); *James A. Story & Associates* (mechanical); *Bullard Associates* (electrical). General contractor: *Parke Construction Co.*

SECOND FLOOR

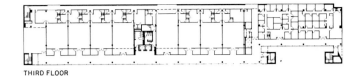

THIRD FLOOR

Commentary: Symbolism in Architecture

"All architecture proposes an effect on the human mind, not merely a service to the human frame."
                                    —John Ruskin

Since the growth of the International Style in the 1920s, the expression of symbols appears to have lost its relevance to architecture.[1] Because symbolism is a major element in the articulation of meaning in architecture, especially in the design of public buildings, its loss must count as a significant factor in any explanation of the serious functional and esthetic shortcomings of so many modern buildings in our towns and cities.

Symbolism plays an especially important role in planning the settings for the judicial system, and the design of courtrooms and courthouses offers a provocative case study for the assessments of its crucial function in architecture. Court procedures are highly formalized and should, in their operation, both uphold and emblemize the tradition and development of our democratic system of government.

Consider courtroom design. The courtroom is the setting for the administration of justice under the law and, as such, is the heart of the courthouse. The layout of a typical criminal courtroom in the United States differs markedly from courtrooms in other countries and reflects our unique system of justice. The American judge is an impartial arbiter and is therefore positioned on a raised podium in the center of the front of the room. Defense and prosecution are equal adversaries and, as such, are each provided with seats at assigned tables in the well of the courtroom facing the judge. The public are silent observers, sitting at the rear of the courtroom, facing the judge. Their role is just as crucial as that of the other parties for, as silent arbiters, they influence the law through the political processes of election and legislation. The jury box is placed at the side of the room, deliberately divorced from the axial relationship of judge, counsel and public. This placement reflects the impartiality of the jurors, who must decide guilt or innocence. The witness box is located adjacent to the judge's bench facing the two parties. This provides the latter with their constitutional right to confront the opposing counsel's witnesses.

In this courtroom layout, symbolism is of paramount importance. Serious consideration of the cultural and social values embodied in the court system is, therefore, a prerequisite to the design or evaluation of any courtroom.[2] The architectural forms should be seen as a "sign system through which society tries to communicate its ideal model of a relationship between judges, prosecutors, jurors and others involved in judicial pro-

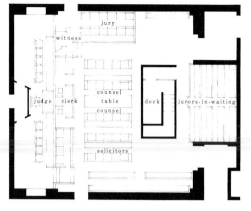

Figure 1. Plan and section of a typical courtroom used for criminal cases at the Crown Court, Dorchester, England (1957). The accused person is seated in a dock, raised above the level of the courtroom and facing the judge. The public seating is in a gallery, and the judge's bench extends almost all the way across the courtroom. The bar area is occupied by the barristers. (Architect: James Hearst).

Figure 2. Plan of a courtroom-in-the-round. Trial participants, with the exception of the court reporter, are seated in a circular arrangement. The judge's bench is slightly differentiated by its geometry and raised platform.

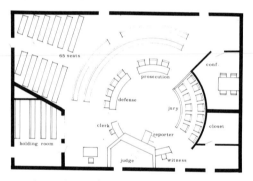

ceedings."[3] In other countries, where social organization and judicial procedures are very different from ours, these differences are often directly reflected in their courtroom designs.[4] For example, in eastern European countries the prosecutor sits on the podium next to the judge, thus leaving the defendant and his attorney alone in the center of the courtroom; in some Swiss courts, the jury sits behind the judge, who may also be a member of the jury panel; and an accused person in England does not sit at a table with counsel for the defense, but is isolated in a dock with a security officer (figure 1). Seen in this light, the traditional American courtroom layout is notable for its marked orientation toward the rights of the accused.

During the past decade, three new courtroom layouts have been proposed. These are the courtroom-in-the-round, courtroom with the judge's bench in the corner, and courtroom with witness located opposite the jury (figures 2-4). In each case, proponents have claimed significant improvements for court procedure and trial participants' ability to see or hear. However, any new courtroom design should be rigorously justifi-

Figure 3. Courtroom with the judge's bench in corner. This remarkable type of plan was developed by Judge George Boldt. Ignoring symbolic criteria, it arranges trial participants so as to give maximum weight to the judge's view of the witness, adjacency of reporters to witness, and to provide space for conferences at the judge's bench.

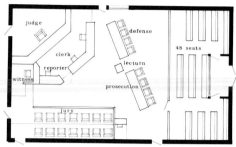

able on grounds of symbolic meaning as well. For example, the appropriateness of a courtroom-in-the-round, especially in serious criminal litigation, is open to question. The equality implied by the circular form fails to differentiate between the trial participants or to express their adversary roles.

The courtroom with the judge's bench in the corner seems to lack a clearly expressed symbolic order, and the courtroom with the witness stand facing the jury is a variation of the traditional courtroom. The witness stand is relocated so as to improve the judge's and the juror's view of the witness. Unfortunately, this move establishes a cross axis of judge-counsel and witness-jury, which has no connection with adversary proceedings and severely undercuts the sense of counsel and client confronting witnesses.

The most important functional criterion is that all the participants in the trial—judge, juror, witness, clerk, court reporter, defense and prosecuting attorney, defendant or litigant, press and public—be able adequately to see and hear everything that occurs and to feel a sense of involvement in the proceedings. This is difficult to achieve in a room of 1,200 to 2,000 square feet in which the focus of attention moves unpredictably from witness to counsel, judge or reporter. Counsel occupies different positions in the courtroom during cross-examination, summation, sentencing and bench conferences, and the jury is often out of the room. The problem is further complicated by the uncontrollable factors of poor enunciation and diction and the use of the same courtroom for trials, arraignments, calling the calendar and sentencing. We are faced with a functional problem whose complex and overlapping requirements preclude the isolation of any dominant set of organizing principles. It is necessary, therefore, systematically to test a series of compromises, none of which can fully accommodate the various needs of all the participants, until layout is developed.

In order to do this, I developed a comprehensive method to evaluate the performance of any courtroom and to compare performance of any number of courtrooms.[6] By establishing principles for good sight lines and acoustics, functional problems can be readily assessed for correc-

Figure 4. Courtroom with witness located so as to face the jury. This plan follows the traditional model with the exception of the witness location.

Figure 5. The traditional courtroom layout imposes some strain on jurors seated farthest from the witness. The angle they have to turn to see the witness can be reduced by careful consideration of jury box location.

Figure 6. The circular courtroom layout imposes severe strain on jurors seated nearest the witness, who have to turn almost 90 degrees to see him or her. Modification of the witness box shape can improve the situation, but the symbolism of the circle is severely compromised.

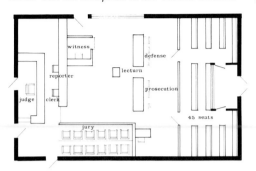

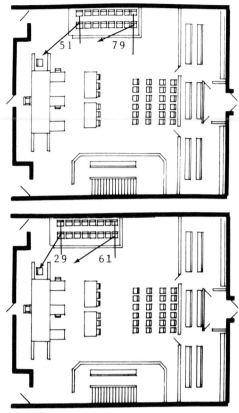

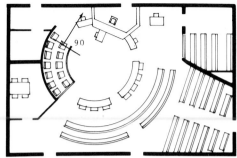

tive action. A point-score system is used to compare and evaluate the performance of two or more courtrooms. However, experience in designing and evaluating courtrooms has made one point abundantly clear: *there is no one optimal functional solution.* Each courtroom's configuration and dimensions have their own set of built-in advantages and problems. For example, the main deficiency of both the traditional courtroom and the courtroom-in-the-round is that the location of the witness denies judge and some jurors a good frontal view of the witness' face (figures 5-6). The courtroom-in-the-round actually worsens the problem for the jurors nearest the witness by increasing the angle they have to turn in order to face the witness. The traditional layout may also create problems for jurors farthest from the witness, who must lean forward to obtain good sightlines to the witness. Both problems can be corrected. In the latter case, the jury box must be moved nearer the witness, and in the former jury box can be modified.

The courtroom-in-the-round reduces distances between some participants, thereby creating a sense of intimacy, but it also increases the sight angles and physical strain.[7] The latter can be alleviated to some extent by using swivel chairs. The courtroom with the judge's bench in the corner keeps the witness between judge and jury but moves the bench into a corner and turns it almost ninety degrees so as to optimize the judge's view of witness and jury (figure 3). These adjustments dramatically increase the distance between counsel tables and witnesses. The courtroom with the witness located opposite the jury optimizes the judge's, jury's and reporter's view of the witness, but limits counsel's to a profile. Counsel must also cross-examine the witness from a lectern to avoid turning his back to the jury (figure 4). The latter two plans optimize sightlines without unduly increasing distances. The traditional plan provides the best relationship between public, counsel and judge.

It is clear that functional analysis yields no ultimate plan, as each type has both advantages and drawbacks. In order to find a way through this maze of ergonomic data and conflicting claims by proponents of different courtroom layouts, I suggest that the most

reasonable design procedure is, *first,* to select a courtroom layout which provides a desired set of symbolic relationships; and, *second,* to optimize ergonomic relationships by detailed consideration of room dimensions and subtle placement of furniture and fixtures. Once a selection of layout has been made, it must be subjected to a rigorous program of testing, adjustment and evaluation by the architect and building committee. Drawings and scale models should be used to optimize all sightlines and distance relationships. The availability of voice amplification and acoustical engineering should ensure that no one in a courtroom misses a spoken word. Having chosen a courtroom for its symbolic attributes, serious study of the functional aspects can then maximize its advantages, and careful placement of the furniture and control of sight angles can minimize the disadvantages of any layout to the extent of virtually equalizing performance factors. It should be clearly stated that advocating a primary role for symbolism in the process of selecting courtroom layout can never be used as an excuse for failing to resolve acoustic or sightline problems in any courtroom, irrespective of size or layout.

It is also important to study the fabric of the courthouse building which houses the courtrooms, as this structure is also imbued with symbolic importance. The exterior articulation of a courthouse and the relationship of the building to its surroundings expresses our concept of the role of the law in society. Similarly, the building's internal arrangement reflects the relative importance assigned to

the transactions and the roles of the various groups using the building. In order to demonstrate the range of meanings and values that can be communicated by a courthouse, let us look at the Virginia State Captiol, which originally included the State Supreme Court, designed by Thomas Jefferson in 1785 (figure 7). Jefferson based the design on that of a Roman Temple. His idea was to express the continuity of the classical ideals of democracy and rule of law now being realized anew in the American Republic, to strengthen the Republic's young roots by demonstrating the intellectual tradition to which it was heir, and to signal to the world the greatness to which it aspired. The organization of the Capitol's plan also has symbolic significance, as the legislative chamber and supreme courtroom were expressed as co-equal branches of the government. The building was sited in a landscaped square in Richmond and elevated on a podium to signify its unique importance as the center of the state's legal, judicial and executive activities. At the time, it was the most elaborately designed and important building in Virginia.

Jefferson's intention was understood by citizen and architect alike, and for the next 150 years so many state capitols and courthouses followed the classical tradition that the United States boasted more large domes and porticos than ancient Rome. Even High Victorian Gothic structures, such as the Connecticut State Capitol at Hartford, are planned to express the independence of the three branches of government.

Buildings like the United States Supreme Court in Washington, D.C., designed by Cass Gilbert in the nineteen-thirties, clearly refer to Jefferson's design and use ambitious sculptural programs, mottos and inscriptions to amplify further the themes of law, justice and democracy, (figure 9). Similar principles underly the design of our greatest public building, the United States Capitol.

Symbolic factors were of primary importance in the design and planning of the interior of older courthouse buildings. The beautiful lobbies indicate—by virtue of their size, rich material and primary importance in the organization of the plan—that public convenience has been an overriding factor in design. Paul Cret, at the Hartford County Courthouse

Figure 7. Virginia State Capitol, designed by Thomas Jefferson. The use of Roman forms suggests that the new American republic is the successor to the ancient Roman republic.

Figure 8. Plan of the first floor at the Hartford County Courthouse (Architect: Paul P. Cret). The lobby, which is three stories high, receives light from high windows between the courtrooms. These windows also mark the entrances to offices on the opposite sides of the lobby.

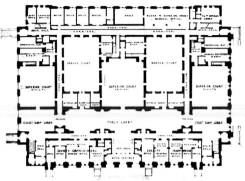

Figure 9. United States Supreme Court, designed by Cass Gilbert. The temple front clearly refers to Jefferson's Virginia State Capitol, and the sculptural program deals with themes related to justice.

Stephen Kiernan

(1926-28), uses light, entering one side of the lobby, to separate courtrooms and mark the location of the entrance to office spaces on the opposite side, (figure 8). The articulation of the lobby in plan and section, which contrasts the large-scale fenestration, murals and doorways associated with courtrooms with the small colonnade and related offices on the opposite side, subtly informs the user that there are one major and two minor courtrooms on one side and office functions on the other.

The grand public spaces and elaborate design found in older courthouses still convey an aura of dignity and, despite current overcrowding and obsolescence, continue to provide a sense of order, orientation and hierarchical importance of destinations. The fact that they provide more than the bare minimum of space is a celebration of human values, a demonstration of concern for user well-being, and a recognition of the fact that people come to a courthouse for the resolution of serious problems and require a setting that confers the appropriate aura of dignity on their deliberations.

Perhaps the most damning characteristic of many new courthouses is the lack of a coherent and symbolically significant relationship with the surrounding buildings and environment. The messages which these buildings communicate to the taxpaying public and attorneys, witnesses, jurors and litigants in the courthouse are that their needs, both functional and psychological, do not warrant attention or expression.

Study of older courthouses often yields valuable data which can profitably be applied to our own work. These buildings' exteriors were monumental, yet did not overwhelm the surrounding environment. They communicated the importance of the venue where society administers laws, metes out sanctions and resolves citizens' conflicts. Entrances were clearly articulated, and architectural forms provided visual pleasure. An analysis of interior spaces in offices in old courthouses also provides a wide range of useful planning information. In this regard, we have much to learn from the Beaux-Art-trained architects who strove to design circulation systems in public buildings so that destinations were obvious and self-evident to the user.

Anything less than this constituted a serious design failure. The shapes of lobbies and foyers, windows, location of stairs and elevators, strategic placement of spacious corridors and decorative elements, were all used to suggest direction of movement, hierarchical importance of destinations, and to provide a sense of orientation at all times.

It is obvious that our idea of what constitutes the most appropriate setting for a courthouse and its various departments has changed over the last two or three decades. Some people argue that the legal process itself is the monument and that the courthouse building is a very secondary concern. This attitude confuses non-design with the need to make visitors, jurors, witnesses and litigants feel comfortable and oriented in the building. This latter, desirable goal can only be achieved, I believe, by recognizing the important role of symbolism and the expression of meaning in architectural design, and by using symbols that are comprehensible to contemporary society in order to communicate with its surroundings and the user.

The design problem is more than simply providing sufficient area and minimal standards for satisfactory operations. A more fundamental question is this: "What kind of environment is appropriate for the particular transaction?" The answer is inextricably involved with cultural and social issues, tradition and process. A design method that ignores these factors, and does not go beyond satisfying minimum needs, results in both the architect and the client neglecting such important considerations as orientation, expression of civic role, and the provision of amenities for the individual. The lack of recognition of the role of symbolism in the courthouse also has the secondary effect of excluding *serious* consideration for provisions both for physical comfort and for psychological comfort as well.

Today, tradition-repudiating doctrines inherent in much Modern architecture compel architects to attempt the development of new design typologies with each new building they undertake. This results in a repeated reinvention of the wheel. The denial of tradition has also led to a lack of serious guidelines for courthouse design which has resulted in poorly informed clients and architects and in

situations where the display of stylistic innovation and formal novelty are confused with the development of functionally appropriate solutions and genuine innovations.

How can this deficiency be remedied? Some obvious answers spring to mind. In the past, architects used a system of building types as the basis of design. Model solutions were based on the accumulated experience of the past (traditions) and constantly revised as new experience became available. There is a crying need now for a rigorous program to evaluate, systematically, the performance of new courthouses as a means of accumulating a body of data dealing with symbolic functional, psychological and physiological aspects of design. The case-study method, which was so pivotal in developing our modern system of legal education, should now be applied to the design of courthouse facilities, as well as other building types. The development of design standards for courthouses and evaluation procedures for architects, clients and users should be a task of our architectural schools and the profession. Without such standards and procedures, experience and knowledge related to courthouse design cannot be accumulated, assessed and transmitted. It is only in this way that the challenging task of incorporating symbolic, as well as functional, concerns can be solved and that as architects, we can rise to meet Ruskin's challenge to service both man's mind and his frame.

FOOTNOTES

1. An early version of this paper was published in *Judicature,* April 1976, pages 422-428 and May 1976, pages 484-490.
2. John W. Hazard, "Furniture Arrangements as a Symbol of Judicial Roles," 19 *ETC: A Review of General Semantics,* pages 181-188 (July 1962).
3. Robert Gutman, *People and Buildings,* (Basic Books), 1972 page 229.
4. Sybille Bedford, *The Faces of Justice: A Traveller's Report* (Collins), 1961.
5. C. Theodore Larson, "Future Shock Hits the American Courthouse: Opportunities for Parameters of Design," *American Institute of Architect's Journal,* July 1975, page 38.
6. Allan Greenberg, *Courthouse Design: A Handbook for Judges and Court Administrators.* American Bar Association Commission on Standards of Judicial Administration, 1975, pages 43-52.
7. *Ibid.,* pages 64-65.
8. *Ibid.*

The county courthouse: rediscovering a national asset

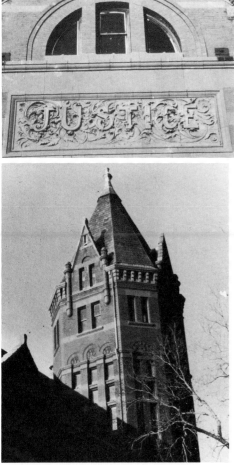

Details of the Marshall County Courthouse in Marysville, Kansas, one of nine Midwestern county courthouses selected for feasibility studies at the University of Illinois Chicago Circle Campus.

Courtroom in the Warren County Courthouse, Warrenton, Missouri. Below, Trumpeters of Justice adorning the clock tower of the Stark County Courthouse in Canton, Ohio.

It is appropriate in a time of growing historical interest to study the American courthouse as a functioning building type of the highest symbolic order. Certainly no other building type has such wide-spread impact on local history, because of its monumental quality and its location, which make it a real symbol of the physical and social organization of countless American communities.

During the last half of the nineteenth century and the first few years of the twentieth, particularly fine court buildings were erected by many counties, especially in the Midwest, which was just then coming into its own economically as well as politically. The county's judicial and administrative offices were housed in a centrally located building in each county seat. Thus county seats were important locations, and the courthouse was carefully sited on the highest hill or the most prominent central square where often their cupolas and towers could be seen from the farthest reaches of the county. In their pomp and style, the courthouses represented a visual locus surrounded by the region's chief commercial buildings. It is because of these factors that the monumental older courthouse cannot be replaced, for without it the town itself loses definition and cohesion.

During the past ten years, nevertheless, we have lost scores of these majestic structures. Throughout the Midwest, noble and opulent reminders of the civic pride of our forebears have fallen to the wrecking ball. Numerous courthouses are threatened today, and more will become endangered in the next few years.

On the surface, there are two reasons for the recent number of courthouse preservation problems. In many cases, generations of deferred maintenance have finally taken their toll, and the buildings have developed serious code violations as well as deplorably seedy appearances. Oftentimes, however, maintenance-related problems are cosmetic in nature, and comparatively easily remedied when objectively approached.

More serious are problems caused by the changing functions of modern county government, coupled with rising county population. Courthouse architects of the nineteenth century could not foresee the changes which have taken place in recent years in county services. Buildings which quite adequately housed governmental services of county courts, clerks, recorders and tax offices are today stretched to the bursting point by the addition of county health departments, welfare offices, motor vehicle license offices, veterans' affairs offices and agricultural extension agents. Some counties in the path of urbanization have added personnel to the point where the old building is overwhelmed.

Nevertheless, why is one county able to rearrange and accommodate its growth and changing needs in a refurbished old courthouse, while another with identical problems ends up replacing its majestic showpiece, its monumental heart, with a faceless, standardized one-story office building devoid of civic dignity? The very fact that this is happening in some counties and not in others calls for more coordinated study of a problem which lends itself to literally thousands of analogous situations, not just in the Midwest but throughout the entire country.

It is our contention that the key element in the preservation of courthouses is the attitude of the architect and the people involved. For too long, architects and citizens have looked at these older buildings as white elephants— liabilities instead of assets. It takes imagination to find solutions to the vexing problem of accommodating modern needs in an older space, and too often architects have taken the easier path of starting from scratch. But in an age of increasing visual standardization in which we are daily losing our sense of time and place, we must begin to find ways to keep our very important landmarks.

This, then, was the rationale behind the Historic Courthouse Project, a cooperative effort involving the National Endowment for the Arts, the National Trust for Historic Preservation, the University of Illinois Chicago Circle Campus and Harry Weese & Associates. Over 1000 counties in 13 Midwestern states were surveyed and asked to participate in the study. From the responses, we were able to narrow the scope of the project to a study of courthouse space management in counties experiencing both increasing and decreasing growth. We elected not to become involved in eleventh-hour hopeless cases, nor was stylistic excellence a major factor in the selection process. While each possesses its individual problems, all nine courthouses chosen for intensive study represent fairly typical conditions, so the results should have wide application everywhere.

Each courthouse was assigned to teams of fourth- and fifth-year architecture students at UICC, acting as "paraprofessionals" under the supervision of a group of professional advisors, including Mr. Michael Lisec and myself, of Harry Weese & Associates.

Prior to the teams' field visits to the subject courthouses for interviews and on-site investigations, the entire group made a joint field trip to seven counties in Illinois to develop a background understanding of the problem. Team visits to the selected courthouses involved interviews with all county officials, onsite photography and data gathering, meetings with local historical societies, interested individuals and inevitably the local media. A wealth of data was brought home, sorted and weighed, and mutual problems were compared. Repeat trips were made when necessary. One county required a special visit by Don Anderson, of The Engineers Collabo-

Marshall County Courthouse, Marysville, Kansas

UICC students Richard Latkowski and Gerhard Rosenberg, under the direction of Ben Weese (and with the advice of The Engineers Collaborative, Ltd.), developed a renovation proposal for the Marshall County Courthouse that, according to current growth projections, will be able to satisfy the County's space needs through 1990. The study, which advocates a versatile adaptive use rather than precise historical reconstruction, begins with a thorough replanning of existing floors in the building, and then proposes either the construction of new annexes or a conversion of existing adjacent buildings to accommodate ultimate space requirements.

The Courthouse, which was built in 1891, is a brick and sandstone faced structure with terra cotta trim, and it was designed by the Milwaukee architectural firm of Henry C. Koch and Company.

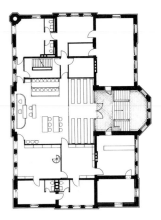

rative, our consultant structural engineer. The students were then asked to develop preservation action strategies which could be returned to their para-clients, the county commissioners, as completed feasibility studies.

Although in the beginning these architecture students were not necessarily committed or interested in questions of preservation strategy, they have made a very mature response to a complex, difficult, and sometimes negative situation. These 19 emerging professionals have received their first in-depth training in a highly skilled but largely uncharted area: that of professional architectural preservationist. The training they have received will help them meet the growing demand for knowledgeable and sympathetic professionals in this field.

One of the chief goals of this effort was to find out what it will cost to save buildings. Unwise counsel in the past has called for major surgery that bankrupts and compromises the patient beyond recognition.

Rule One is that the old building, con-structed in an era of cheap labor and high quality craftsmanship, was better built than new buildings, given reasonable maintenance (or even none!). Old buildings withstand the test of time.

Rule Two is to not intervene beyond what program and common sense require. Naturally, accommodations to public safety and codes must be made, but an overzealous effort at "sanitizing," automatically dropping ceilings, closing off the grand stair or the central cupola are misguided. "Compensatory" code requirements can be negotiated so that public safety, access for the handicapped, etc., can be accommodated without losing the original grandeur and concept of the building. Minimal intervention is a hallmark of a competitive final cost.

As mentioned earlier, it is possible for court functions to continue to be accommodated in these buildings. In some cases, however, a series of unplanned changes over the years had resulted in too much space devoted to dead storage (election machines, old records, etc.) or completely unused areas such as attics. Here, a comprehensive plan was developed that focused on the total space available. Minimal alterations resulted in greatly increased space. In other cases, light steel mezzanine floors were added between floors (often 10-20 feet clear) with no structural problems, because of the massive masonry walls.

A word here about extensively modifying the interiors of an historic building: in many counties all the resources were spent on the exterior shell and thus the buildings have virtually no internal decor. In these cases sympathetic embellishment is appropriate to sensibly renovate a building. In general, exterior maintenance on these axial, symmetrical buildings is the prime need. Most often additions—unless underground or sensibly linked—are a defacement. In all our records and data on courthouses, we cannot unqualifiedly recommend one successful example of an addition.

In the first place, expansion should be considered within the interior of the courthouse itself through better space utilization,

Warren County Courthouse, Warrenton, Missouri

In their feasibility study for the renovation of this building, students David Lencioni and Wayne Miller first tackled minor structural problems like a sagging second floor and a wobbly cupola on the roof. Then they turned to replanning the space inside, and to developing a courthouse "campus" plan by renovating the buildings on Warrenton's Main Street. They confidently predict that the county's space requirements can be met in this way.

Stark County Courthouse, Canton, Ohio

Because of the unusual enthusiasm with which their initial feasibility study was greeted by county officials, students Robert Klute, Thomas Meredith and John Pohl continued their work and submitted a second-phase proposal in March 1975, and a final proposal in June 1975.

The Stark County Courthouse, as the adjacent photographs attest, has already gone through a series of renovations. The original building was begun in 1868; by 1893 it was no longer large enough to accommodate all of the court and clerical functions of this growing county, and it was more or less completely remodeled by Cleveland architect George F. Hammond. Further minor alterations brought the building to its pre-renovation state.

Klute, Meredith and Pohl's scheme called for preservation and restoration of the building's exterior, its main lobby and at least one courtroom; the remainder of the interior would be remodeled in a contemporary manner. All county functions not directly related to the courts would be removed from the courthouse and housed in existing adjacent buildings or new ones.

mezzanine construction, or attic expansion. Secondly, many county services unrelated to the traditional court functions do not have to be housed under one roof and can easily be physically separated. This is the basis for the "campus" concept, already practiced successfully by numerous counties throughout the country. Through this method, counties expand into available nearby commercial buildings which are often themselves of architectural merit. This commitment to the traditional central downtown location is critical, for the alternative is to move to the edge of town or to an off-center location where the whole pattern of historic community growth is abandoned and a devastating suburbanizing influence takes hold. Gone is the memorable image of the majestically imposing building, replaced by a courthouse, which is easily confused with any new shopping center.

With an arsenal of strategies, a sympathetic "client/user," and a dedicated and sensitive professional, I submit that the clarification and solution of the courthouse problem is possible. In our Bicentennial era, it is the American people who benefit from the daily presence of the historic courthouse as a continuing symbol of our heritage of justice and democratic government.

This joint project involving the University of Illinois Chicago Circle Campus, Harry Weese and Associates, and the National Trust for Historic Preservation represents the first attempt to find broadly applicable answers to a wide-spread problem: making the grand, impractical and extravagant courthouse of another era suitable for the vastly changed conditions of modern life. The results of the study clearly show that most courthouses can be preserved if people are motivated. But county commissioners are a conservative lot who generally have little experience or understanding of historic preservation. They rely on their paid expert, the architect, to render a professional judgment. We hope the methods we have developed will motivate both architects and county officials to explore fully and imaginatively all possible ways in which the architectural gems of the past can remain in service for the future.

As important as the preservation of these civic monuments is the sensitizing of the student architects to view the architectural extravagances of the past as essential anchors to keep us steady in an ocean of prefabbed standardization. Even if they are never involved again in a courthouse, the students who participated in this exercise have had their eyes opened to the possibilities for imaginative reuse of many older buildings to enrich the fabric of our lives.

To call further attention to the preservation of historic courthouses, county officials and architects were invited to a national conference on the subject, sponsored by the National Trust in December 1975, and a summary publication of the project results was published for wide distribution in 1976. Perhaps the emphasis that was placed on the noble ambitions of previous generations during the Bicentennial years will stimulate all of us to assure the preservation of our temples of justice.

WILLIAM MORGAN'S COURTHOUSE IN FORT LAUDERDALE

The progress photos shown here already indicate the strong urban qualities of William Morgan Architects' design for a major intersection in this loosely-knit Florida city. Like Morgan's police station for Jacksonville, this Federal court facility manages to combine the seemingly incompatible images of monumentality (a client mandate) and public amenity. Here, the public amenity takes the form of what will be lushly planted water gardens, visually contained by a peristyle. The intersection gains a major pedestrian space that—because of its visual inclusion within the volume of the building—is appropriately urban. Parking spaces are provided on grade under the building, and this plan allows the relatively low massing shown here—in contrast to the tower and separate garage originally implied in the GSA program.

The concrete "tree" construction is similar to the Police Center's, as described on page 78. The project is completed after five years, and and is well under budget. According to the report of the Public Advisory Panel: "The result is a project design of ingenuity, structural and energy efficiency and total integrity. It has the potential of achieving a new high in Federal architecture dedicated to a democratic ideal."

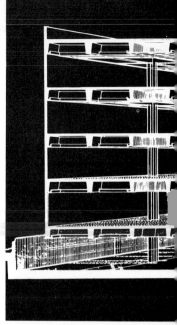

Dan Forer photos

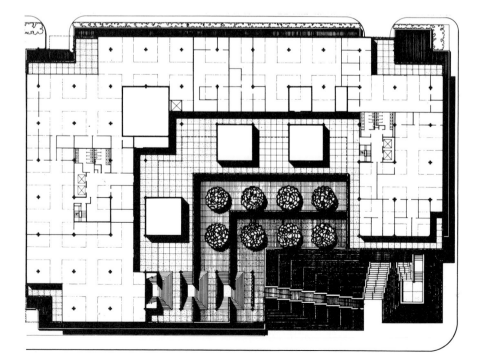

TANGIPAHOA PARISH COURTHOUSE
AMITE, LOUISIANA
DESMOND-MIREMONT-BURKS, ARCHITECTS

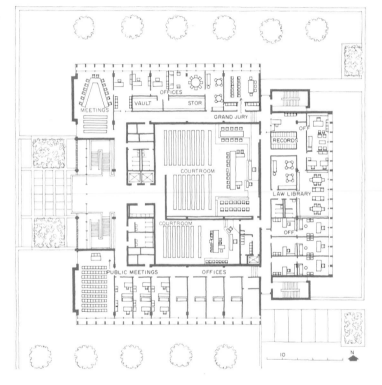

To those who associate courtrooms with scarred wainscoting and chipped terrazzo, these interiors provide a welcome contrast. Part of a contract that included interiors, the two courtrooms, which double as fallout shelters, are set side by side and acoustically isolated on the building's second floor.

Both spaces are panelled in white oak, with silverwood ceilings, and each has white oak furnishings and brown wool carpeting. Ceilings are relatively low in both spaces. In the large courtroom, however, a section of the ceiling has been raised to provide a visual release while sharpening the focus on the area of the bench. Finish materials are generally smooth except for slatted wood screens (shielding entrances at either side of the bench) which offer a textured counterpoint. Both courtrooms are windowless but avoid any sensation of entombment by skillful use of artificial light.

Courtroom furnishings are detailed with an exemplary consistency that helps to give these spaces a clarity, unity and dignity too often absent from courthouse design.

Engineers: J. C. Kerstans & Associates (structural): Ingram-Barbay, Inc. (mechanical and electrical); contractor: Polk Construction Company; fallout shelter analyst: L. E. Miremont.

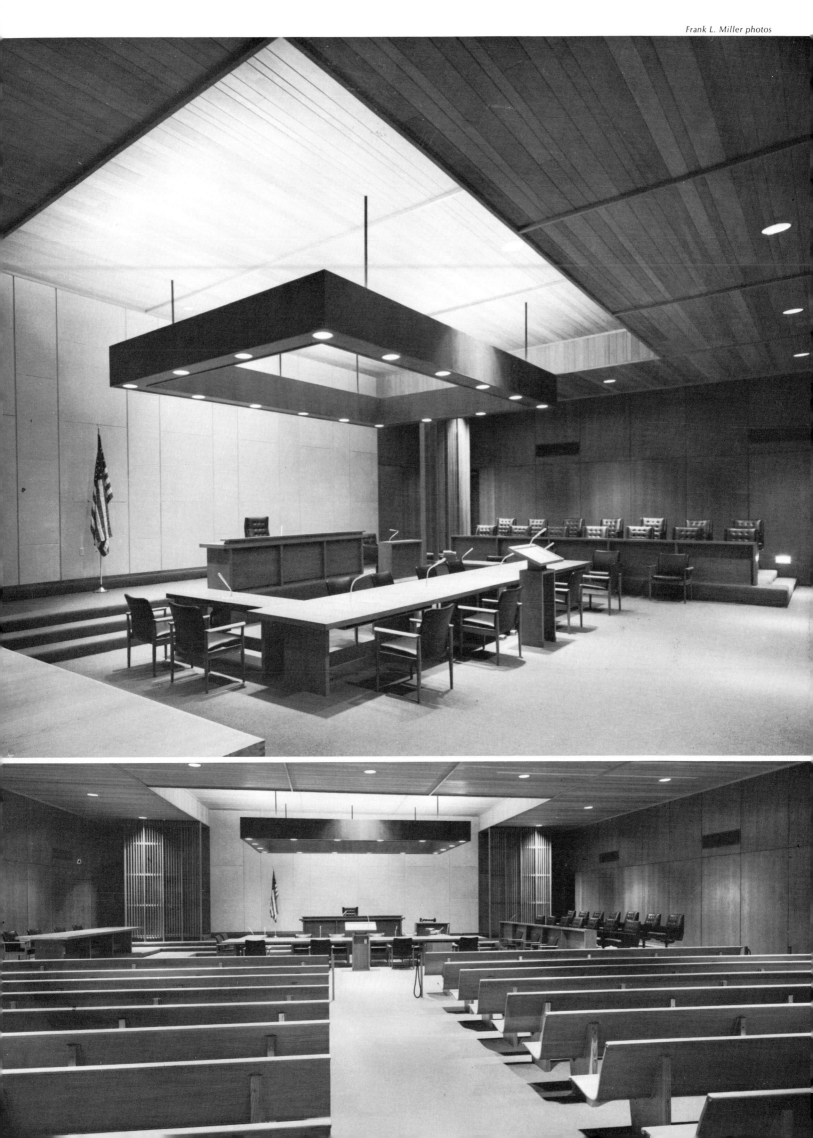

BREAKING DOWN THE BATTLEMENTS: JACKSONVILLE'S NEW POLICE HEADQUARTERS

Police Memorial Building

In designing what is officially known as the Police Memorial Building in Jacksonville, Florida, architect William Morgan has produced two unified civic facilities that would seem by traditional standards to be incompatible: a functioning law enforcement agency and a public park. But it is exactly this skillful marriage of the two normally distinct faces of government's responsibility that makes this building significant. The park is located on the stepped levels of the agency's roof, and it lends a totally new and humane image to normally stern and forbidding functions. But such innovation is nothing new to Morgan. The two-part use of the site is consistent with his innovative design approaches for all sorts of buildings. Morgan's buildings are in harmony with their surroundings — or sometimes with what their surroundings might be in the most considerate of worlds. Truly, he is telling us something about the nature of what architecture can be all about — and in this case what government might be all about.

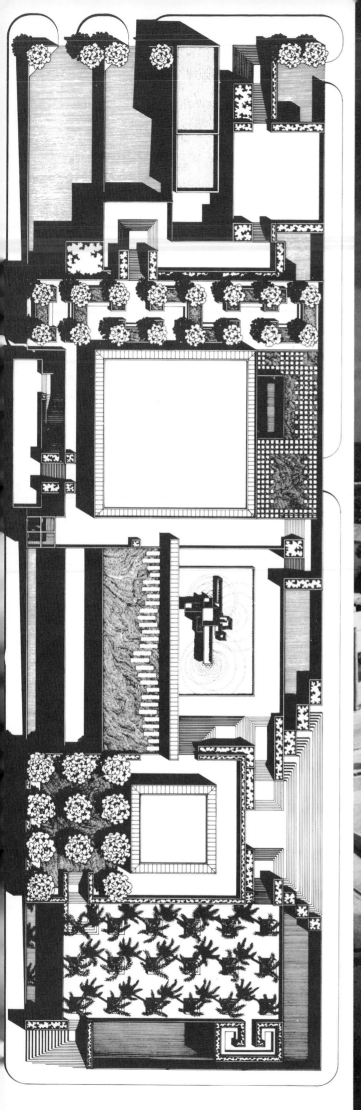

In the past, some police stations have been designed as civic monuments (in the spirit of the great nineteenth century railroad stations), others as examples of hardheaded efficiency. It requires an appreciation of both design approaches, and it requires the spirit of the most recent times, to produce the adventurous design shown here by architect William Morgan for Jacksonville, Florida's Police Memorial Building.

First of all, the building is monumental—but in two very different senses from the overbearing connotation of that description. It is a monument to a new concept of civic responsibility, wherein the barriers between government's function and the aim of that function, human amenity, are broken down. The building is monumental because its symbolic values go far beyond its day-to-day purposes, and boost humane sensibilities. (Another monumental quality is the visual recall of the ancient Indian architecture of northern Florida—a subject that has fascinated Morgan for many years.)

The design was the winner of a competition sponsored by the AIA, and the jury report stated that the selection was based on the need for breaking down the barriers of isolation, unpleasantness and resentment that have recently become attached to the image of law enforcement. In an understatment, the jury said "we tried to choose a design with an airy rather than eerie atmosphere." The jury also said that the design was selected for visible "ease of approach and efficiency in handling day-to-day business."

And the building does handle business. Police functions are distributed over two floors, which are elevated above a subgrade parking area. The parking level also accommodates service functions such as mechanical equipment rooms, and provides space for future expansion of the building. (The utilization of the current 208,000-square-foot building is approximately 70 per cent). The main floor is surprisingly straightforward in plan for a building with the apparently complicated volumes that are seen from the exterior. All spaces are organized around two interior courts, which are respectively centers of public-related and internal functions. Accordingly, the main entrance (see photos page 81) leads to the smaller court (see section), around which are public services and records, and facilities for public transactions—such as paying parking tickets. The sheriff's office and the offices of other police officers are located around the larger court, with such functions as detention.

Architect Morgan was determined to create a building in which people's sense of location would be quick and easy, as they traveled from place to place. Accordingly, the two courts are connected by a two-story-high gallery (photo top). Here hang banners created by artist Anne Emanuel, whose designs are derived from paintings by local school children transferred onto canvas. The building's exterior walls (as seen in the photo above) are poured-in-place concrete with a fluted, bush hammered finish that is interrupted by smooth concrete bands at the floor levels.

POLICE MEMORIAL BUILDING, Jacksonville, Florida. Architects: *William Morgan Architects*—associate-in-charge: *Thomas McCrary*. Engineers: *William Le Messurier* (structural theory); *H.W. Keister & Associates* (applied structural); *Haley Keister & Associates* (foundation and soils); *Roy Turknett Engineers* (mechanical/electrical). Consultants: *William Lam Associates* (lighting); *Ed Heist, Jr.* (interiors); *Hilton Meadows* (landscape); *Meyer/Lomprey & Associates* (graphics). General contractor: *Orr Construction Company*.

MAIN LEVEL

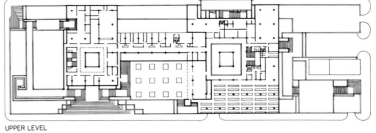

UPPER LEVEL

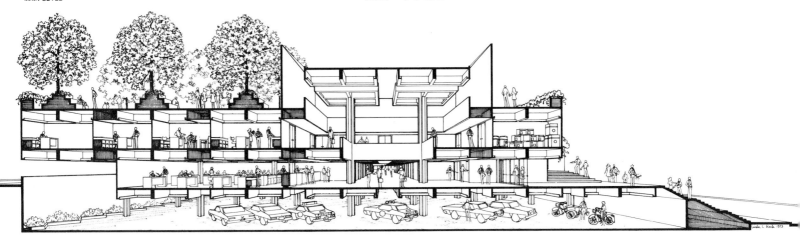

Despite the building's open appearance, security was a strong consideration in the design. Accordingly, there are few windows, and skylights take on great importance. The skylights are located over the two courts and the connecting gallery. The larger court (photo opposite) rises four stories from the parking level to the underside of a helicopter landing pad, which is elevated above the roof. Architect Morgan calls these courts "inverted pyramids of space" in reference to his interests in the ancient architecture of the local Indians. As the development of downtown Jacksonville moves in its direction, the roof-top park (photo left) will gain increasing importance as both open space and as a place for people to relax. Consistent with his interests in urban context, the preservation of a nineteenth century firehouse on the site was successfully urged by Morgan. The building has been converted to a museum for historic fire-fighting equipment (photo bottom).

Otto Baitz Photos

SCHENECTADY POLICE HEADQUARTERS

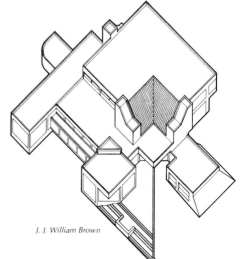

J. J. William Brown

Joseph W. Molitor photos

This police headquarters building—designed by architects Werner Feibes and James Schmitt—was built to accommodate the activities of a 150-person police force, and also to create a handsome and visible image for the law enforcement profession in this upstate New York town of 81,000 people. The site is adjacent to the Schenectady County Public Library and close by the central business district, city hall and post office, since it was thought that such contiguity with the everyday public life and affairs of the community would aid the morale of the police force even as it indicated to the public the force's role.

The form of the building, according to the architects, resulted from the complexity of ac-

tivities that make up a modern law-enforcement facility; they allowed each of these elements proper expression and then organized them all in their most natural and immediately identifiable way, so that, according to Schmitt, the building "emerged as a village cluster of interconnected forms." The diagram on the right shows how security areas, administrative areas and public areas are related.

SCHENECTADY POLICE HEADQUARTERS, Schenectady, New York. Architects: *Feibes & Schmitt.* Engineers: *John T. Percy and Associates* (structural); *Robert D. Krouner Consulting Engineer* (mechanical/electrical); *Thomsen Associates* (soils). Consultant: *Bristol, Hiser & Leaver* (landscape). General contractor: *Hanson Construction Corporation.*

☐ PUBLIC
☐ STAFF
☐ SECURITY

10

CHAPTER THREE

Buildings for the Mentally and Physically Disabled

MENTAL HEALTH FACILITIES:

IMPROVEMENT THROUGH MANAGEMENT AND MONEY FOR ARCHITECTURE

Syracuse State School of Mental Retardation
Architects: Sargent-Webster-Crenshaw & Folley

Kings Park Rehabilitation Center
Architect: Edgar Tafel

Hudson River Rehabilitation Center
Architects: Cadman & Droste

Buffalo Rehabilitation Center
Architects: Milstein, Wittek, Davis & Hamilton

As the public client at every level of government has poured increasing billions of dollars into construction of all kinds, two important effects have emerged. First, the sheer volume has called for fresh approaches to management of both design and construction processes. Second, the response of the architectural profession has been to reach for new dimensions in practice commensurate with the size and complexity of new work.

Health facilities demonstrate these changes more aptly than some other building types---partly because of the increasing penetration of the public client into programing and design development, and partly because of the rapidly changing medical techniques new facilities are called upon to accommodate. In the field of mental health, especially, new therapies have had a two-fold effect on architects' involvement. One effect has been the rapid obsolescence of existing facilities, which has called for new client sophistication in programing and new administrative approaches to reconstituting state facilities. A second effect has been the emergence of entirely new kinds of mental health facilities for which few design precedents exist.

The facilities described on following pages have been designed (with one exception) under a construction program initiated in 1964 by the New York State Department of Mental Hygiene and implemented by a funding and management agency called the New York State Health and Mental Hygiene Facilities Improvement Corporation, now renamed the Facilities Development Corporation. The facilities shown are a sampling of the following kinds of work handled by the Corporation:
 Rehabilitation centers. As tranquilizers and other modes of therapy permit a more truly psychiatric interchange between physician and patient, rehabilitation becomes a major activity replacing the mainly custodial care of former programs. Hence, a new series of some 15 rehabilitation centers is being developed for the New York system. Characteristically, these are separate day-centers located on hospital grounds and designed to implement training for return to outside communities. See page 94.
 Schools for the mentally retarded. In 11 new designs for these schools, the architectural goal, again, is to reinforce development of the maximum capacities of the retarded rather than simply provide custodial housing. See page 112.
 Psychiatric hospitals for children. There are seven such planned for New York's mental hygiene program. In addition there will be a series of some six hospitals newly designed for mentally ill adults. See page 98.
 Narcotic addiction rehabilitation centers. These are commissioned by the state's Narcotic Addiction Control Commission, and the design and construction management are handled through the Corporation. See page 107.
 Research facilities. At least two separate facilities for scientific research in psychiatric problems are in work. One of these, the Institute for Basic Research in Mental Retardation, was initiated prior to 1964, but is being completed under the Corporation's management program. See page 109.

The article beginning next page describes the role of the Corporation in fostering a working climate in which new dimensions of architectural and construction practices may thrive.

Architects in private practice, mustered by enlightened public policy, are upgrading New York's health and mental hygiene facilities

One public agency that has been a proving ground for methods of maintaining architectural quality while meeting unprecedented demand for new kinds of health facilities is the New York State Facilities Development Corporation. That name, cumbersome though it may be, grew to its present length as visible testimony of the Corporation's success in handling some 1500 projects valued at over $855 million.

The agency started out simply, in 1964, as the Mental Hygiene Facilities Improvement Fund. It was created by the New York Legislature, on behalf of the Department of Mental Hygiene, as a means of accelerating the flow of money and construction know-how into updating old and developing new kinds of mental health facilities. Success of the fund's operation led to new assignments, first for the Narcotic Addiction Control Commission and later for general health facilities. The latter assignment was launched by a $700-million appropriation by the 1968 State Legislature in a bill directing the Corporation to help cities and counties in the construction of general hospitals and changing the Corporation's name.

The funding methods established in the charter of the Corporation in 1964 are essentially self-sustaining. Money for a given mental health project is appropriated by the State Legislature. Bonds through which the money is repaid are sold by the Housing Finance Agency. When the facility is completed and in operation, fees from patients are used to pay off construction bonds and the program continues as a self-funded agency without excessive load on the state tax structure. As a public agency, the corporation is accountable to the State Bureau of the Budget, but otherwise maintains substantial freedom of action in the management of its own affairs.

Selection of architects is flexible and fair

The role of the corporation is not only to administer funding but also to award architectural commissions and to manage construction of facilities for clent agencies.

The procedures for selection of architects are substantially more flexible than those of some other public agencies. For example, there is no "approved list," so the whole membership of the architectural profession is available to the program. The scope of work is such that there are opportunities for all. Firms do have to qualify for a given project by showing capability to produce quality work within restrictive budgets. And they must have the capacity in manpower to design the proposed project without adding considerable staff. Since the design and development staff of the Corporation, consisting of staff architects, engineers and construction experts, operates in the New York office of the Corporation where development meetings at regular intervals are held, the architects responsible for design must be able to be present at those meetings.

On mental health projects, for example, the process might work as follows. The Corporation's director of design development may receive a letter of request from the State Department of Mental Hygiene. He or she will review a number of available firms, considering scope and location of the project, and discuss these firms informally with the executive director of the Corporation. The executive director then puts a recommendation for some of the firms on an agenda for consideration at the next meeting of the client department. For general health services, architects are similarly proposed and are finally chosen with the consent of the local agency for whom the facility is being designed. At the invitation of the client, city or county, the Corporation may identify three firms which have demonstrated abilities. Or the client municipality may itself suggest three or more prospective architects who are invited to make presentations to the various officials involved and to the Corporation staff. The Corporation seeks strong assurance that the project architect assigned to work commissioned to a particular firm is at an executive level and fulfills the requirements of responsibility implicit in the firm name.

Corporation staff architects and engineers review plans and specifications at various stages of development as a check against omissions or errors that could eventually develop into change orders. This review process as well as much of the follow-up on construction schedules is done under the administration of the coordinator of construction management.

Construction management: one key to quality and cost

One of the decisions of the corporation has been to commission an independent construction manager accepted by the architect to work on each project. The construction manager is usually a representative from one of the large contracting organizations which have elected to participate in management consultation rather than bid on any of the basic contracts involved in the job. By law, jobs are bid under at least four contracts: one each for general construction, HVAC, electrical equipment and plumbing.

The larger general contractors are not always available or willing to bid on the multiple contract basis, but their skills in overall construction management are brought to bear on Corporation projects by inducing them (with a moderate percentage fee) to assign some of their top people to act as construction managers. The caliber of management personnel is checked at approval interviews with the Corporation's board.

The selected construction managers are sophisticated not only in the wide variety of technologies involved but also in the practices employed by certain marginal bidders in making up for extremely low bids by encouraging the proliferation of change orders and other opportunities for profit. The Facilities Improvement Corporation sought for many years to coordinate the required four contracts under the general surveillance of the prime construction contractors. In many cases, however, the construction contractor was not equal to the task. Moreover, he often had a self-interest in disputes that involved other contractors.

The answer to this quandary was the establishment of the construction management program.

As projects increased in size and complexity, difficulties emerged in obtaining responsible bids even under the four-contract system. The Corporation decided to make greater use of its well-developed construction management potential and to further divide bidding into as many as 30 trades involved on a given project. The results of this ultimate diffusion of the bidding process are not all in, but on those few projects to which it has been applied, it seems to be working well.

One of the encumbrances on earlier process involving four prime contractors had to do with the flow of money. Now smaller contractors who may be of good quality but not substantially capitalized have an opportunity to participate as primes and can be directly and promptly reimbursed by the corporation rather than being subject to the delays of transfer between prime and sub-contractors. The rate of payment has been accelerated to three-week intervals so that the demands on resources of smaller contractors are alleviated.

Regular meetings help solve communications problems

One of the major advantages of the construction management operation has been the ability of the Corporation to involve the construction managers in design develop-

ment conferences among architects, Corporation personnel, the client agency and various consultants. The advantage to the architect is two-fold. First, he gains assurance that his own administrative time will not be dissipated in coordinating and scheduling problems. Second, he gains some feedback of the manager's familiarity with local conditions in the region where the building will be located. This pertains not only to the resources of local contractors but also to the capabilities of local trades in using optional materials that vary in availability and cost from one locale to another.

In design meetings which (for a major hospital, for example) are regularly held at the New York headquarters of the Corporation, there may be as many as a dozen agencies represented, including the client agencies. The Department of Mental Health may be brought in at both city and state levels, because most large general hospitals now are introducing substantial mental health facilities. The medical personnel of the hospital will also be represented either by the administrator or various department heads.

This technique of large preliminary meetings seems cumbersome at first, until it is realized that one of the most inhibiting conditions that has slowed the process of development and construction has been the increasing multiplicity of agencies and bureaus with some stake in the outcome and some responsibility for review during the development process. This overview process has reached the point where it is quite normal for a ten-year lapse between the emerging need for a facility and its ultimate completion. Further, the facility design itself not only suffers compromise for the mere sake of expediency in getting it approved, but is likely to be obsolete, or at best inadequate in scope, by the time it reaches completion.

There is some temptation to castigate the burgeoning process of overview as bureaucratic empire-building, but the fact is that the growth of multiple surveillance has been a direct response to public pressure. The consequences of direct action by individual public officials in the expenditure of public funds for construction have often been dire, politically, for responsible officials whose aim was only to "get things done." The human response of inviting multiple backup to share responsibility is at least understandable.

Historically, from the architect's point of view, the result has been an increasing proliferation of basically architectural deci-

sions made, or at least controlled, by non-architectural bureaucrats. But, under the state system, with face-to-face presence of all parties concerned at preliminary meetings, the review homework has already been done at the end of each meeting, and the understanding of the purposes and cross-purposes of participating bodies is aided by verbal exchanges, heated or otherwise, rather than cumbersome and lengthy exchanges of correspondence.

One of the side effects of this conference process has been an educational interchange among parties involved. A city official from, for example, the Bureau of the Budget may not only increase his own comprehension of a project but may also get quick answers, without political repercussions, to some of the technical or costing questions that might have encumbered his approaches to a purely documentary presentation of the project.

Not the least contribution to this educational process is an opportunity for everyone present to rationally evaluate cost figures of a particular job rather than superficially compare square-foot-cost records of previous and not necessarily comparable projects. The essential components of the square-foot cost can be simply explained, and the realities of the particular situation brought to bear.

On the subject of square-foot costs, the Corporation has made detailed analyses of comparable mental health facilities. They have turned their attention to categorical analyses of the costs of recreational space, therapeutic space and dormitory space; this analysis then becomes a guide, but not a constraint upon, the emerging cost figures as the project develops. It is a useful tool of the estimating technique rather than a catalogue of limits.

Endless details of invention and control have made of this whole program a demonstration of how money, management and architecture can unite in new dimensions of public benefit.

Middletown Rehabilitation Center is the first completed of 15 such centers New York State is building at existing mental hospitals. The design objective is to bring together and express, in community-related rather than austerely institutional buildings, new programs in pre-discharge therapy that had become fragmented and poorly housed in state hospitals during recent years.

The Middletown center is designed to actively enhance mental rehabilitation procedures in advance of patients' return to

New centers at state hospitals
designed for rehabilitation, not custody

their own communities. For that purpose, the architects sought to achieve the effect of a busy small town. The building's one-story and two-story elements enclose two courtyards that contain towering oak trees. Patient traffic traverses the larger courtyard that is partially sunken and has an outdoor dining area that functions as a miniature town square (see page 96). Glassed arcades that surround this courtyard lead to workshops, classrooms, the cafeteria and to other parts of the building. The second courtyard is a quiet grassy space (right) surrounded by a terrace that provides access to the library, classrooms, and therapy areas. The superstructure in the photo is the cooling tower. Photo at bottom, opposite, is a high-bay exercise game room near the swimming pool and joined by glass arcade to the gymnasium. The vocabulary of brown brick and yellow fascia is sustained throughout.

Entrance to the complex through the "town square" courtyard is approached from the outside through a passage bridged by second-story offices (top, opposite).

Directly across the "town square" from the bridged passageway is an entrance to the lobby of a 400-seat, multi-purpose chapel-auditorium. This lobby also has a terraced entrance from the grounds outside the complex and another door leading to a gymnasium and other recreation facilities which extend around the south end of the town square and terminate in a cafeteria to the left of the bridged entrance passage.

The rehabilitation program seeks maximum development of each patient's capacities for self-sufficiency. For this, the center offers medical, counseling and testing services and a variety of educational and vocational activities.

REHABILITATION CENTER, Middletown State Hospital, Middletown, New York. Architects: *Helge Westermann/Richard Miller Associates;* mechanical engineers: *Caretsky & Associates;* structural engineers: *Lev Zetlin & Associates;* landscape architects: *Robert Zion & Harold Breen.*

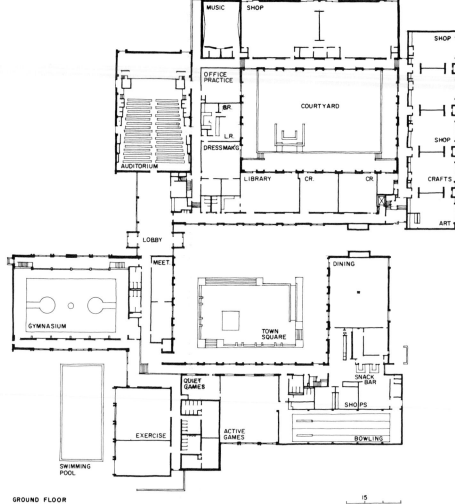

GROUND FLOOR

Labels on ground floor plan: MUSIC, SHOP, SHOP, OFFICE PRACTICE, COURTYARD, SHOP, BR., CRAFTS, LR., DRESSMAK'G, AUDITORIUM, LIBRARY, CR., CR., ART, LOBBY, MEET., DINING, GYMNASIUM, TOWN SQUARE, SNACK BAR, SHOPS, QUIET GAMES, EXERCISE, ACTIVE GAMES, BOWLING, SWIMMING POOL

15

Designed around courtyards to function as a cluster of buildings rather than as a single building, the Middletown Rehabilitation Center has many features in common with other community centers. The large court (photo top left) is called the town square, and the arcade surrounding it gives access to classrooms, gymnasium and meeting rooms. The administration offices are on the second level bridging vehicle and pedestrian access to the larger court. Interior rooms such as the secretarial space (left) have clerestory windows facing the court side. Activities are carefully zoned but are related visually across courts and sequentially in terms of patient traffic. The objective has been to enhance the sense of scale and place with reference to ultimate community experience.

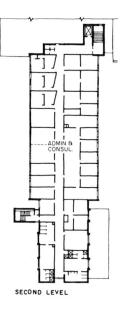

ADMIN & CONSUL.

SECOND LEVEL

A great house for children
copes with the urban scene

Houses for 192 psychotic children 5 to 16 years old have been designed and scaled to relate not only to the residential experience of their occupants but also to the massive urban scene surrounding their site on the grounds of the Bronx State Hospital. The urban scene is not new to these children. But the overwhelming presence of high-rise, and the street canyons from which many of the patients come, have been counteracted in this facility by design emphasis on residential aspects and human scale. This was done in spite of the enormous problem of housing almost 200 children in what is, in fact, a single building.

The planning concept involves clusters of domicile units in which small-group living will be enriched by easy access to central facilities reflecting community participation within the scope of the young patients. It is enlivened by an irregular succession of courts in which colorful sculpture and wall decorations enhance the sense of childhood participation. The children are housed in a series of eight two-story buildings. These buildings are arranged to permit each group of eight children to live in some semblance of family relationship in four double bedrooms opening on a living room. Three such 8-member groups will live on a ward floor with common social and dining spaces on each floor.

The first floor of each two-story living unit will adjoin diagnostic, evaluation and therapy sections as well as educational and administrative spaces. Each second floor will contain a small infirmary and some educational spaces.

In addition to the central courtyards, there are ample spaces for outdoor recreation with playing fields and picnic areas as well as sheltered play terraces adjacent to the complex.

The exteriors are of brick bearing wall construction with steel joist framing, concrete plank roofs and concrete floor slab.

Although interior materials and decoration had to be selected for durability, the architects strove for warmth in color and texture by the use of painted block walls and vinyl asbestos floors with accent colors.

BRONX CHILDREN'S PSYCHIATRIC HOSPITAL, Bronx State Hospital, Bronx, New York. Architects: *The Office of Max O. Urbahn;* structural engineers: *Wayman C. Wing;* mechanical enginers: *Tizian Associates, Inc.;* site engineers: *Seelye Stevenson Value & Knecht.*

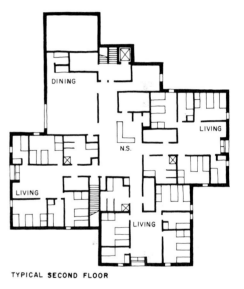

TYPICAL SECOND FLOOR

Plan of the Bronx Children's Psychiatric Hospital encompasses the huge problem of handling almost 200 boys and girls of varied diagnoses in a single giant complex with a full panoply of interdisciplinary psychiatric, medical and educational services. Division of the children into family-sized residential groups with opportunities for interaction are aspects of the design intended to pre-adjust the children for return to the outside communities from which they come. The use of sculpture and decoration was a strong design component—inside and out—and was implemented by the architects' personal visits to the brick-yard for design and casting of gay figures into brick walls and the Nivola sculptured animals and relief in concrete as shown in photos above. The plan shows division of the complex into three main categories of space.

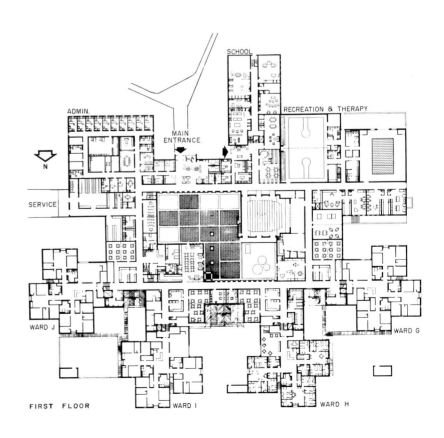

FIRST FLOOR

A GUIDANCE CLINIC AT THE CHILDREN'S HOSPITAL OF PHILADELPHIA

The Philadelphia Children's Mental Health Center, designed to relate to—but to function independently of—the Children's Hospital of Philadelphia, is located on the southwest corner of the 34th and Civic Center Boulevard site. The building (total area: 79,500 sq ft) was designed so that its materials, scale and over-all milieu would relate to children in as intimate—almost residential—feeling as possible; in contrast to the more clinical environment of a general hospital. To help emotionally disturbed children to run and to play and to lead, so to speak, normal lives, all of the major children's services in this facility are related to outdoor play areas. Even though this facility is large in itself and attached to an enormous building, every consideration was given to defining functions as clearly as possible and breaking up the immensity of the project with smaller, more comprehensible parts, each related to a child-scale activity.

The Children's Mental Health Center has its own entrances and driveways along with several outdoor courts and play areas. It has a main, grade-level driveway and "drop off" which allows children or adults to go directly into the school at grade level or to go down some convenient stairs to a courtyard to the nurseries or main entrance and lobby which are one level below grade. Besides this entry, there is a driveway ramp and turn-around, one level below grade which directly serves the main lobby and also the nurseries.

The reason for these different entrances was to separate the very different flows of traffic to the over-all facility and the school, and to give the precious grade-level outdoor areas to the traffic of children instead of cars and parking.

Basically, the four-story facility purposely appears as a two-story building and those two stories which are the first and second floors are for the main children's functions. The first floor at grade level houses the school and has its own entrances for the children, with the main entrance to the facility being one level down below grade; see grade drawings at right.

....

PHILADELPHIA CHILDREN'S MENTAL HEALTH CENTER. Architects: *Office of Bruce Porter Arneill*. Engineers: *A.W. Lookup Company* (structural); *Leonard Weger Associates, Inc.* (mechanical). Consultants: *Sylvan R. Shemitz & Associates* (lighting); *Robert A. Hansen Associates* (acoustical); *Louis Audette* (TV); *Office of Dan Kiley* (landscape); *Raymond Doernberg* (interiors). General contractors: *Baltimore Contractors, Inc.*

The second level is the living level for children and two families. These two floors which resemble a standard urban row house layout (the school being the living level and the inpatient being the sleeping level) are sandwiched between the "adult" levels. The lowest level (Level A) under the school provides the main entrance by car, bus or elevator from parking below, and it contains all of the main outpatient consultation rooms.

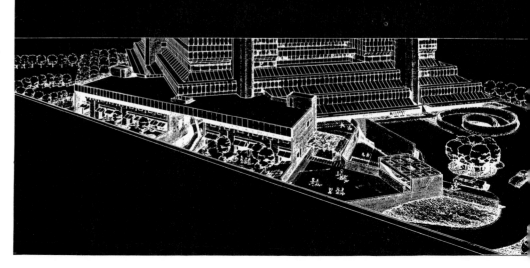

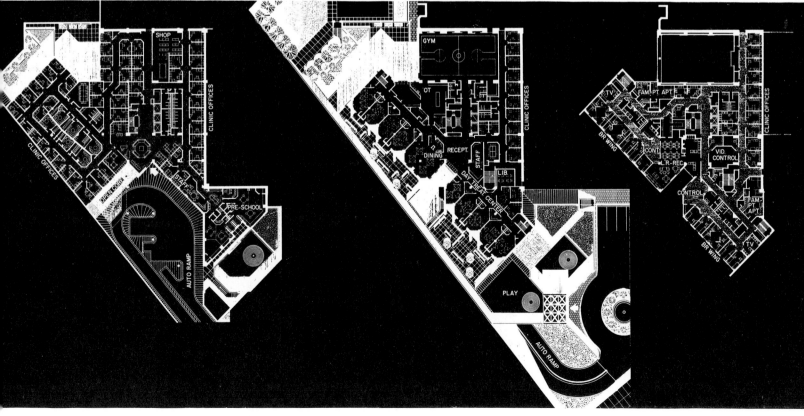

Center for child development and rehabilitation

■ Highly specialized though this study-diagnostic-treatment center is, its design, and the medical premises on which it is based, have broad implications for other such facilities. The Center, a part of the Crippled Children's Division of the University of Oregon Medical Center, is a complex of three buildings in whose carefully controlled environment the physical, mental and emotional needs of handicapped children can be evaluated, and where multi-discipline teams can be trained to treat the "whole child." Each structure has a different function—administration and recreation; research, diagnosis and treatment; residence for out-of-town patients, special-observation patients and a few parents—but all structures have in common the fact that the first two floors are basically patient areas, with the third floor for staff and students.

Essential to the Center's program is the process of unseen observation, by doctors and students, of children in real-life situations. A mezzanine "spine" or viewing corridor solves this difficult three-dimensional problem: from the mezzanine there is a view down to the "holding areas" and from the "alleys" on the first floor there is direct observation of the patient work areas on that level. Intricate electrical and electronic connections make possible a variety of communication systems, including lecturing a distant class during observation, video and audio tape recordings, etc. As many as 200 doctors, professors, and students can observe more than 50 rooms without being seen by those they observe.

The Center was jointly funded; the Public Health Service contributed 75 per cent, the State of Oregon 25 per cent. Per square foot cost, including equipment and furnishings was amazingly low, possible, the architects say, through orientation of the buildings to north and south which eliminated the locally difficult east and west exposures and greatly reduced the cooling load, and through use of brick bearing walls and poured pan joists.

CHILD DEVELOPMENT AND REHABILITATION CENTER, Portland, Oregon. Architects: *Campbell-Yost & Partners.* Engineers: *R. R. Bradshaw Consulting Engineers of Oregon, Inc.,* structural; *Keith Krucheck, Inc.,* mechanical; *Klawa-Mehlig & Associates,* electrical; *Robin M. Towne & Associates,* acoustical. Laboratory program consultants: *Earl L. Walls & Associates.* Interiors: *Campbell-Yost & Associates.* Contractors: *Todd Building Company,* general; *Imperial Plumbing & Heating, Inc.,* Portland; *Bohm Electric Company, electrical.*

Edmund Y. Lee

Photo Art Commercial Studio

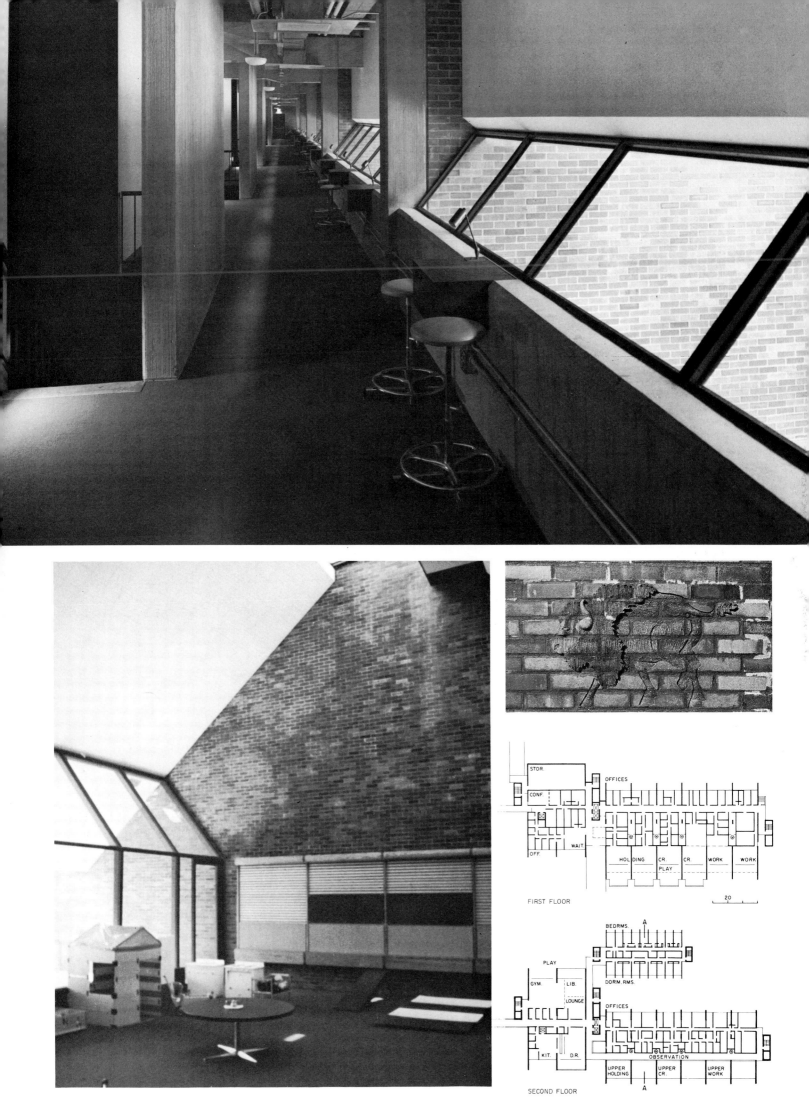

FIRST FLOOR

STOR.
CONF.
OFFICES
OFF.
WAIT.
HOLDING
CR.
PLAY
CR.
WORK
WORK

20

SECOND FLOOR

BEDRMS.
A
PLAY
GYM.
LIB.
DORM. RMS.
LOUNGE
OFFICES
KIT.
D.R.
OBSERVATION
UPPER
HOLDING
UPPER
CR.
UPPER
WORK
A

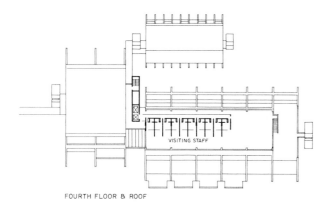

SECTION A-A

FOURTH FLOOR & ROOF

UPPER DORM. RMS.

THIRD FLOOR

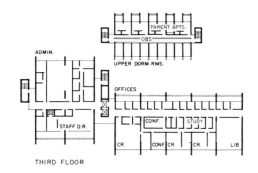

The sloping brick bearing walls are not only strong visual elements and a means of breaking up the mass of what is a sizable building, thus mitigating its institutional look and humanizing its scale; they also act as acoustical buffers between the holding rooms and outdoor play spaces. (The angle of slope evolved from the angle needed for photographing the holding areas from the "spine" observation corridor.) The architects commissioned a wood relief by LeRoy Setziol (below) and a tapestry (not shown). In addition, designs in the brick along the patient corridors were conceived and carved by the architects' staff (page 103). The broad scope of the Center's work resulted from the success of a demonstration clinic based on the hypothesis that "children with mental retardation must be in as near normal a state of health as possible for learning at maximum potential."

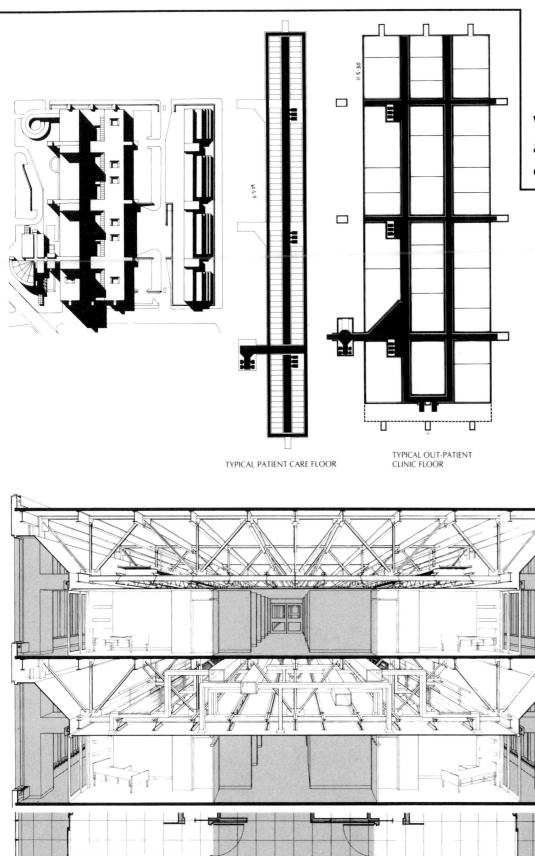

TYPICAL PATIENT CARE FLOOR

TYPICAL OUT-PATIENT
CLINIC FLOOR

Woodhull medical and mental health center, Brooklyn, N. Y.

Done in association with Russo & Sonder and now nearing completion, this hospital program of 850,000 square feet is accommodated in three lower levels of service, ambulatory care and treatment, above them a parking level, a level for mental health care and over the eastern track five levels of in-patient care. Each floor is served by a level containing the mechanical services.

Plan organization

In this scheme the simple, horizontal arrangement of spine and served volumes is replaced by a more complex linear matrix. On both patient care levels and on the much larger lower three floors circulatory routes of varying widths alternate with broader use zones. The system can expand horizontally at the lower levels to provide another track of use zone and circulatory spine and upward growth of two more levels for inpatient care is possible. At the ambulatory care level, clinics are accommodated in three column-free tracks 68 ft 10½ in. wide.

Movement system

In so deep a building complex the major circulatory routes are developed beyond the function of access, into major orienting devices providing amenity beyond the purely clinical function of the building. At significant points the circulatory route is distended to invade the use zone to provide places for sitting, gathering, etc. Such places form points of reference in an otherwise anonymous matrix of regular interior streets.

Urban form

The linear tracks of space served by glass roofed indoor streets and the visitors daylit corridor suggest an affinity to street patterns of the neighborhood. The eventual addition of housing for staff parallel and close to the west boundary of the site will reinforce the existing street pattern, and, in addition will create a linear park running north-south.

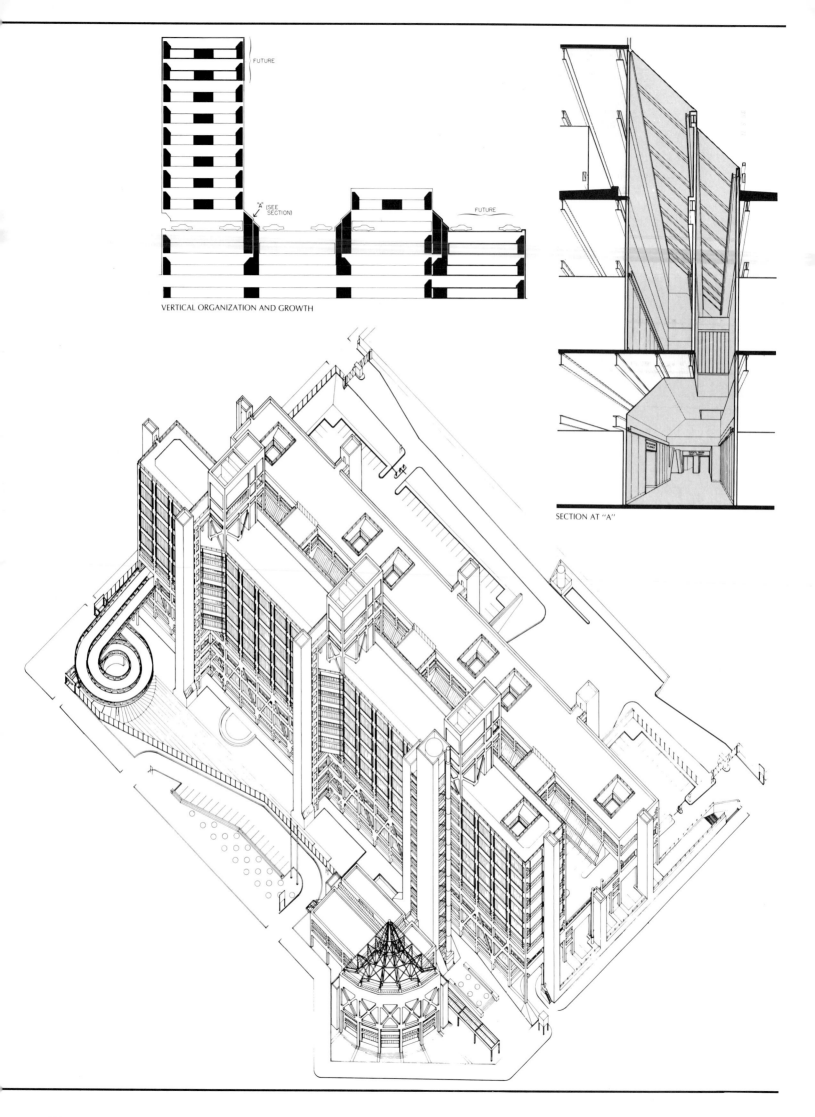

VERTICAL ORGANIZATION AND GROWTH

FUTURE

"A" (SEE SECTION)

FUTURE

SECTION AT "A"

Architecture to help drug addicts calls for speed and inventiveness

The response of architects and the Facilities Improvement Corporation to program requirements of the New York State Narcotic Addiction Control Commission has been prompt and varied. Facilities tend to center in the environs of New York City where the majority of the state's addicts are located. The pressures of time and urban location have demanded that architects and commission programers use great inventiveness in the design and rehabilitation of urban facilities.

This Manhattan Rehabilitation Center, designed by Gueron Lepp and Associates, demonstrates some of that inventiveness. It is a 400-bed narcotics rehabilitation facility for women and consists of three separate buildings served by common mechanical and kitchen facilities. The two buildings which form the treatment portion of the center were existing structures which were extensively renovated. One of these is an old public library which was converted to a treatment center. The other was a motel building which was converted for dormitory and activity uses.

The third building is an entirely new structure (right and page 108) which serves as a reception and administration building. This building also has facilities for housing 50 patients during detoxification.

One major problem in conversion of the motel was to screen the view from the street and provide some security at windows. This was solved by the addition of a bronze-tinted aluminum screen on the street side of the building. There are bedrooms for 350 women in addition to classrooms and sanitary facilities on converted motel floors. The ground floor and the basement (formerly lobby and parking garage) were converted to administrative support offices, infirmary, visitors' lounge, food services and mechanical spaces.

The library building completes the interior court on this site and provides additional classrooms and vocational training areas as well as a library and gymnasium.

The architects and commission programers were able to discern the general potential of the existing buildings as more or less conventional spaces to which addicts might respond. The special problems of early confinement and analysis were handled appropriately in the new structure.

MANHATTAN REHABILITATION CENTER, New York, New York. Architects: *Gueron, Lepp and Associates;* mechanical engineers: *William Kaplan & Associates;* structural engineers: *Zoldos & Meagher;* construction contractors: *George Rosen & Son Inc.*

Exterior of the new building at Manhattan Rehabilitation Center is an expression of the concrete frame with splayed walls of dark brown brick to harmonize with a bronze-colored aluminum security screen on the adjoining dormitory building, a converted motel. Spaces in the new building include combined dining and recreational rooms, doctors' offices, treatment rooms, admissions facilities and an exercise room.

A small multi-faith chapel (above right) was included in the rehabilitation of the existing library, which now adjoins the new building. All patient "activities" are housed in the sturdy, turn-of-the-century structure including classrooms, vocational training shops, library, gymnasium and beauty shop. Large story heights in the building permitted addition of mezzanine floors for the patients' library and two additional classrooms.

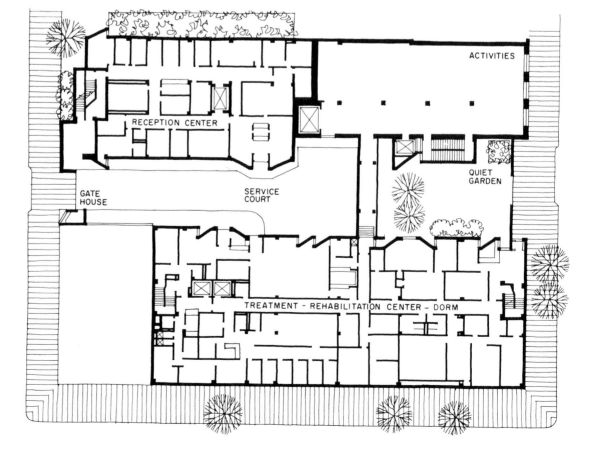

ACTIVITIES

RECEPTION CENTER

QUIET GARDEN

GATE HOUSE

SERVICE COURT

TREATMENT - REHABILITATION CENTER - DORM

Retardation research lab has
total flexibility for basic sciences

Robert Damora photos

The $12-million Institute for Basic Research in Mental Retardation, located on Staten Island adjacent to New York's Willowbrook State School for the mentally retarded, is the first institution in the state (and perhaps in the world) to focus programs in eight to ten disciplines in the basic sciences entirely on mental retardation with all facilities housed in one structure. The building has been finished and construction and outfitting of its laboratories are now under way.

The structure is of steel and prestressed concrete, and stone panels. It consists of a 5-story concrete research tower, to which are joined three single-story wings. One wing contains administrative offices. Another has wards for 40 patients. The third wing houses experimental animals.

An important element in the design of the building is the flexibility that has been built into the laboratory spaces to accommodate changes in research techniques and the diversity of procedures of many disciplines. The structural module is 25 by 10 feet, and each laboratory floor is laid out in 40 such modules. Movable walls allow rearrangement of space within the module system as research presses in new directions.

Also serving flexible layout of laboratories is a vertical distribution system for utilities at module intervals (see page 91). Further, each laboratory floor has a 5-foot mechanical space above its walk-on ceiling, with many knockout panels for access so that utility lines can be serviced without disturbing laboratory work.

Laboratories have been laid out so that any scientist can get from his work area to the administration section or to the wards without passing through any other scientist's work area.

The same principle of flexibility is built into the wards which are designed so that patients selected from the Willowbrook population for specific research projects can be studied under controlled conditions in groups of two to forty. These wards are solely for patients under observation.

In the administration area, there is a divisible multi-purpose room for scientific meetings in addition to interview rooms specifically designed and equipped with instruments and projectors.

INSTITUTE FOR BASIC RESEARCH IN MENTAL RETARDATION, Staten Island, New York. Architects: *Fordyce & Hamby Associates* (now Hamby, Kennerly & Slomanson); consulting engineers: *Syska & Hennessy, Inc.*

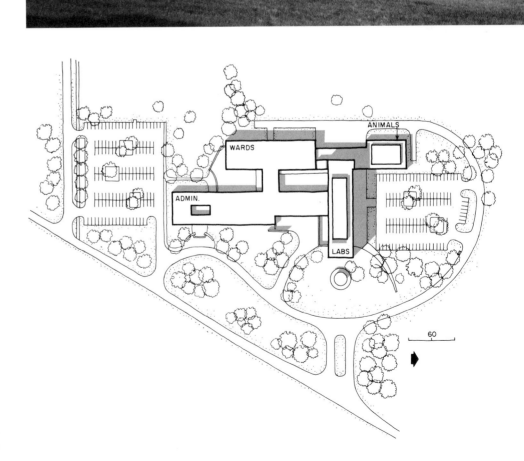

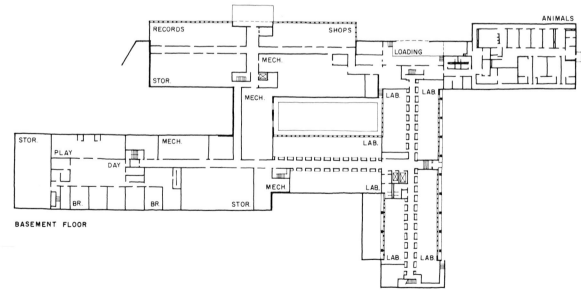

RECORDS

SHOPS

ANIMALS

LOADING

STOR.

MECH.

MECH.

LAB.

LAB.

STOR.

PLAY

MECH.

LAB.

DAY

MECH.

LAB.

BR.

BR.

STOR.

MECH.

LAB.

LAB.

LAB.

BASEMENT FLOOR

Virtually total flexibility in laboratory design was the objective of architects and engineers at the Institute for Basic Research in Mental Retardation. The basic design module is 10 by 25 feet with wide ceiling span as shown in the photograph above for unlimited options in placement of partitions according to discipline requirements. Mechanical spaces over ceilings and vertical service cores with a variety of piped fluids placed at ultimate module intervals (opposite) further support flexibility. The two-level support facilities house general administrative and operating spaces and a small patient wing in which selected patients from nearby Willowbrook State Hospital for the Retarded are housed during some phases of research. Special rooms for controlled atmospheres and pressures aid patient research.

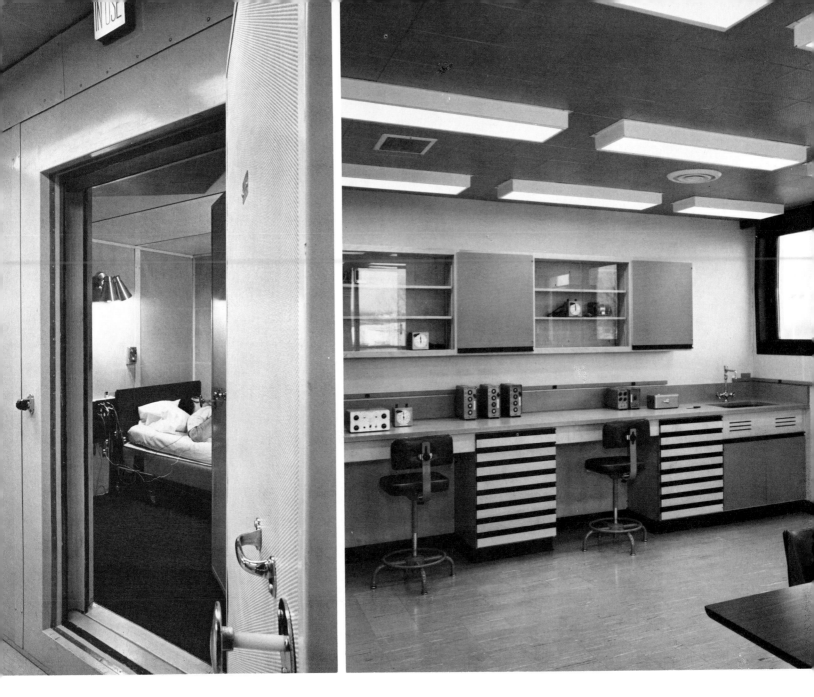

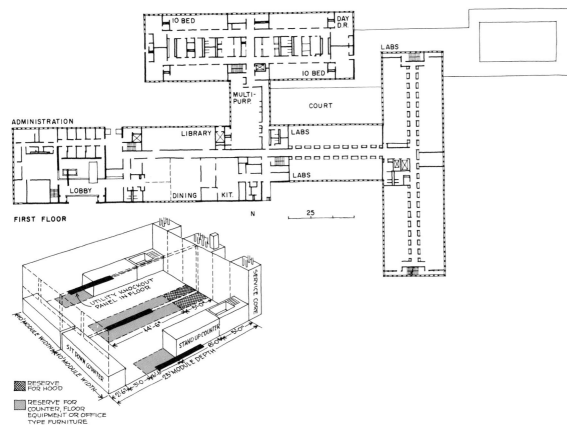

IO BED

DAY D.R.

IO BED

LABS

MULTI-PURP.

COURT

ADMINISTRATION

LIBRARY

LABS

LABS

LOBBY

DINING

KIT.

N

25

FIRST FLOOR

UTILITY KNOCKOUT PANEL IN FLOOR

SERVICE CORE

5'-0"

14'-6"

STAND UP COUNTER

5'-0"

10' MODULE WIDTH

10' MODULE WIDTH

SIT DOWN COUNTER

2'-6"

3'-0"

4'-6"

8'-0"

25' MODULE DEPTH

▨ RESERVE FOR HOOD

▦ RESERVE FOR COUNTER, FLOOR EQUIPMENT OR OFFICE TYPE FURNITURE

Architectural stimulus and response in a school for the mentally retarded

The Wilton State School for Mentally Retarded, the first of 11 such new facilities planned for New York State, houses a population of 500 mentally retarded children and adults. The program of the school calls for each resident to be scheduled for activities suited to his needs and capacities. Training includes activities of daily living and a full program of educational and prevocational training for those who may be able to develop personal independence.

The architects' interpretation and development of the program, in cooperation with the Department of Mental Hygiene, took into account the fact that the inhabitants would be indoors for nine or ten months of each year, so that the concept was directed to provide a complete community experience indoors. The over-all plan, therefore, simulates a system of streets and houses with as much diversity as those terms imply.

A sense of residence is generated in living units which are arranged in four clover-leaf clusters of four structures each. One structure in each cluster is a two-story unit so that there is a total of five house-size patient floors in each cluster.

Each floor is divided into three corner-groups of four two-bed rooms opening onto a two-part living room made up of a central activity area and a glazed corner. Each two-bed room has built-in storage for personal belongings and a round plastic window designed to relate to the outdoors while preserving a sense of security. Each 24-patient floor has a common activity area and dining space and each cluster hub is a two-story high space called an environmental center which serves as a near-home gathering plaza and directional clue to the passageway connection to the central activities building. Each cluster looks out on a peripheral play area and in toward its own environmental center.

The main building has learning spaces connected by "streets" and divided into quadrants allocated to identifiable categories of activity. Quadrants for recreation, education, medical services and occupational shops and kitchens are arranged around a central square which students identify as a main plaza and to which the four "streets" from living quarters enter on diagonals at the corners.

WILTON STATE SCHOOL, Wilton, New York. Architects: *Conklin & Rossant*; structural engineers: *Zetlin Desimone & Chaplin*; mechanical engineers: *Caretsky & Associates*.

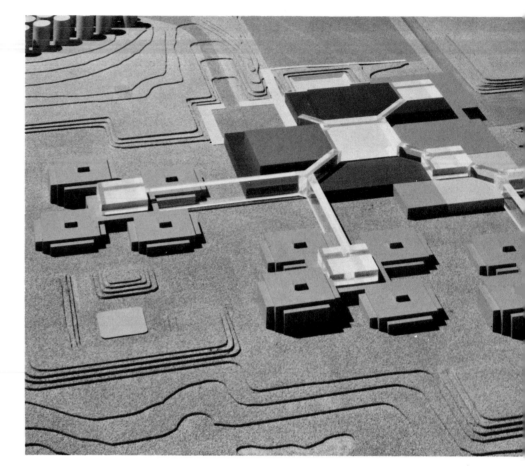

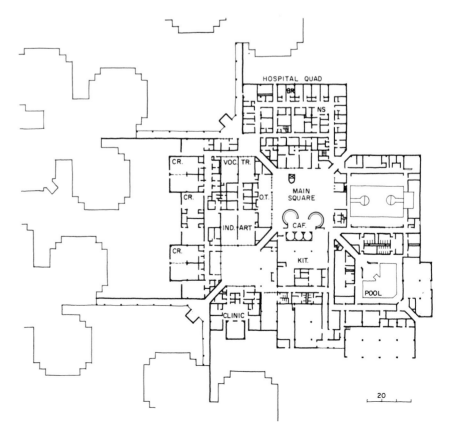

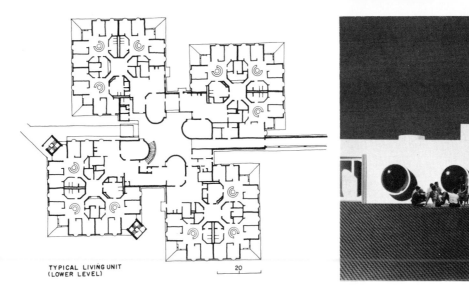

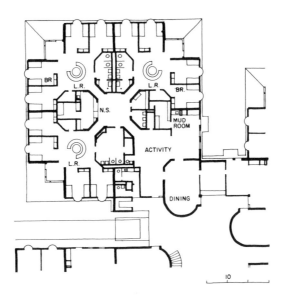

TYPICAL LIVING UNIT
(LOWER LEVEL)   20

BR   L.R.   L.R.   BR

N.S.

MUD ROOM

ACTIVITY

DINING

10

The street idea in the Wilton school plan is reinforced by four smaller squares peripheral to and visible from the main central square. Two of these sub-squares identify linkage to the corner meeting points of pairs of living-unit passageways. The other two relate to and identify activity areas which are grouped as recreational, educational, clinical or occupational in quadrants of the central building. Each sub-square can be readily identified by a characteristic drug store, barber shop, or other street-corner aspect. The main plaza has a cafeteria for noon meals which is laid out to include three smaller circular dining areas intended to preserve some aspects of residential scale. The main plaza also has "teaching walls" with lively lights and sound devices to stimulate outgoing responses of residents as shown in elevations on page 114.

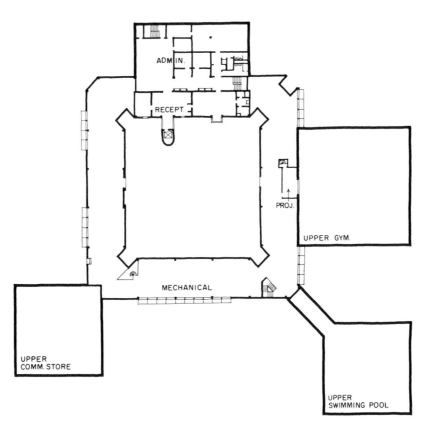

ADMIN.

RECEPT.

PROJ.

UPPER GYM.

MECHANICAL

UPPER COMM. STORE

UPPER SWIMMING POOL

113

North

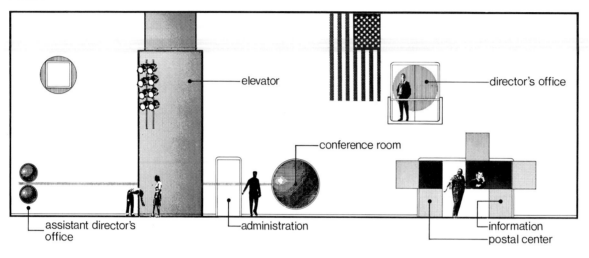

assistant director's office — elevator — director's office — conference room — administration — information — postal center

West

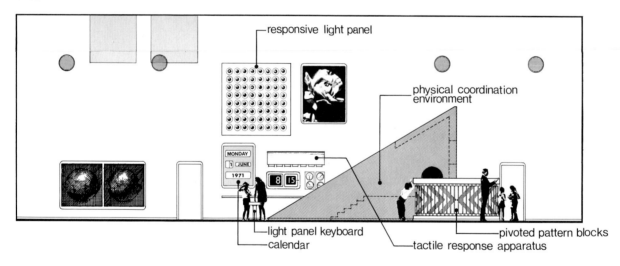

responsive light panel — physical coordination environment — MONDAY 1 JUNE 1971 — 8 15 — light panel keyboard — calendar — tactile response apparatus — pivoted pattern blocks

East

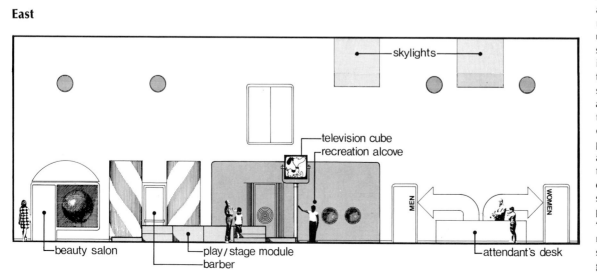

skylights — television cube — recreation alcove — MEN — WOMEN — beauty salon — play/stage module — barber — attendant's desk

Rendered elevations of three of the walls of the main square in the central building at Wilton State School for the mentally retarded restate and underscore fundamental design objectives: to increase innate capacities of residents to the fullest possible extent so that they may not vegetate as their affliction inclines them to do in the purely custodial situation. For example, the overstated graphics and human presence at the toilet-training station on the east wall, the physically responsive light panel and apparatus on the west wall, the "establishment-oriented" reminders on the north—all stimulate and guide the outgoing response.

Alexandre Georges photos

JACKSONVILLE BUILDS FOR ITS EXCEPTIONAL CHILDREN

Because mental retardation occurs with predictable frequency and cuts impartially across all racial and socio-economic lines, every large community can predict with surprising accuracy the incidence of retardation it can expect among its young. Jacksonville's school authorities, intent on helping such unlucky youngsters, commissioned a separate facility for 150 children to replace the special classes they had previously attended at various dispersed locations. Utilizing a heavily wooded site, set well back from the road, William Morgan developed a plan that pivots four classroom clusters around a central assembly area. Most of the children suffer from hypertension. They are easily excited by unexpected sights or sounds. And because such hypertension is infectious, each classroom is fitted with a small "time-out" room (see plan) where an excited youngster can be isolated until he regains his composure. Other special adaptations include a therapy pool centered in the administration spaces and the deliberate installation of a wide variety of door and window hardware. The advanced pavilion includes a family living area and model apartment where girls learn domestic skills and a shop where older boys receive pre-occupational training.

SCHOOL FOR EXCEPTIONAL CHILDREN, Jacksonville, Florida. Architect: *William Morgan*; structural engineer: *H. W. Keister*; mechanical and electrical engineers: *Evans & Hammond, Inc.*; contractor: *Newman Construction Company.*

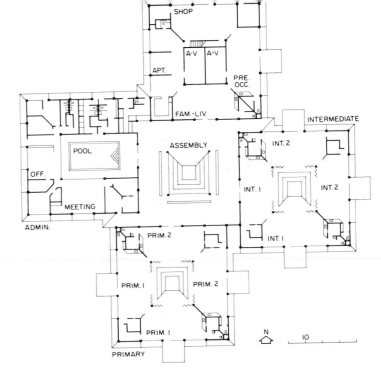

The classroom clusters, each with its pyramid roof, give the plan its visual order and reflect the school's domestic, non-institutional character. The central assembly area (photo below) doubles as a cafeteria and is used in the evening for adult education. The structure is concrete frame, exterior walls are light brown brick, ceilings and soffits are heavy pine plank. Orange carpeting, set against a generally neutral background gives these spaces an uncommon warmth and unity.

Loomis-Shade photos

Horizon House,
a place for readjusting
to community living

■ A place in which to readjust to life in the community is an essential part of mental health programs. Horizon House in Philadelphia, a non-profit voluntary social agency, provides for this in-between program in a three-story building designed for the four aspects of the program: administration, research, case and social program, vocational counselling. Zoning restrictions limited building height to three stories (35 feet), and lot coverage to 80 per cent of the site, but these restrictions actually played into the design solution. The area on which the building is located is a single-family redevelopment area, with new and rehabilitated houses and residential facilities and since the intent of the design was to fit the building into its neighborhood in scale, character and materials, the limitations implied what was actually desired: a non-institutional building. Built to the property lines, like its neighbors, the building was "purposely underplayed," say the architects, to "prevent it from being a discordant element in the area. We wanted the people who use the building to feel like people—not patients."

SITE PLAN

HORIZON HOUSE, Philadelphia, Pennsylvania. Architects: *Francis Cauffman Wilkinson & Pepper, D. Hughes Cauffman,* partner in charge, *John R. Caulk III,* project design. Engineers: *Rothbaum & Davis,* structural; *Sharpless & Whiting,* mechanical; *Louis Moxey,* electrical. Contractor: *McCullough-Howard.*

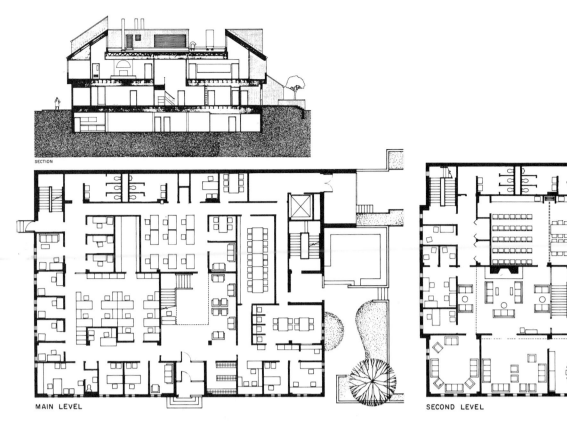

SECTION

MAIN LEVEL

SECOND LEVEL

The role of the building is, in effect, to "substitute for the home, the club, the workshop," and its facilities reflect these needs. In the basement are the restorative vocational activities—a clerical workshop, pre-vocational evaluation rooms, the transitional and terminal shops. On the first floor are administrative and research offices, meeting rooms and library. Social areas are on the second floor, and include meeting rooms of various sizes, for classes, film showings, etc.; lounges; and a kitchen-laundry which is actually part of the vocational program. The pleasantly landscaped garden court adjoins the on-site parking.

ELMCREST PSYCHIATRIC INSTITUTE

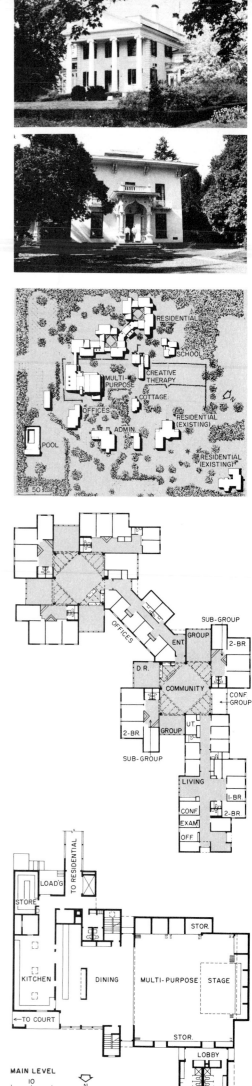

The design of spaces for psychiatric services cannot be codified into universal solutions any more than can the design of spaces for people in general. Certainly, the so-called "indeterminate" spaces seem to work well for in-patient residential activities, but spaces for structured programs such as patients' schools or workshops enter into therapeutic programs by reflecting the atmospheres of discipline and endeavor the patient is likely to encounter in the real world outside.

Elmcrest Psychiatric Institute is a 99-bed private facility for adults and adolescents in Portland, Connecticut. The buildings to accommodate recent doubling of capacity are sited on the cultivated 14-acre semi-rural grounds of three former mansions. The mix of early-American styles of the original buildings, which have housed the operation since its founding in 1938, is shown at top right. The new buildings are designed to introduce a compatible but not imitative vocabulary of a more contemporary aspect.

Architect Jonathan Foote, head of the New Haven based Environmental Design Group, describes the genesis of the project. Medical Director Dr. Louis B. Fierman brought together a group of psychiatrists, architects, administrators and interior designers to create an environment in keeping with strongly developed therapeutic programs with a high level of clinical intensity. Components of the program include mileu therapy which calls for a capability of reproducing the community while sustaining an atmosphere of small self-governing patient groups as well as some of the aspects of family therapy, encounter groups and also some elements of behavior modification techniques of treatment.

The design process itself had many of the aspects of the encounter group. The entire program evolved with many long sessions of interchange among the various specialists. These exchanges were guided at key points by the group member most responsible. Herbert McLaughlin, who was architectural and psychiatric design consultant to the project, was a leader/facilitator in matters relating to his experience in psychiatric design at Marin, Buffalo and other mental health facilities. Dr. Fierman, Elmcrest administrator Allen Cohen, nursing director Joan Schmidt and representatives of the design department of The Psychiatric Institutes of America (a Washington based association representing institute owners) each played a role in the procedure.

There was a particularly active interplay among the design group members in their approaches to the admitting-residential building (center plan at right). Various basic design approaches were considered. These included conventional inpatient nursing unit configurations, some of the proposals of Osmond and other psychiatric workers—and, of course, the "indeterminate" spaces of Marin CMHC (see pp. 126–129) and other mental health facilities.

The indeterminate idea gained precedence with the group, and physical plans were prepared demonstrating degrees of structured organization within the indeterminate concept and responding to specifics of the institute program. A moderately structured plan evolved, as shown, and was fitted into the EDG master plan for this and other buildings of the complex—the school, therapy center, etc.

Designs for the other buildings were similarly generated out of design group interplay but were more straightforward in conventional terms. That is, for example, the multi-purpose building (bottom plan, right) developed out of a need for spaces for eating, meeting and team play. The double-story multipurpose room serves for games, parties, theater and other uses, while a second level over the dining area serves for group encounter meetings and other clinical activities that may be noisier than would be desirable in the communal group spaces.

Similarly, the design for the school rooms sought a more conventional discipline than was applied to the indeterminate inpatient building. Here, on diminished scale, are straighter lines and harder furnishings to foster concentration for whatever attention spans may be available without communal distractions. To preserve a sense of benign discipline, the school corridors are richly warm in color, while classrooms are cool and diligent without being forbidding or austere.

Following is Jonathan Foote's description of the process:

"The architecture of the new Elmcrest is the direct result of a design process which itself is a reflection of the attitudes of the therapeutic community (as previously described).

"The architects, who took an active part in all these phases, were then left with the responsibility of developing architectural continuity within the limits of the program and budget—in short, 'to get it all together.'

"In the new facilities, the two-bed room is the territory of two roommates who, with the occupants of three other two-bed rooms, form an eight-person group. They have their own sub-group territory defined by space change, while remaining an integral part of the forum space, which is group territory for three such 8-patient sub-groups housed around it.

"The sky-lighted forum, central to the community, is the space for the bulk of community activity. This space is extremely flexible and conducive to ambulatory activities and is at all times visible from each of the private two-bed rooms.

"The nurses' station is a major social gathering point and is therefore treated as the kitchen table might be, where patient, family, staff and visitors can interact, rather than feel intimidated by the traditional barrier approach to the nurses' station.

"Isolation of each unit from the whole is minimized by emphasizing the connections between inside and outside, developing a campus plan which focuses on the grounds and the creative therapy center and by the development of centrally located 'meeting places.' From the inside, there will be a con-

Lautman photos

Western cedar siding and pitched roofs give the new buildings at Elmcrest a character with which patients can identify. Both the wood and variations in height are carried to the interior providing accents of rough wood colors and telephone pole columns in contrast to vinyl chairs and plaster walls in tones predominantly yellow and orange. The roof angles permit volume variation and ·skylighting to help identify transitions of space. The central community space, above, is surrounded by alcoves for smaller group activities and by four-bedroom pods of dormitory space, each with its own subgroup alcove — a kind of eight-member family room.

stant awareness of weather, light and season.

"As a member of the community goes from his unit to the creative therapy center, he is made aware of the whole and of the constant activity of the community."

All of the interiors at Elmcrest were the special concern of the design department of Psychiatric Institutes of America. Marge Thomas, director of the department, and Marcia Lacy, project designer, emphasize that "indeterminate," in their parlance, does not mean "indefinite" but has a special character for its own uses in the community. "Each space within the new facility," says Marge Thomas, "was planned and furnished to meet specific needs and perform certain functions. Through experience with other psychiatric facilities, we have learned that large, ill-defined, multipurpose spaces do not work for therapy. Consequently, the over-all facility was designed to create a progression of varied spaces to foster a therapeutic setting for the hospital's program." For example, patient bedrooms (center photo at right) were furnished with specifically designed modular furniture for ease of maintenance without institutional appearance. Colored tackwalls permit individual displays. The rooms are comfortable but not for lounging or nesting. This is in keeping with a treatment philosophy of interaction rather than isolation.

Furniture designed at PIA for community and lounge areas includes sturdy vinyl chairs that can be moved about like giant building blocks (bottom photo, right) and coffee tables strong enough to serve as stages for psychodrama. In smaller subgroup areas, carpeted small platforms strewn with pillows encourage casual sitting to observe the open area.

Patients return from outside activities through an entrance near the kitchen and snack-bar area (top photo) where they can help themselves within usual family limits. Spatial transitions and variety of light and color are enhanced by varied ceiling treatment, pitched or flat, so there is identity and even a sense of privacy despite almost total visibility.

Evaluation programs outlined for Elmcrest include ongoing work by an internal staff committee to develop information for both current use of spaces and for future design guidance. EDG is also working with an environmental physiologist to see if the physical impact of spaces on staff and patients can be measured.

ELMCREST PSYCHIATRIC INSTITUTE, Portland, Connecticut. Architects: *Environmental Design Group—Jonathan L. Foote*, project architect; *Barun K. Basu*, project coordinator. Program and design consultant architect: *Herbert McLaughlin, Kaplan/McLaughlin Architects*. Engineers: *John C. Martin* (structural); *Hubbard, Lawless and Osborne* (mechanical/electrical). Interior designers: *Design Department, Psychiatric Institutes of America—Marge Thomas*, director, *Marcia Lacy*, project designer. Elmcrest Design Group: *Louis B. Fierman*, clinical director; *Allen Cohen*, hospital administrator; *Joan Green* and *Lou Perlin*, unit directors; *Joan Schmidt*, chief of nursing; *John Silverman*, PIA representative; *James Green*, group facilitator. General contractor: *J.H. Hogan, Inc.*

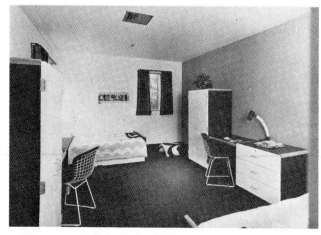

Adventures in architectural services on the frontiers of change

Programming, client education, user research, systems analysis and post-design evaluation are five pillars of support for design at Kaplan and McLaughlin's small office.

A primary objective of design excellence confronts—in today's architectural practice —mounting barriers of budget, competition, technical changes and increasingly complex program requirements. Many clients do not themselves fully understand these requirements or are unable to convey them adequately to their architects. Design of new building types, particularly those in research and medical fields, is especially hampered by limited architectural research and a scarcity of successful examples.

Kaplan and McLaughlin is one firm that has recognized these barriers and done something to surmount them. They have committed themselves to an exceptional degree of client-related activity so that the best design obtainable within their considerable scope of basic talent is in fact the end point of supportive processes which allow good design to flourish.

"Good design," says Herbert McLaughlin, "is useful design in the full sense of the word. Useful denotes, in our mind, not only the functional adequacy of a building, but also its capacity to enhance the enjoyment of both its occupants and its beholders.

"This often means that a useful building is innovative. Conservative wisdom would have it that most innovative buildings do not function well, having too many 'bugs' in their systems. However, in the contradictory mass culture through which we push our way, innovation is certainly necessary to deal with rapid change."

Response to change has been one of the outstanding characteristics of the Kaplan and McLaughlin firm since its inception as a two-man office in January, 1964. The two principals, Ellis Kaplan and Herbert McLaughlin, had been working as designers in the office of another architect. The emergence of new building types, in particular community mental health centers, engaged their interest and Kaplan set up a one-man office to implement and describe some of the emerging criteria under development by the National Institute of Mental Health. When the Marin County Community Mental Health Center (described on pages 126–129) developed as a commission, the two decided to execute it together as a firm. The work increased until today the staff averages 75 people.

Now good design has five supports

The adventures of Kaplan and McLaughlin on the frontiers of change soon brought realization that genuinely architectural involvement would require supportive activities in addition to those conventionally associated with extended services. The questions confronting them in new pre-design problems had no ready method of solution by conventional consultation and coordination processes. There was, in fact, a need for creative architectural participation in developing program concepts which clients themselves agreed were in the vanguard of their own disciplines.

For example, in the Marin County Community Mental Health Center project, architectural translations of therapeutic objectives called for an educational exchange between the disciplines involved as a necessary preamble to both program and design.

Within the architects' office, then, there emerged a category of activity called client education. This was not so much a didactic posture of expertise as it was a gearing up for information exchange with clients on a practical and continuing basis. How this has worked in one case is described in connection with the research facilities for New York Psychiatric Institute on following pages.

Similar client-involvement procedures were developed for design-augmenting purposes in four other categories: in-depth programming (related to but not identical with client education), user research, systems analysis, and post-occupancy project evaluation.

The choice of examples illustrating these supporting services on these pages should not imply that they are used separately on one project and not on another. In some degree, each is enlisted as circumstances indicate on any or all projects. Further, the predominant presence of medical-related facilities in these examples is not construed as indicating special appropriateness for these fields. The processes are, in fact, universally applicable throughout the diverse architectural practice of this firm.

RESEARCH BUILDING PROGRAMMING VIA CLIENT-ARCHITECT EDUCATION

This research addition to the New York Psychiatric Institute is physically and programmatically related to the Columbia-Presbyterian Medical Center and is also a part of the New York State mental health system. It was designed by Kaplan and McLaughlin with Morris Ketchum Jr. and Associates as associated architects.

In early user-interviews, researchers did not anticipate rapid growth or change and felt that interdepartmental relationships were not very important. These responses seemed quite contrary to prior basic program research and were perhaps being overstructured by researchers' present experience with extremely cramped quarters. Therefore, two lines of inquiry into future operations were pursued.

A series of interviews was developed to analyze the types of contact, both casual and structured, which researchers were already having and would desire to have in the future. Careful analysis was made of the interaction patterns which existed in terms of corridors, elevators, conference rooms, lounges, public outdoor spaces, dining facilities, offices and labs with particular emphasis on unstructured interaction.

The initial attitude of skepticism changed as various potentials were explored, and the plan shown here reflects that change.

The second line of inquiry was developed around the possibility that the researchers had, either consciously or unconsciously, been limiting the size and scope of projects due to limited existing physical facilities.

Characteristically, animal experiments using large or middle-sized animals had not been conducted. After considerable questioning, researchers remained firm in their opinion that they would probably not want to do experiments with human subjects involving large-scale spaces, and also they could not conceive of a circumstance in which they would wish to experiment on elephants.

In the course of research on the attitudes of scientists towards the buildings they use and, arising from this, attitudes of architects towards researchers, it was found that all too often laboratory planning practice has been to enclose the scientist in a windowless box. At the same time the researcher tends to place a relatively low value on the importance of the visual quality of his environment.

The educative process, then, sought common ground on which sensible and sensitive architecture and a reasonable respect for visual values on the part of the researcher could meet. Then detailed analysis of functional space requirements and relationships developed on a firm base of user-architect communication.

Engineers: *Joseph R. Loring & Associates (mechanical); Severud-Perrone-Sturm-Conlin-Bandel (structural).*

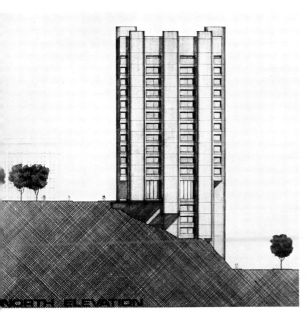

NORTH ELEVATION

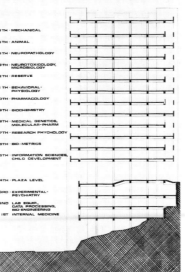

15TH · MECHANICAL
15TH · ANIMAL
14TH · NEUROPATHOLOGY
13TH · NEUROTOXICOLOGY, MICROBIOLOGY
12TH · RESERVE
11TH · BEHAVIORAL · PHYSIOLOGY
10TH · PHARMACOLOGY
9TH · BIOCHEMISTRY
8TH · MEDICAL GENETICS, MOLECULAR · PHARM
7TH · RESEARCH PSYCHOLOGY
6TH · BIO·METRICS
5TH · INFORMATION SCIENCES, CHILD DEVELOPMENT
4TH · PLAZA LEVEL
3RD · EXPERIMENTAL · PSYCHIATRY
2ND · LAB EQUIP., DATA PROCESSING, BIO·ENGINEERING
1ST INTERNAL MEDICINE

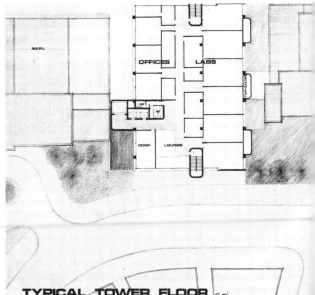

TYPICAL TOWER FLOOR

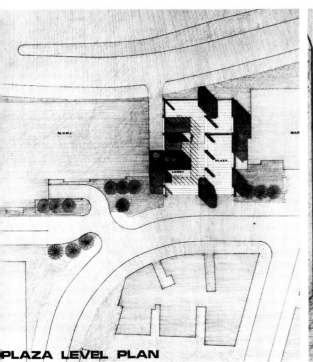

PLAZA LEVEL PLAN

LOUNGE

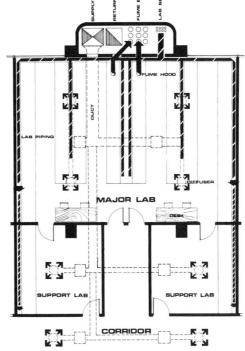

MAJOR LAB

SUPPORT LAB

SUPPORT LAB

CORRIDOR

The building has 16 floors (about 180,000 gross square feet) of research space with emphasis on the behavioral and biological sciences.

The site is an "unusable" portion of New York's 168th Street which plunges down a cliff from the medical center above to Riverside Drive below (plan opposite). Before the site provided a visual release at the end of 168th Street and was one of the few open spaces for the neighborhood.

The design develops an open plaza at 168th Street which maintains the westward view from the neighborhood to the Hudson. The plan emphasizes possibilities for unstructured interaction by maintaining an extremely simple circulation system and a series of interlocking, two-story lounge spaces adjacent to each elevator. These offer maximum opportunity for casual meeting and communication between the various disciplines represented in this facility.

The plan is zoned into four areas of use: offices, circulation, subsidiary lab and major lab. The location of circulation on each floor is able to be shifted considerably to adjust to the ratio of space types within each department.

Mechanical elements are given clear expression in the projected design. Vertical shafts for elevators, stairs and mechanical services are all located on the exterior for maximum flexibility of space arrangement and use on each floor.

MENTAL HEALTH CENTER REVISITED
TO EVALUATE DESIGN EFFECTS

In an attempt to evaluate the success or failure of design methods applied to a new building type, Kaplan and McLaughlin twice revisited the Marin County Community Mental Health Center; once for staff conferences just after completion and again a few months after it had been put in operation. The purpose was first to articulate for the staff the design response to the therapeutic program and second to examine the immediate interaction of the architecture and the people it houses under operating conditions. The third phase was another series of interviews held after the center had been in operation long enough to see how the building performs under changing conditions (see page 128).

The response by patients and staff to the evaluation procedure, the architects report, was unusually organized, perceptive and generally enthusiastic. As might be expected it turned out that some details of design might have been done differently (closet space, food service lines, meeting rooms, security devices, etc.). The over-all conclusion, however, was that the building works well and clearly demonstrates that architectural design can and does enter actively into the therapeutic milieu and that the mentally ill respond positively and in an unusually structured way to innovative, complex architecture. Further, and unexpectedly, a quality of non-rectilinear openness is highly valued and contributes to group interaction. (Code writers, please take note.) The image sought was that of a benign institution rather than a home and appears to be correct for this type of center.

The evaluation process, the architects point out, is necessarily subjective, since there are few ways to quantify the reactions of individuals to space. The method used was to set up a series of interviews with staff and selected patients, develop group interaction sessions and to collect information in the form of behavior reports, statistics and other data considered as useful indicators.

Evaluation was conducted by a team of architects, psychologists and sociologists who were experienced in building evaluation. Kaplan and McLaughlin participated in the process to the extent of organizational and review meetings and joined in some of the interviews and group meetings. Most of the actual evaluation work, however, was done by the independent firm of Building Program Associates of San Francisco. This firm, headed by architect Gerald Davis, is now The Environmental Analysis Group.

Details of the findings are not really the subject here so much as the extension of the architectural function into the evaluation process. The confirmation of specific architectural effects on patients and staff lays ground for improving future design.

Engineers: G. L. Gendler & Associates (mechanical); Rutherford & Chekene (structural).

UPPER LEVEL

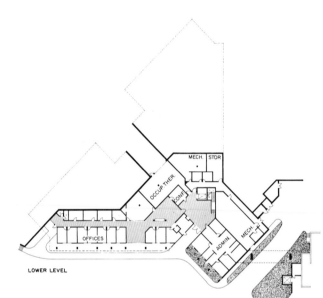

LOWER LEVEL

The Marin C.M.H.C. was completed in 1968 at a cost of approximately $1,250,000, excluding site work, furnishings, and fees. It is a two-story, poured-in-place concrete structure with full air conditioning. Interior finishes are generally exposed, painted concrete, acoustical tile ceiling, plaster walls and carpeted floors. The area of the building is approximately 39,500 square feet.

The building consists of four essential elements: Two triangular treatment units for inpatients and day patients; a bridge linking these units to the existing Marin general hospital and containing a medical library and conference rooms; administration and reception area; and a mechanical floor below the two treatment units.

The center was sited on a steep hillside. This allowed it to have a horizontal organization and a close relationship to the ground. A noticeable aspect of the design, seen in the section, features high triangular spaces with clerestory lighting around a low, large, square central space. The result is an irregularly defined space with a character of openness to which light from clerestories provides changes throughout the day.

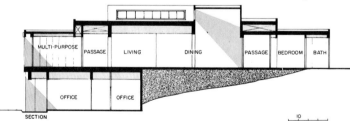

SECTION

Interior views of Marin County Community Mental Health Center
show unconstrained variety of space and light
in common rooms in treatment areas.

The underlying drive and philosophy of this firm of Kaplan and McLaughlin may be best conveyed in the following paragraphs from a statement by Herbert McLaughlin on the occasion of opening a New York branch office: "It is too easy to blame failure on the pace at which the world moves and on the rigidity of construction. Certainly the architect's task is difficult, keeping up with both social and technological change, but it is made more difficult by the fact that many architects have not developed enough techniques to enable them to analyze their work well, both before and after it is built.

"The profession is now making very promising efforts in the field. User research and multi-disciplinary design teams are gaining new applications. Building evaluation and the use of systems analysis in architectural design are rare, but there is a very real drive to make use of these techniques.

"There should be an equal drive to make sure that we use them with the client. We feel the tools we have used at Kaplan and McLaughlin in programming, evaluation, systems analysis and design are of particular value to us as architects, because all are designed for use *with* the client. We have a long way to go in making this relationship more effective, but I think that it is a beginning.

"Useful buildings of any complexity require client involvement and client education. We have found that the traditional approach of a brief period of programming which establishes space needs and the general operational pattern of the client, followed by a retreat to the selected studio and a presentation of a scheme to be approved, simply is not adequate in most complex and innovative buildings. Programming and design are inextricably linked. Operational concepts will change as design reveals new opportunities, and the client must play an informed role in this process. Both architect and client must have wide knowledge of each other's traditions, tools and operation.

"The client who really does not have a firm idea of what he wants—and clear understanding of what he is getting—is in the majority; and he is the one to whom we must devote considerable attention. If the world is moving awkwardly fast for the architect, architecture is also moving in frequently incomprehensible ways to the client. Answering the layman's questions as to why a building functions or looks a certain way is often difficult. But it is necessary and can be done well only if the layman has some knowledge of the language, limitations and potentials of architecture.

"I would say further that using these techniques does seem to work. This is not fancy flim-flam designed to snow the client. These techniques have helped us turn out better buildings. Evaluation thus far tells us that the buildings do work, and are flexible enough to allow significant adaption."

The Kaplan/McLaughlin evaluation program for this county facility is updated in this fifth-year report by Herbert McLaughlin.

The Marin County CMHC design focuses on a large, irregularly shaped room with sunlight spilling in from clerestories above and through large windows—a splendid landscape is readily apparent. Clearly visible on the periphery are bedrooms, offices, and multi-function spaces. This central space is usually full of people in low comfortable chairs talking, playing games, reading or making snacks.

It is an extremely innovative design in which spaces are in some ways purposely ambiguous and changing. The architects refer to this as "indeterminate" design. This concept negates the philosophy that rigidly defined spaces are appropriate for patients—or others—who are learning to define themselves and deal with a world of change. Rather architecture should create spatial variety.

The criteria for this fifth year evaluation were the well articulated original design and treatment programs, tested by activities that have stayed relatively close to the original conception in one unit and a drastically different program inaugurated during 1972 in the other unit.

Many variables exist: the quality and attitude of the staff and of the patients at any one given time, the competence of the valuators, the techniques used which did not stress direct comparisons with other facilities—although there was a very brief simultaneous evaluation of another mental health center that has a program and patients similar to Marin but a pleasantly conventional Spanish style single-story, U-shaped design. This center is identified in this report by the fictitious name of Carehaven.

The basic intent of "indeterminate" design is to encourage many different behaviors. This runs contrary to most designs for mental health which are structured to provide the strongest possible behavioral messages of conformity—whether to a medically powerful doctor-patient relationship, or an equally pervasive home-away-from-home status.

Not that this design is unstructured. An exposed structure and a clear hierarchy of spaces exist; but within those clarities, complexity of spatial relationships, variety of routes and of surfaces and experiences exist. Geometries are superimposed on one another but expressed directly in plan and section. In this case, square is laid upon triangle. The resulting atmosphere is one of great openness and a real range of clearly different spaces in which one can occupy, and express oneself in very different ways.

The Center is very much like a village under one roof. There is the village's hierarchy of a major public space surrounded by semi-public and private spaces. The Center is a village microcosm preparing individuals to return to the larger community.

In order to create an environment that fosters positive involvement between patients and staff and among the patients themselves, Kap-lan and McLaughlin believed that a radically new type of design was called for, a spatially indeterminate environment that was emphatically non-linear and non-boxlike, an architecture of irregularity that consistently emphasized change and choice. Stimulation, change and challenge to the patients would make them feel independent. This was not just to be a home, but a school of sorts, from which one graduated as soon as possible.

This second evaluation, by a sociologist and an architectural psychologist, was a study of the long-term use of the building after the original program had been in operation for five years in Unit A, with however, a patient population that was considerably more acutely ill than the one originally designed for. In unit B, a radically different program of emergency crisis intervention had been substituted in 1972. This was an ideal set-up for the evaluation team to see how well the building responded to a different program.

The 1969 and 1974 evaluations reveal that in the unit used as conceptualized in the original design, the communal space dominated patient and staff awareness. When patients were asked in 1969 if the unit's design was "free," or "bossy," more than two-thirds said "free," 14 per cent said "both," and 14 per cent said "bossy." That distribution holds in 1974. Further, 95 per cent of the staff described the Marin design as the best in which they had ever worked. There was more patient activity and interaction at Marin than at Care-haven. Staff at Carehaven who had also worked at Marin preferred the Marin design.

All were keenly aware that the Marin space was unusual and stimulating. In 1969, 39 per cent of the inpatients and day patients said the space was relaxing. Forty-eight per cent said it was both relaxing and challenging. The staff felt it definitely increased socializing and decreased a strong feeling of territoriality, both physicially and psychologically. Except for room-to-room trips the patients had to pass through or pass by the communal space and virtually all activities take place there: games, preparation of foods, meals and meetings. As one patient put it: "With any brains at all, you can find something to do (in the communal space)."

Activities in the communal space overshadowed the secondary public areas: the music, sewing and TV rooms. Those areas quite literally languished due to the attraction of the communal room. In 1969 and 1974 the over-all response was very favorable. Staff noticed patients emerging from group therapy sessions in rooms away from the communal space seemed to lose their moods of anger and aggression soon after their return.

How well does Kaplan and McLaughlin's design concept work for more severely disoriented patients? Though the staff of unit B liked the openness and spaciousness of the communal space, it was less used by patients, according to observation in 1974. The communal space seemed unfocused and sparsely furnished to the evaluation team. According to the clinical staff, the communal space worked well for the day patient program; however, the staff did think the communal space and plan of the unit was overly challenging to severely disoriented patients. Those patients rarely used the communal room, but then this patient type seldom mixes well in any setting.

For crisis patients, perhaps design emphasis should be on control and supervision with small scale simple spatial experiences and undemanding environmental details. As the staff of Unit B put it: a more "home-like atmosphere" with familiar and clearly defined spaces is best for crisis intervention work.

There would seem to be much to learn from the design, and from the evaluation of it.

MARIN COUNTY COMMUNITY MENTAL HEALTH CENTER, Greenbrae, California. Architects: *Kaplan and McLaughlin—Ellis Kaplan, partner-in-charge; Herbert McLaughlin, programming and design; Fred Lee, construction supervisor.* Engineers: *Rutherford & Chekene* (structural); *Ben Lennert & Associates* (foundations); *G.L. Gendler & Associates* (mechanical). *Lenore Larsen & Associates,* (interior design consultant). Landscape architect: *Douglas Batus.* General contractor: *Christenson & Foster.*

Joshua Freiwald photos

Herb McLaughlin observes a developing line of continuity in the concept of indeterminate space from the communal spaces at Marin, left, to the design for renovation of the Christiana factory for informal office use, right and below. Some of these concepts were carried forward to the Elmcrest facility on page 120, which Herb McLaughlin thinks is more successful than Marin because pitched roofs permit more varied spaces.

AN INDUSTRIAL MEDICAL CENTER DESIGNED FOR HUMAN BEINGS

Unlike most new medical buildings which function primarily as antiseptic containers for their frightening equipment ,left and below. this new clinic has been designed to educate and relax the patient as well as treat him.

Were it not for the figures in white coats it would be hard to tell what the elegant model (opposite page) is meant to be. The remaining photographs and drawings give no additional clues and for once words are really needed to buttress the visual language of an architectural project. This is because the Columbus Occupational Health Center to be constructed in Columbus, Indiana will be like no other, and has no precedents as an image of medical treatment.

The interior planning concept of the center challenges the commonly held theory that a clinic is merely a series of individual self-contained boxes connected by corridors. During careful examination of the services the clinic would perform and the kinds of activity it would engender, the architects discovered that not all functions require the same degree of privacy. It was found that only examination rooms need the degree of aural and visual privacy provided by walls extending to the ceiling and conventional doors. Activities such

as physiotherapy, eye examination, cardio-pulmonary testing and dressing can be performed in alcoves enclosed by door-height partitions and folding screens. Slight testing, weight and height recording, exercise areas and nurses stations are in the open.

The architects believe that many of the activities of a medical center are essentially interesting to the waiting patient who will take advantage of the opportunity to educate himself. The laboratory area has been encased in glass but is visually open to the waiting area. The latter consists of two gently sloping ramps and a large flat space which connects all three levels of the building. Circular seating pods, which can be seen in the models and plans, will be equipped with audio-visual devices to disseminate educational medical information and to record individual medical histories. The sequence of events which occur along the waiting ramps has been planned to occupy the entire duration of the waiting cycle in order to reduce boredom and anxiety.

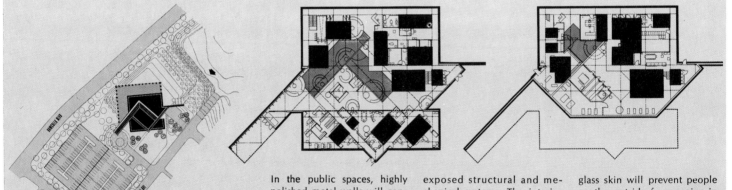

In the public spaces, highly polished metal walls will contrast effectively with the rougher surfaces of textured concrete block. The perimeter wall will be of black glass affording a smooth background for the exposed structural and mechanical systems. The interior face of this wall,which will be supported by open web joists will be illuminated from above by a continuous skylight. In the daytime, the black reflecting glass skin will prevent people on the outside from seeing in while providing excellent views from within the building. At night, when the building is empty, its interior will be visible from outside.

Gil Amiaga

Gil Amiaga

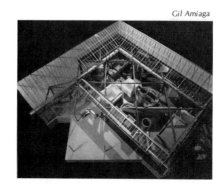

High school for the deaf creates special living, teaching and research facilities for disabled

This model school, created by federal action, was designed to explore and demonstrate teaching methods for high school students whose hearing is impaired. In a sense, it is a basic research facility with two major aims: "to improve educational opportunities for handicapped students by providing a secondary teaching-learning environment comparable to that available to hearing students, and to demonstrate the feasibility of such a program nationally."

The school was built in two phases: the first was the academic building for 600 students, and the second was the on-campus residential facilities for 450.

The academic building, beyond providing spaces for an extraordinary variety of curricular needs (liberal arts, business, vocational, technical, etc.), varies from the usual school for the deaf in two major ways. One is the use of large open teaching spaces to facilitate easy change and experimentation. Since the openness posed acoustical problems, provisions were made to control sound within ranges critical to deaf persons by using amplification systems and absorbent materials which cut down reverberations.

The second big difference is the use of balconies for observers, instead of the more usual one-way mirrors or tv monitors. In addition there are unobtrusive observation points planned so circulation can occur around classroom areas without being a disruptive force.

Housing is provided in six units, of one to four stories.

MODEL SECONDARY SCHOOL FOR THE DEAF, Washington, D.C. Owner: *Gallaudet College.* Architects: *HTB, INC.—principal-in-charge and project architect: James N. Freehof; consulting architect: Bertram Berenson.* Landscape architect: *CR-3.* Engineers: *Smilsova, Kehnemui & Associates (structural); Schnabel Engineering Associates (foundation and soils); Herbert L. Arey (mechanical); Richard H. Freidin (electrical); Dr. Arthur F. Niemoeller (acoustical); David A. Mintz, Inc. (lighting).* General contractor: *Phase I—American Construction Co. Phase II—A.A. Beiro Construction Co.*

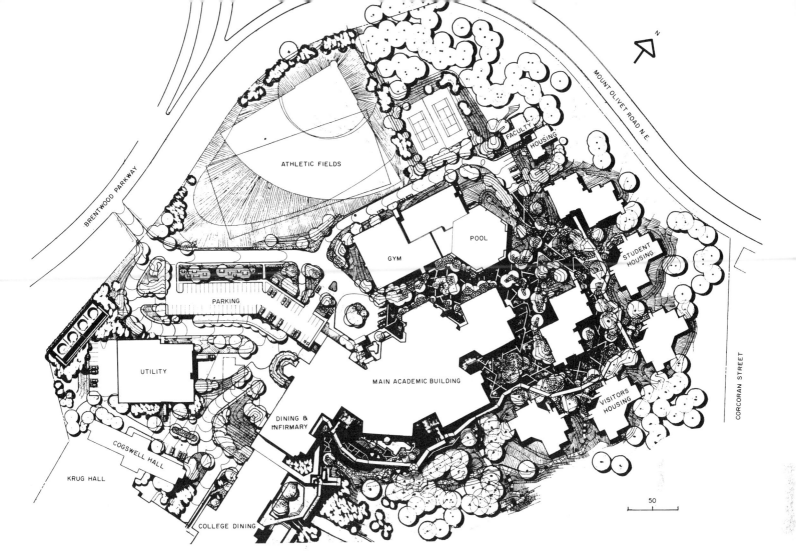

The complex, as a model school, was not designed for duplication elsewhere as a complete facility, but to research and experiment with ideas that may be adapted. As such, it is a demonstration program with provisions for extensive visitation and observation, for the education of professionals and parents, and as an information and testing center. And, of course, it is intended as an exemplary, innovative program for deaf students, with a campus-full of living, learning and recreational facilities.

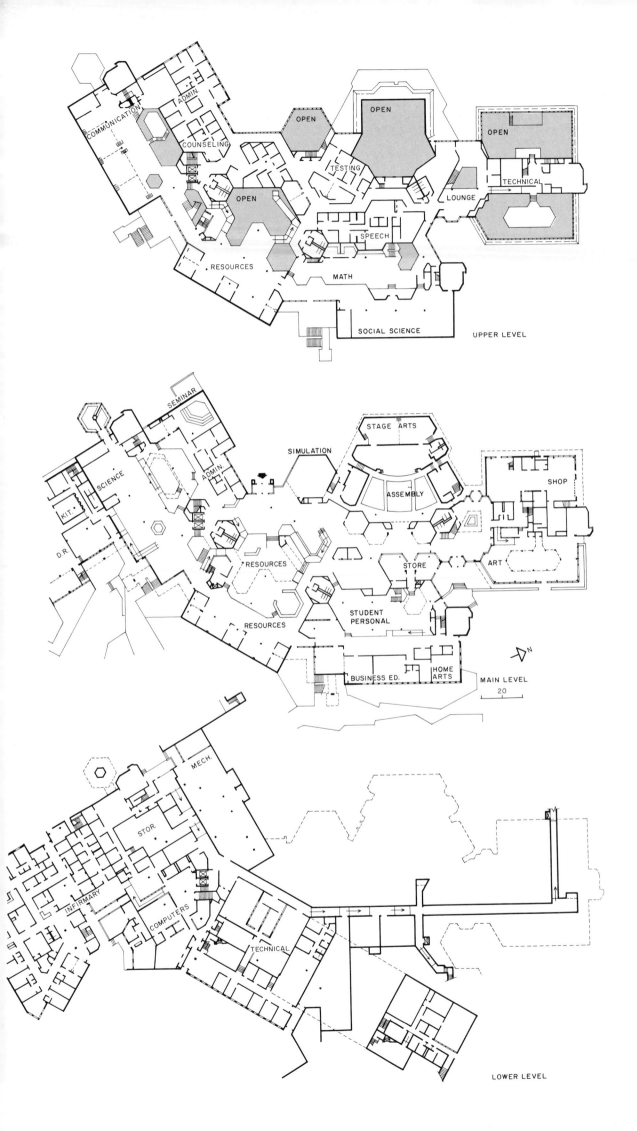

UPPER LEVEL

ADMIN.

COMMUNICATION

COUNSELING

OPEN

OPEN

OPEN

OPEN

TESTING

TECHNICAL

LOUNGE

OPEN

SPEECH

RESOURCES

MATH

SOCIAL SCIENCE

SEMINAR

SIMULATION

STAGE ARTS

SCIENCE

ADMIN.

ASSEMBLY

SHOP

KIT.

D.R.

RESOURCES

STORE

ART

STUDENT PERSONAL

RESOURCES

N

BUSINESS ED.

HOME ARTS

MAIN LEVEL

20

MECH.

STOR.

INFIRMARY

COMPUTERS

TECHNICAL

LOWER LEVEL

The hub of the academic building, shown here, is the big, multi-level resources center, which winds its way up the core of the building. In addition to books and magazines, the center contains a large selection of filmstrips, slides and videotapes.

Most of the classroom areas are large open spaces, but provision has also been made for privacy and closed classrooms where appropriate. Each student has an individually — designed program for speech and auditory testing and training. All courses are taught using "total communication" (a combination of speech, fingerspelling and sign language). In addition to a full range of high school courses, facilities are provided for training in a number of vocational areas (metalworking, woodworking, automotive repair, drafting, electronics and photography).

ARCOLA LAKE ELEMENTARY SCHOOL
SPECIAL EDUCATION BUILDING

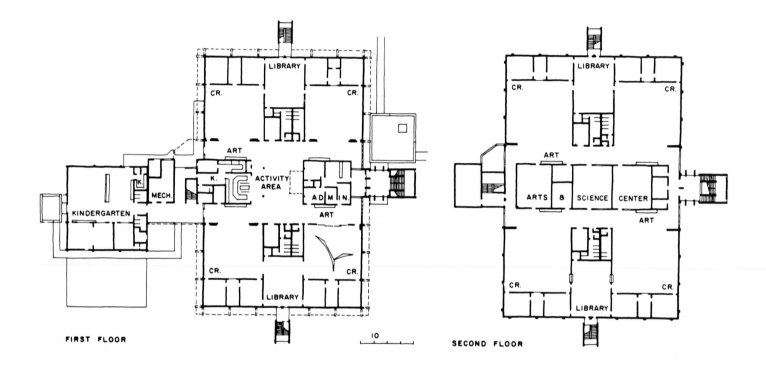

FIRST FLOOR

SECOND FLOOR

A SPECIAL EDUCATION BUILDING ANNEX provides extensive facilities for the instruction of the handicapped at the Arcola Lake Elementary School. The main school is identical with that of the Olinda School shown above, and was constructed simultaneously with it in 1968.

The annex is similar in design spirit to the main school, though smaller in scale, and is surrounded by covered walks which extend to link with the school.

ARCOLA LAKE ELEMENTARY SCHOOL SPECIAL EDUCATION BUILDING. Architect: *Murray Blair Wright.*

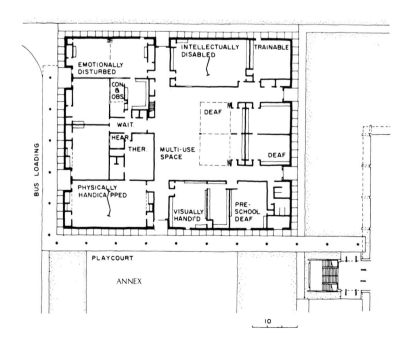

ANNEX

ILLINOIS REGIONAL LIBRARY FOR THE BLIND AND PHYSICALLY HANDICAPPED

Probably the very best building Tigerman has ever done—and surely the most sensitive—is this Illinois Regional Library for the Blind and Physically Handicapped on Chicago's West Side near the Circle Campus of the University of Illinois.

In this building, Tigerman's curved shapes, which in other work might be considered fanciful, are completely functional, everywhere working to assist the blind or wheelchair-bound to use the library on their own with a minimum of assistance from the staff.

And perhaps more completely than in the other work shown in this article, Tigerman has developed his "reversals" or "oppositions and inversions." For example:

▪ Where the building is tallest—on the hypotenuse and short side of the triangular building—the space is in fact one story inside; a tall "people space." In the center, where it is lower, are layered three low (7½-foot-high) levels of stacks.

▪ The building is brightly colored inside and out. The metal exterior panels are a Mondrian-red baked finish; all structural members are painted yellow; and all of the mechanical elements, exposed inside and on the rooftop, are blue. Why the color? Tigerman gives three reasons: "Some of the users, while legally blind, are not totally blind—and light and bright colors are the only things they are able to see. It's

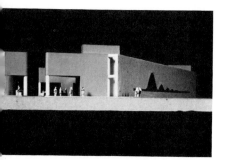

whimsical and playful—and it's good for a library to be thought of as 'fun' instead of as 'a serious place for serious learning.' Finally, the building will be used by people with other physical disabilities, by friends and relatives of the blind, and by the community residents. I wanted to design a building that gives everyone who uses it a lift. . . ."

▪ The final "inversion" is perhaps the most striking: The solid portions of the wall (drawing lower right) are made of lightweight metal panels. Yet it is the one dense wall—the poured concrete wall of the longest side—that is made transparent with an extraordinary window (drawing at right). The window is 165 feet long, butt-glazed without columns or support of any kind—which of course requires the wall above the window to act as a massive beam. "This is irrational," Tigerman would agree. "But so is blindness irrational. . . ."

Significantly, the window is set at such a height that only those in wheelchairs and seated staff members at service desks can really see outside.

The shape of the great window reflects in elevation the beautifully thought-out circulation system just inside the window. Using the curving shapes (easier to "read" than tactile changes in surfaces), the blind visitor will be able to "feel" where he is. The circulation system is also (see caption on facing page for details) entirely linear—"easier for a blind person to remember," says Tigerman, "than any system with freestanding elements. And everything has rounded corners—there are no surprises."

ILLINOIS REGIONAL LIBRARY FOR THE BLIND AND PHYSICALLY HANDICAPPED, Chicago, Illinois. Architects: *Stanley Tigerman and Associates* and *Jerome R. Butler, Jr., City of Chicago Bureau of Architecture—Stanley Tigerman, design; Robert E. Fugman, associate-in-charge.* Engineers: *James L. Mitchell, Inc.* (structural); *Wallace & Migdal, Inc.* (mechanical/electrical). Estimating consultants: *Hanscomb Associates, Inc.* General contractor: *Walsh Bros., Inc.*

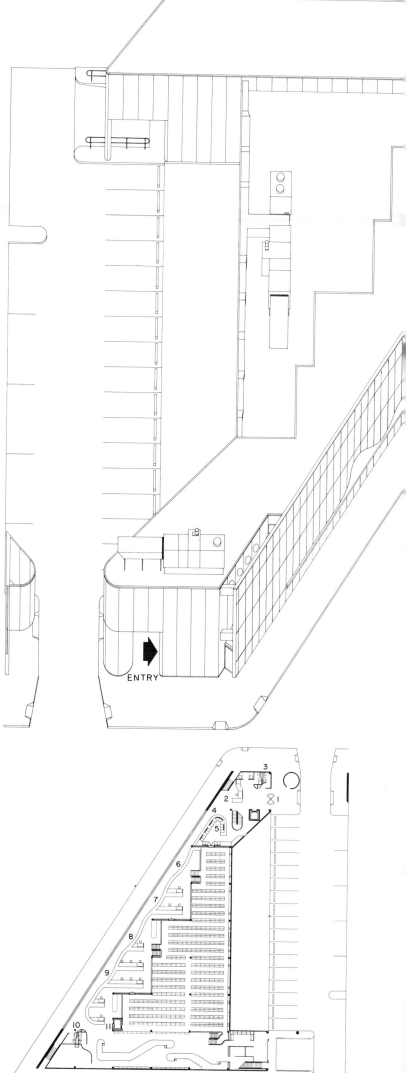

ENTRY

GROUND LEVEL

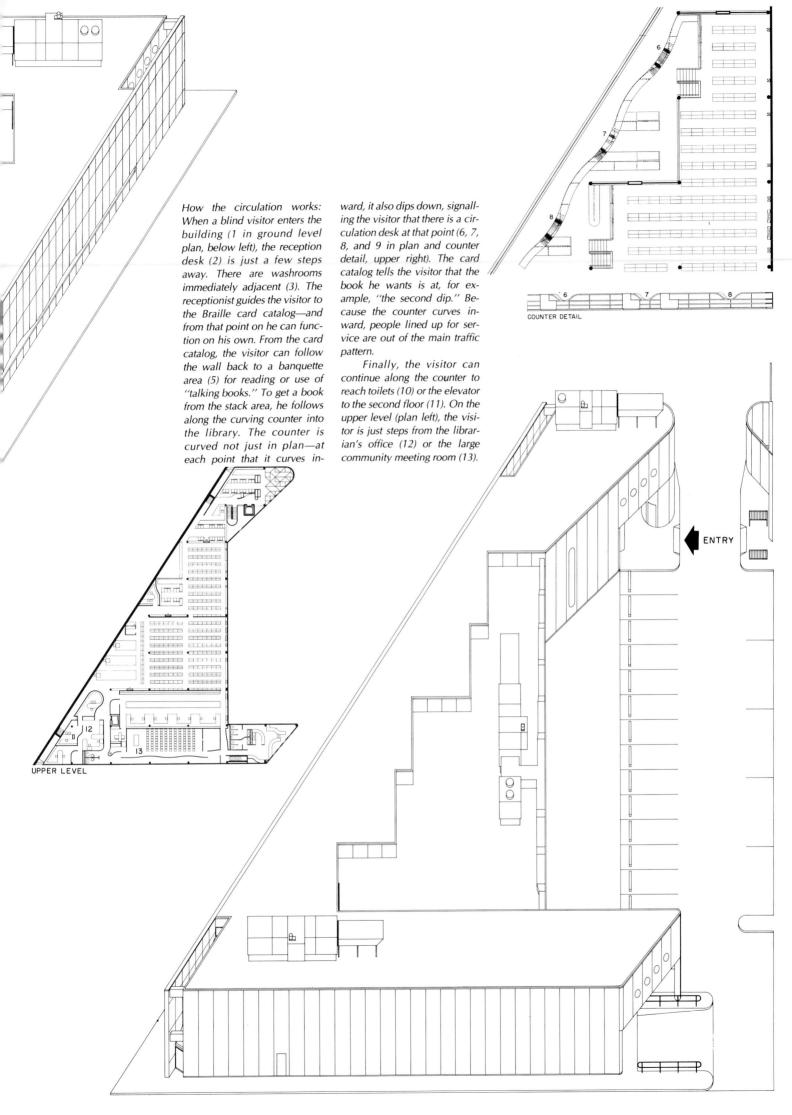

How the circulation works: When a blind visitor enters the building (1 in ground level plan, below left), the reception desk (2) is just a few steps away. There are washrooms immediately adjacent (3). The receptionist guides the visitor to the Braille card catalog—and from that point on he can function on his own. From the card catalog, the visitor can follow the wall back to a banquette area (5) for reading or use of "talking books." To get a book from the stack area, he follows along the curving counter into the library. The counter is curved not just in plan—at each point that it curves in-

ward, it also dips down, signalling the visitor that there is a circulation desk at that point (6, 7, 8, and 9 in plan and counter detail, upper right). The card catalog tells the visitor that the book he wants is at, for example, "the second dip." Because the counter curves inward, people lined up for service are out of the main traffic pattern.

Finally, the visitor can continue along the counter to reach toilets (10) or the elevator to the second floor (11). On the upper level (plan left), the visitor is just steps from the librarian's office (12) or the large community meeting room (13).

COUNTER DETAIL

UPPER LEVEL

ENTRY

139

CHAPTER FOUR

Housing for the Elderly

HOUSING THE AGING

The living conditions suffered by many people over 65 urgently point toward the need for both construction of better physical facilities *and* more positive attitudes about a national problem. The fast-growing portion of the population that will be pressing their needs on us demands radical change—and better answers. For the design professions, this will mean a re-examination of everything that has been built for the elderly—and it will mean hard work coupled with a search for knowledge.

The current statistics on the aging point to a field of construction that could be more promising and more challenging to architects than the Middle East. Toward solutions for what has become an increasingly apparent problem, there has been some rhetoric and very little action in meeting the needs of a steadily growing part of the nation's population. While the 22 million persons now over 65 at present form a relatively large 10 percent of the population, the average life expectancy of everyone alive today is now well above 70, and increasing. Of course, this means that over half of the enormous number of people who are in our currently crowded environment may eventually need and expect some type of housing tailored to specifications that have been little met so far.

Today, there are only some three million units designed specifically for the aged, and these include everything from apartments to intermediate and advanced medical-care facilities. Yet, in New York City alone there are over one million persons over 65, and—according to a study by the National Council on the Aging—a large percentage almost never leave their homes because of physical or psychological reasons.

It is estimated that less than 10 per cent of those aged considered chronically ill are housed in *any type* of suitable long-term-care facility. There are only slightly over one million units for such purposes in the whole country, and only three-quarters of these are qualified by either Medicare or Medicaid as having adequate programs. Last year's 25 per cent increase in the construction of medically related facilities (as reported by F.W. Dodge) may mean that the "catching up" is about to begin. So may the fact that Jimmy Carter included demands for better elderly housing among his campaign promises, although nothing has been initiated yet. The pressure is on: The growing numbers of aging are clearly becoming better-informed, better-educated and more vocal in fighting for common goals.

What is wrong with what *is* being built?
Except for the lack of facilities of all kinds, the biggest problem today may be the separation of the sorts of care that an older person can

receive in *any* facility. Not only is this separation confusing to those who may already be confused; it can lead to disaster for exactly those persons who are supposed to be helped. Currently, facilities are generally categorized for those who are fully independent, totally dependent, or partially dependent; apartments, nursing homes or something in between. Thomas Byerts of the Gerontological Society says experts see rough ranges: "It's go-go (ages 65-75), slow-go (75-85) and no-go". The obvious implication is that residents—at a time that they are already having difficulty in adjusting—frequently have to move repeatedly to a different kind of housing, at a time when it is increasingly difficult. Indeed, according to a study by Professor Leon Pastalan at the University of Michigan, changing the environment for persons in advanced old age can quite literally kill them.

There are vast differences between facilities in every category of care. Normally the apartments are managed by non-profit groups, such as churches, which may well have built them under the only currently active Federal program, Section 202, for persons of limited income. Inherent in the often-minimal medical facilities provided by these apartments is the concept that tenants will have to move when they can no longer take care of themselves (as is the case in most of the examples on pages 156–157). The next step is usually a choice between care in non-housekeeping residences that provide communal meals and limited medical aid, or straight to the nursing "home."

About 75 per cent of the nursing homes are run for profit. The remainder are run by non-profit groups and tend to be larger, have better rounded facilities and programs, and larger staffs per patient—but not necessarily more nurses. Because of the rising costs of providing basic services and facilities, nursing homes are getting larger—and often more impersonal. The average now has over 60 patients, while almost a quarter has 100. There are about 6.5 employees, including four nurses (usually "aides") distributed over an around-the-clock schedule for every 10 patients. The average charge nationally is over $500 per month, with regional variations reaching around $750 in the Northeast. But in a Kafka-like situation, charges tend to rise in larger establishments, because of the more elaborate facilities and programs.

Even in the best of the nursing facilities, the environment tends to be sterile and hospital-like, clearly designed for efficiency and *not* for independent living—or even the vestige of it. There is little hope of mental growth and stimulation here.

In the "residences" for those needing only partial care, there have been many misunderstandings of what is to be provided. Persons entering are often asked to give substantial parts—if not all—of their assets in return for what they believe to be life-long care, when such care is not the purpose of such institutions at all. The criteria for continued tenancy is often the ability to make a daily trip through a cafeteria line. (This situation is exemplified by example 2 on pages 156-157). The atmosphere can be little better than in a nursing home.

While there are some institutions which do provide life-long care for a continuous residency by older persons in every physical condition, "there are too few to even test the side implications" according to Byerts. There are several examples on the following pages that provide some variation—usually geared to the advanced-care end of the spectrum. Only the Givens Estates (page 144) promises to provide a continuous environment for persons who should be in their "golden" years.

The basic question: Are institutions ever the right answer?

Perhaps the greatest mistake that has been made is to lump together wholesale the problems of many people with no more in common than age. One of the foremost rationalizations for institutionalization is the desire to be with companions of the same age. But, according to Margaret Bemiss (see article, page 156) companionship was the *last* of four major reasons given by voluntary residents. The first three reasons involved the practical necessities of security and physical aid—sorry comments on society's failures. It is obvious that the "experts" have sometimes been confused. And it is also obvious that many people who would otherwise be happy and useful, deteriorate quickly in institutionalized environments with nothing to do.

According to Jacob Reingold of the American Association of Homes for the Aging, early institutionalization can be like "shooting a fly with a cannon," in terms of creating a dehabiliting overdependence. According to architects Byerts and Don Conway of the AIA: "The most desirable level of assistance is *only* that which the elderly person is unable to provide for himself." They stress a maximum choice in types of available facilities—which is not necessarily incompatible with the concept of life-long care in one campus-like arrangement.

The whole concept of care has too often been custodial. The attitude has produced role reversal between young and old that brings over-reliance in child-like ways. It is largely a question of how the residents perceive their environment. Is it run for them, or for the convenience of the administrators? The fact that there may not be options does not have to be accentutated.

And the whole concepts of institutionalized care may be misused. According to Byerts: "20 to 30 per cent of people in institutions do not need to be there"—while of course many more people who do need help cannot find it. Often such facilities are used as a dumping ground for family problems (again, see Bemiss article).

To many people involved with the aging, the best solution is care in their home—or an approximation of it. Here—with proper help—the person remains a person, able to pick and choose among companions and activities in the widest ranges of choice. This situation rates an A on the motivation scale. But there are obviously many problems with this approach. To explore this solution, the "Triage Program" has been funded by the Federal and Connecticut state governments in a demonstration program to test both the cost and psychological effectiveness of caring for persons in their own homes. It provides services ranging from skilled medical care to companionship and housekeeping, according to needs. According to Director Joan Quinn: "institutionalization should be an alternative to home, and not the other way around."

Then, why are there institutions at all? If there are strong questions about age-segregated communities, the best answer should be something in-between the "home" and a real one—possibly an almost-new building type. The fact remains that many older persons will really need some form of constant care for medical, financial, and even social reasons. Even if the Triage program is expanded, the real home may often just not be good enough because of its physical condition or because of the family or the community situation. According to one woman interviewed by Bemiss: "I would rather be here than be a built-in baby sitter for my daughter while she looks for a job." According to an article in *Business Week* on February 7, 1977, a question frequently asked by families is: "Is one visit a month enough?" Indeed, the traditional family roles here *have* broken down. To add incentive to why the aging may be institutionalized, the social problems that bring older people to institutions for security continue; almost all older people currently in facilities for advanced care *do* show real mental and physical deterioration from mainly arterial disorders, which they cannot control by self motivation; they need constant care that is usually not affordable—even under a Triage program. Apparently, at some point people are happy to just give up the struggle—no matter the conditions. But the architects' responsibility to produce better environments can only become greater because their real clients—the elderly—have no options.

Are design professionals missing their responsibilities to the aging—not to mention real opportunities for business? The answer has to be separated into mostly a "no" on the responsibilities and probably a "yes" on the opportunities. No matter how humanitarian the concerns of an architect or design-related professional, the fact is that facilities for the aging, like most forms of construction, are built to the requirements of clients—clients who in the case of housing for the aging are mostly owners who may never live in their project. (Herein could lie one good idea for change: the users could become the developers.) These clients may or may not have good ideas of what the facilities could or should be. It is then the professional's obligation to produce the best solutions within the framework that the client dictates—and to possibly educate that client a little further toward a real goal: a basic concern with humanitarian concepts. And it is these concepts that *should* create the new business in this field—as is described on page 154. Still, the business will come for those who make any effort, because of the sheer pressure.

While—according to Byerts and a director of one of the projects on the following pages—the hospital mentality continues to prevade boards of directors, progress in understanding the problems of the aging is evident on the part of everyone involved from design professionals to administrators. This understanding will affect all levels of design, although it may not produce fundamental changes as quickly as we would like. The effects range from the way in which space is distributed in a building, to concern over details. While most living quarters for those with even less severe geriatric problems tend to be rooms with one and two beds in them, a study by architect Bettyann Raschko has established that a separate living room and bedroom are held to be minimal requirements by the occupants (as any thoughtful person might have known all along). The bedroom allows space for hobbies and projects, that the aging disastrously abandon in one-room environments. According to Byerts and Conway, elderly couples ideally should have two bedrooms, because sleeping patterns become increasingly less fixed with old age. On details, designers and manufacturers have been even more imaginative. Recent advances include everything from devices that counter the aging's increasing fears, such as improved handrails to hardware for fire safety, including pneumatic door closers that impede free swing only when a fire is present. There has been good work in the field, and there is much more to be done. **None of the projects that follow have yet answered all of these questions, but they do represent thoughtful work by skilled architects for clients with real constraints. . . .**

Individual lifestyles are to be encouraged in a stimulating nearly rural environment that will enhance independence—but not reject those who finally cannot take care of themselves. The concept is a nearly normal community without the stigma of institutionalization

What are the real advantages here? While residents will be physically separated from completely normal lives, a majority who enter as active persons are expected to provide a positive and diverse influence on the less able. The initial attraction will be a "country-club" environment, and the long-range attraction will be the assurance that the need for care will never force moving on at an advanced age. Activities will range from regular participation in the life of the nearby downtown, to fishing in the streams which converge on Givens' man-made lake. All who are able will meet for at least one communal meal each day.

THE GIVENS ESTATES, INC., Asheville, Carolina. Architects: *William Morgan Architects.* Associate architects; *Moore-Robinson Associates.* Engineers: *H. W. Keister Associates, Inc.* (structural); *Ray Turknett Engineers* (mechanical/electrical). Consultants: *Meyer/Lomprey & Associates* (graphics): *The Cathedral Foundation of Jacksonville, Inc.* (management). General contractor: *Buncombe Construction Company, Inc.*

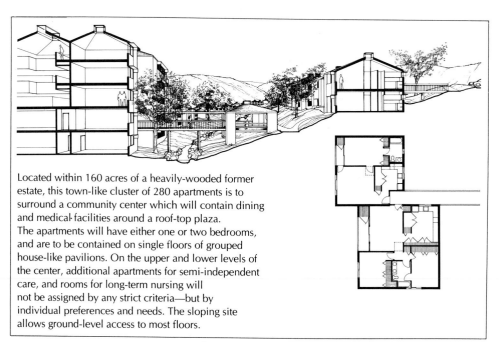

Located within 160 acres of a heavily-wooded former estate, this town-like cluster of 280 apartments is to surround a community center which will contain dining and medical facilities around a roof-top plaza.
The apartments will have either one or two bedrooms, and are to be contained on single floors of grouped house-like pavilions. On the upper and lower levels of the center, additional apartments for semi-independent care, and rooms for long-term nursing will not be assigned by any strict criteria—but by individual preferences and needs. The sloping site allows ground-level access to most floors.

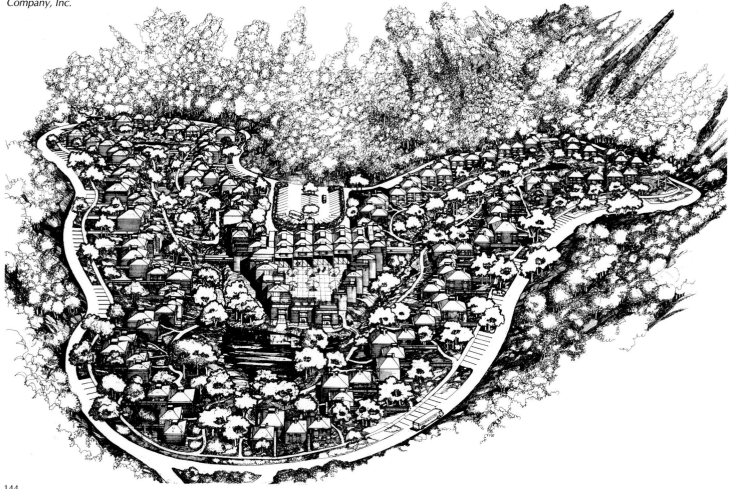

An advanced-care facility shows that it can be a continuation of community-life, and by doing so recognize the needs of a particular group of users, here older persons of Puerto Rican descent.

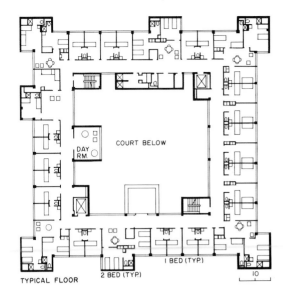

TYPICAL FLOOR   2 BED (TYP.)   1 BED (TYP.)   10

Both intermediate and skilled care is provided for 180 persons in one- and two-bedroom units, which open on corridors and day rooms around a central atrium. Ground-level facilities are planned for older persons in the neighborhood and include a dining room and clinic.

What are the real advantages here? The concept is, both through necessity and through philosophy, to keep residents in their own homes as long as possible. And when patients are admitted, different philosophies become effective. Aside from creating an on-going relationship with older persons in the community through its out-patient care facilities, C.A.B.S. is designed to attract inside a broad range of neighborhood residents—families and friends of the infirm and general community groups. The courtyard is not only reminiscent of ethnic architecture, but accommodates all sorts of activities. Of course, the most important result is that otherwise isolated residents are lured onto the surrounding balconies "to know and to help each other."

C.A.B.S. NURSING HOME, New York, New York. Owner: *Consumer Action Program of Bedford Stuyvesant.* Architect: *William Breger Associates— project architect: James Terjesen.* Engineers: *Paul Gugliotta* (structural); *Batlan & Oxman* (mechanical/electrical). Consultants: *Leeds Associates* (interiors); *Luis Villa/Lois Sherr* (landscape architects). General contractor: *Dember Construction.*

Gil Amiaga photos

Care for those with advanced geriatric problems can lose much of its institutionalized overtones by good physical and social planning—even on a restricting urban site. The Palisade is part of a continuing project which goes a long way toward doing just that

Nathanial Lieberman photos

Part of a 12-year-old master plan for the Hebrew Home for the Aged, that is gradually being completed, The Palisades Nursing Home has been designed to accommodate 348 residents, most of whom need long-term care for serious geriatric problems. But the Home as a whole does not segregate those needing care from those who are able-bodied. There is no need for a major change of lifestyle, friends, or surroundings with each change of physical condition. There are three main buildings at the institution, all of which overlook spectacular views of the Hudson River. They are physically linked by a large central terrace (see photos) and by corridors under the terrace. Program participants who may live "off-campus" are linked to the daily social and therapeutic programs by daily transportation.

What are the real advantages here? Chief administrator Jacob Reingold is primarily a sociologist, and he has "revolutionary" ideas. One of his primary missions is to maintain the spirit of self motivation that comes from an ability to make choices for a group whose average age is 82. Accordingly, the new building includes (besides a full range of facilities for usual activities) a coffee shop which is convertible into a "night club"; at night, there is entertainment and a bar. Other evidences of the normal life created: there have been marriages between residents, and couples that have chosen to live together.

The new building's eight stories include five for an infirmary, with 34 single and 116 double rooms; and two stories for intermediate care in both single and double rooms (each with a separate sitting room). Extensive medical facilities occupy a large part of the ground floor, and reinforce the concept of life-long care. The new building offered an opportunity to incorporate improvements to re-examined details over Gruzen's earlier Goldfine Pavilion on the same campus.

PALISADE NURSING HOME, New York, New York. Architects: *Gruzen & Partners—partner-in-charge: Peter Samton; director of technology and construction: Charles Silverman.* Engineers: *Harwood & Gould* (structural); *Batlan & Oxman* (mechanical/electrical). Consultants: *M. Paul Friedberg & Associates* (landscape architects); *Bill Bagnall Associates* (interiors); *Romano-Gatland & Associates* (food). General contractor: *Starrett Brothers & Eken, Inc.*

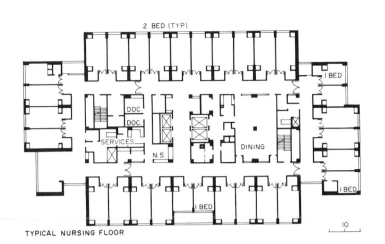

TYPICAL NURSING FLOOR

2 BED (TYP.)

1 BED

1 BED

1 BED

DOC.
DOC.
SERVICES
N.S.
DINING

10

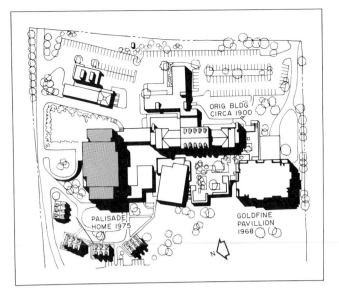

ORIG. BLDG CIRCA 1900

PALISADE HOME 1975

GOLDFINE PAVILLION 1968

N

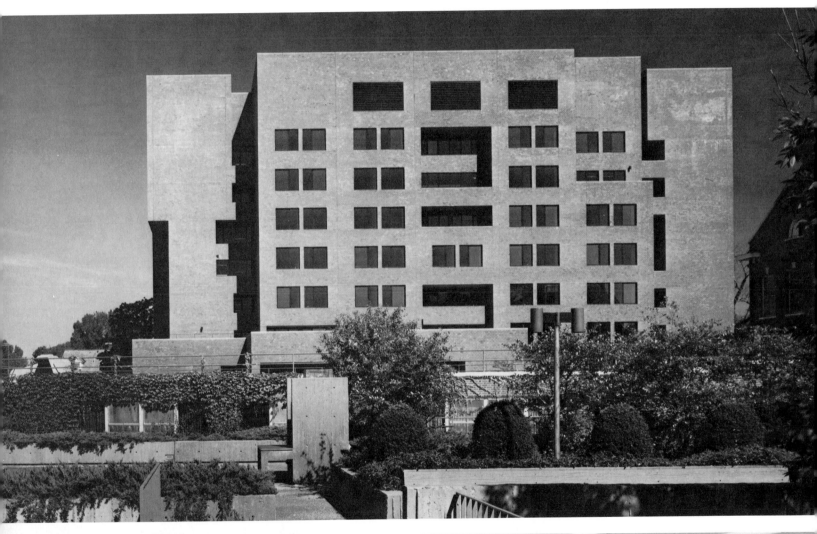

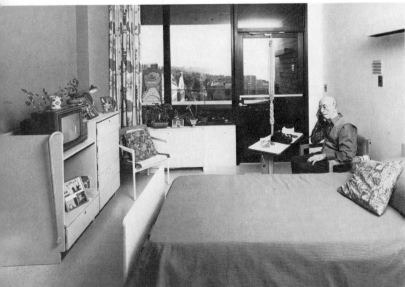

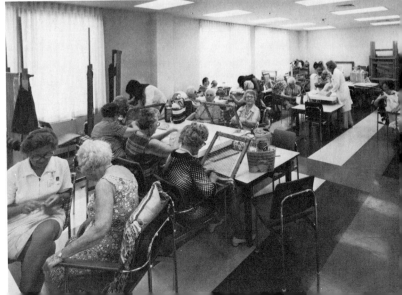

Located in an imaginatively handled urban renewal area, this public housing keeps residents in their revitalized neighborhood, and keeps them active through familiar contacts, aggressive social programs—and better design

Norman McGrath photos

Monument East is part of a 35-block urban renewal area. But there is little old style "renewal" here. Old Town Mall (photo, opposite) was created by a renovation of existing stores that face onto a previous street, now a walkway. Examples of Baltimore's famous "homesteading" plan are one block away. Many original businesses and residents remain in the neighborhood.

What are the real advantages here? Monument East has 187 apartments, of which more than half have one bedroom (the rest are efficiencies). But the building does far more than just house people. It has been designed to meet the requirements both of its largely black tenants and a very progessive office of the Baltimore Department of Housing and Community Development. The philosophy here has been to keep the elderly in their own neighborhood, close to normal lifestyles, and therefore independent as long as they can manage it. Programs managed by DHCD include organized recreation and housekeeping and medical and therapy services within apartments—all designed to keep those who need such services away from more institutionalized care as long as possible, or indefinitely.

The apartments were planned according to comments by a committee headed by one of the current residents. Spaces are large (by government standards), and made to seem even larger by taking advantage of diagonal views through the relatively open plans. The kitchen was identified by the committee as a major space in previous living patterns, and was accordingly made into a full room—normally with adjacent corner balconies. The round openings from most of these balconies and the correspondingly smaller windows were planned by the architects because they felt that not all of the older residents would feel psychologically comfortable in a tall building without some sense of confinement. Furniture and kitchen arrangements were closely scrutinized by both the architects and the committee during planning.

MONUMENT EAST APARTMENTS, Baltimore, Maryland. Owners: *The Department of Housing and Community Development.* Architects; *Conklin & Rossant—personnel-in-charge: Ray Longwell, George Taft, Gerald Li.* Engineers: *Ewell Finley* (structural); *Charles Creswell* (mechanical/electrical). General contractor: *Leimbach Construction.*

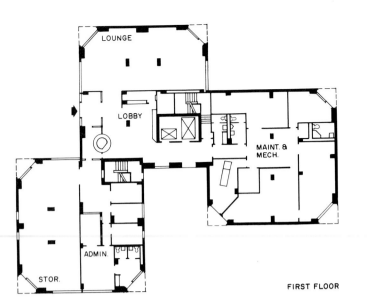

LOUNGE

LOBBY

ADMIN.

STOR.

MAINT. & MECH.

FIRST FLOOR

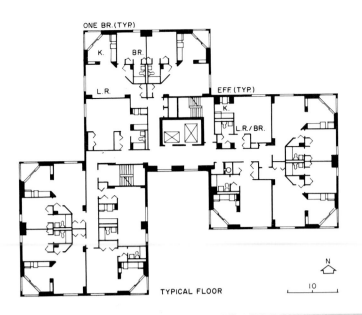

ONE BR. (TYP.)

K. BR.

L.R.

EFF. (TYP.)

K.

L.R./BR.

TYPICAL FLOOR

N

10

For those who are fully independent, this apartment tower provides an interesting example of a self-governing community

Otto Baitz photos

Built by a private developer as a turnkey project for the Bucks County Housing Authority, these apartments are intended for able-bodied, low-income persons—many of whom, in this community, had earlier owned their own homes. The Authority does maintain an active social-affairs department, which provides aid during temporary illnesses. According to Executive Director Carl Gabler, the Authority is amending its policies on current projects to include some sort of long-term care, but will continue to consciously avoid an institutionalized environment: "to the residents, these are just good apartments." The building is named after Senator Joseph Grundy, whose foundation supplies extra monies to such projects for amenities not included in the basic government financing.

What are the advantages here? Although many residents may have to look forward to moving on to institutions, while they are at Grundy they have better facilities than they might expect—even under the project's restrictive financing. The apartments are small, but Sauer has tried to overcome this disadvantage by using a stepped perimeter to the building, which visually expands the spaces by providing views in two directions. The fenestration also allows cross ventilation for the majority of rooms which will not be air conditioned. Sauer states that the cost increase for the stepped perimeter was held to 5 per cent. Although the building follows the convention of a double-loaded corridor, the configuration avoids the usual lack of a "sense of location" by providing natural light and recesses for individual apartment doors.

One of the most interesting aspects of the life at Grundy Tower is the way in which social programs and even tenant government are managed—not by the Authority but by a resident committee with elected members from each floor. The common backgrounds of the residents, coupled with the interest in self-government, produce a much more active community than could any imposed program.

GRUNDY TOWER, Bristol, Pennsylvania. Owner: *Bucks County Housing Authority.* Architects: *Louis Sauer Associates.* Associate architect: *Frank Schlesinger.* Engineers: *Joseph Hoffman and Associates* (structural); *Michael Garber and Associates* (mechanical/electrical).

ONE BEDROOM

BR.

LIVING

K.

K.

BED

L.-D.

EFFICIENCY

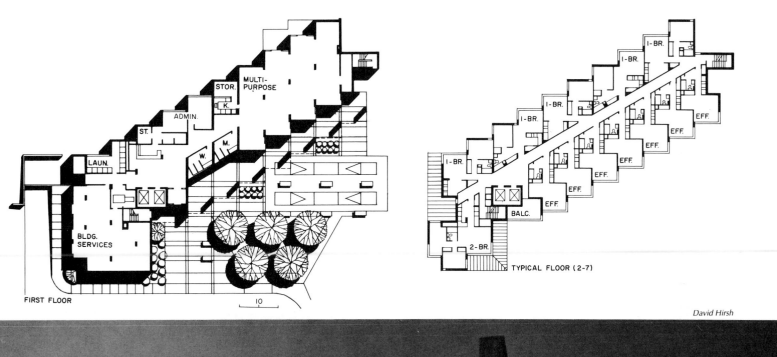

FIRST FLOOR

LAUN.

BLDG.
SERVICES

ST. ADMIN.

STOR. MULTI-
PURPOSE
K.

W. M.

10

TYPICAL FLOOR (2-7)

1-BR.

1-BR.

1-BR.

1-BR.

EFF.

EFF.

EFF.

EFF.

EFF.

EFF.

EFF.

BALC.

2-BR.

David Hirsh

Acknowledging particular lifestyle patterns, this apartment building is like locally popular "luxury-style" developments, but accommodates the needs of a community of elderly in subtle and non-institutionalized ways

Built under HUD's Section 236 program, this first phase of construction contains 180 apartments. With its six-story height and its segmented mass, it represents something in-between a "home-like" image and that of the many new "luxury" high-rises that dot the area. The angled configuration of the wings (and of a proposed addition, bottom of the plan shown below) conforms to a curved site boundary and provides a smaller scale than the building would otherwise have. Types of apartments are separated in respective wings and—on upper floors—occupy the spaces assigned to common uses on the ground floor plan shown here.

What are the real advantages here? According to architect Peter Rumpel, the FHA 236 financing was not particulary encouraging to the concept of life-long care in a continuing environment. Nor is he certain that the concept is right—when it involves mixing the relatively well with the relatively sick. Still, the 180 apartments are served by a completely separate nursing unit on the grounds, and a planned second stage of construction (dotted lines on the plan) would accommodate persons with more serious geriatric problems. The building's poured-in-place and precast concrete walls are an unusual departure from normal practice in Florida, and add greatly to the strong sculptural appearance.

The greatest advantage here may be that the building meets the expectations of retired middle class persons with limited incomes. Aside from the building's non-institutional appearance, the apartments contain ample dressing, bath and storage facilities, although the units are not large—in keeping with the FHA restrictions. Natural light and views of activities in the corrdiors are seen upon leaving elevators at each floor, and are among the advantages of the planning of public spaces. The project is within easy walking distance of stores, theaters, churches and public transportation in an urban setting.

THE FLORIDA CHRISTIAN HOME APARTMENTS, Jacksonville, Florida. Owners: *The Christian Church (Disciples of Christ).* Architects: *Freedman/Clements/Rumpel—designer: Peter Rumpel.* Engineers: *H. W. Keister Associates* (structural); *David Bruce Miller* (mechanical/electrical). General contractor: *Wesley of Florida, Inc.*

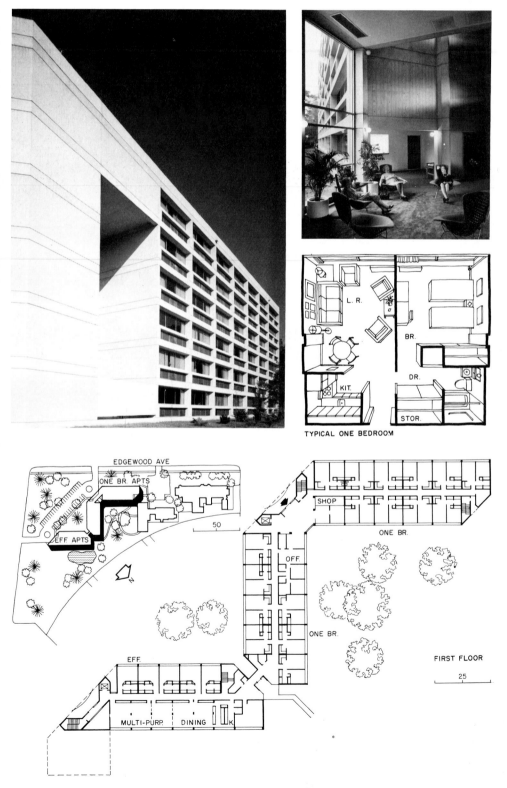

TYPICAL ONE BEDROOM

EDGEWOOD AVE

ONE BR. APTS

EFF APTS

SHOP

ONE BR.

OFF.

ONE BR.

ONE BR.

EFF.

MULTI-PURP. DINING

FIRST FLOOR

WHAT ARE CONCERNED ARCHITECTS DOING ABOUT THE AGING'S PROBLEMS?

While there is much to be done before living conditions for most of the aging will live up to real possibilities, there are architects who have led the way toward a brighter future.

This study raises serious questions about the sort of buildings and indeed the sort of lives that we have been producing for the aging. The questions are most especially evident in Madge Bemiss's article on the following pages. The projects in the Study point to answers, and here is what their architects and others have and will be doing to produce increasingly better facilities:

First they will identify the real problems. The issues which are sometimes perceived to be most important are not necessarily so. Whether a building will be high-rise or low-rise and whether it will be in a city or in the country has meaning only *after* the particular needs of the particular residents are identified. These needs are just as diverse as those of all younger generations, and are results of on-going life styles as much as they are of physical conditions.

Accordingly, Peter Samton of Gruzen & Partners worked on the design of the "mid-rise" Palisade Nursing Home (page 146), but he has also worked on the village-like design for a more rural project in Ohio. In the latter, many low buildings are grouped along an internal "street" which wanders around a green. Samton describes the physical differences between the two projects as being deliberate and direct responses to different philosophies of the administrations, to the different backgrounds of the inhabitants—*and* to the different surroundings. As extreme examples of how particular needs can affect design, the Palisade and the C.A.B.S. home (page 145) are designed specifically for respective ethnic minorities which are often at opposite ends of the economic spectrum, and—while they are of similar heights and are located in surroundings that are equally urban—they offer interesting contrasts. Housing older persons of mainly Puerto Rican descent, C.A.B.S. is arranged around a courtyard that recalls typical construction in the "homeland" (which—according to architect William Breger—becomes increasingly important in the minds of aging immigres). The courtyard also provides a sense of location in the building to those who might otherwise be confused—and most importantly it provides a space that is large (and pleasant) enough to accommodate the traditional big groups of relations and an ambitious program of community activities. Residents here are drawn from neighboring houses, and may find such spatial relationships more meaningful than, say, the residents of the Palisade who usually come from apartment buildings—which the Home resembles.

These architects realize that they are designing something more than hospitals—or repositories. Breger has done extensive research in geriatrics care—part of it in conjunction with specialist Dr. Michael Miller. He says: "Most funds are spent on facilities that promise to cure people. There is no cure for old age." Among this architect's contributions to the field is the complete current section on nursing homes in *Time*

Saver Standards. This includes a categorization of the physical implications for the various stages of care—including idealized models of nursing units. "We should be better to them than we are to people who spend only a limited amount of time in a building"—but how? Most of Breger's models are those for nursing care within traditional standards for the more advanced stages of old age, although C.A.B.S. certainly is not.

According to architect William Morgan (see page 144), the primary goal of facilities for the aging should be to keep residents out of advanced care. He says that the question should always be: "not how sick, but how well?" Like others quoted in the introduction to this article, Morgan feels that institutions can *breed* dependency and hence degeneration—unless the seemingly inherent conflict between the need for physical and mental care is recognized. And he states that just lumping a lot of old people together without stimulus to go on can be fatal. He also recognizes that most current government programs are designed to get the elderly in a wheel chair and keep them there—at disasterous cost to the elderly's well being and younger tax payers' bank accounts.

And there is a strong emphasis on the techniques of better design. Boulevard Temple (page 155) was designed by architect and doctor Nathan Levine, who lectures widely on the subject of gerontology. One of his major concerns is the detailed study of behavioral response. Levine developed elaborate graphs that describe the relationships between various daily occupations for older persons in every state of health. In giving meaning for those whose perceptions are weakened, Levine relies heavily on "redundant cuing"—or the repeated emphasis of the functions of spaces so that they will be used effectively. Aside from the visual emphasis placed on various spaces, he relies on noise, touch and even smell to tell residents their location in a particular building—and to increase their awareness of it, His studies have established favorite colors (at Boulevard, blue) and effective distances for social interaction (about a 6-foot radius) and public interaction (about 12 feet). Levine emphasizes the importance of strong colors in overcoming failing visual perception. (Breger went as far as painting various rooms, in a facility to be demolished, with either strong or pale colors and asking residents about their favorites. Strong colors were preferred—despite the staff's objections.)

One of *the* most active architects in the field is Thomas Byerts of the Gerontological Society. His division generates new ideas and promotes them in practice and education. Among such ideas are flexibility—in planning everything from wall locations in apartments (by movable closets) to variable heights for cabinets. According to a report for (among others) the A.I.A. by Byerts and Conway: "Given the unfortunate choice between esthetic values [and a humane environment] or utilitarian function, the designer should often choose the first." Byerts—like other architects—thinks the field *can* look very bright for the future.

This most urban project, remodeled from a previous "home", embodies strong concepts of continuity—both in its visual associations and in its program of care. It also demonstrates the psychological effects of careful planning

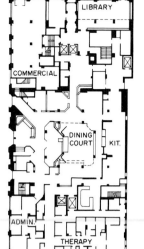
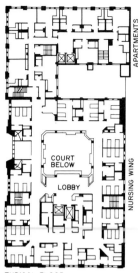

MAIN FLOOR   TYPICAL FLOOR

Greg Hursley

The re-planning of the 1926 Boulevard Temple was initially conceived as a doctoral thesis by architect Nathan Levine. And it embodies many of the concepts that he has developed over many years of research in the field (see previous article). Over the years the residents and the neighborhood had both grown older, and it was only after a feasibility study that it was decided to stay in the same location and remodel the existing spaces. A multi-story chapel became a central atrium (photo, right) by the addition of circulation balconies at each upper floor—giving access to rooms for advanced nursing care. (Apartments for the more able are located in a separate 9-story wing to the top in the plan, above).

What are the advantages of this project?
Boulevard Temple provides an exterior image of tradition for its residents and their on-going relationship to the neighborhood. Within, totally revised uses of space accommodate those with all kinds of needs, and reinforce a feeling of internal community by providing for purposely limited contact between those in advanced care and those who are more independent. Meals are shared by all who are able.

The atrium—besides relieving the image of institutionalized care—provides the strongest instance of what Levine considers the need for repeated sensory stimulation for those in advanced old age. In any of the nursing-care rooms, residents are made aware of where they are by easy reference to the central space, which holds the main dining room with its noises, smells *and* sights. Besides various rooms for quiet activities and gatherings at each nursing floor, main lounges at the elevator entrances provide contact with the nurse on duty, with those who come and go on the floor, and with the activities below—and hence overcome the tendency to not use isolated lounges that has occurred in other projects (see article, page 156). Other cuing devices include the variation of carpet colors (neutral for circulation and vivid for meeting spaces).

BOULEVARD TEMPLE METHODIST HOME, Detroit, Michigan. Owner: *RHODAC.* Architects: *Nathan Levine & Associates, Inc.* Engineers: *William Lefkofsky & Associates* (structural); *Migdal, Layne & Sachs* (mechanical/electrical). Consultants: *Hospital Dietary* (kitchen) Dr. Leon Pastalan (environmental psychology).

155

WHAT DO THE REAL CLIENTS, THE AGING, THINK ABOUT THE CURRENT FACILITIES?

In first of all trying to find out *why* older people move into age-segregated communities, it became apparent that the primary reason was family related. When choosing new housing, the advantages which were most important to them were in order of importance: 1) protection from crime, 2) conveniences to help them live independently in a period of declining strength, 3) the security of having someone nearby that they could contact in an emergency and 4) a community of peers. (The last has often been thought the most important by experts, and it really held even less importance among the poor.) Still, some residents say they did not feel abandoned by their families. As one woman pointed out, "My life is here. I have much more in common with these people, than living with my daughter as a built-in baby-sitter while she goes out and gets a job."

The four particular projects to be described here illustrate the variety of the best options available to the elderly in a metropolitan area. Sites range from urban to almost rural. Three of the facilities are moderate rise (5-9 stories); the fourth is a planned community of one- to three-story buildings. Each offers residents private apartments with kitchens for "normal", independent living; but the quality of the community spaces, the recreation and medical services available on site and in the surrounding neighborhoods all vary substantially. Going from the barest to the most lavish (and coincidentally from the most urban to the most rural), the four subjects are:

Residence 1 was renovated under the FHA 236 program by a private investment company for mostly persons of lower incomes. There are 14 one-bedroom apartments and 78 efficiencies in this downtown location. The average age is 62.

Residence 2 is located in a densely settled suburb, and is newly built under the 236 program by a non-profit, church-sponsored group to house a higher percentage of "fair market tenants." Besides 74 one- and two-bedroom apartments and 136 efficiencies, there is a central dining room where tenants are required to take their evening meal. The average age is 77.

Residence 3 is a "life-care" facility in which residents pay a founder's fee ($18,000 for a small efficiency to $34,000 for a one-bedroom apartment) and a substantial monthly maintenance fee—which covers meals, medical care, recreational facilities and cleaning. Approximately one fifth of the 340 residents receive financial assistance from the "supporting" church group. The average age is 81.

Residence 4 is one of a chain of "leisure worlds" located across the country for persons over 50. There are separate houses, townhouse-style apartments, a medical clinic, golf course, swimming pools and a clubhouse. Security from crime is emphasized, and ownership is on a condominium basis. The average age is about 68.

A few generalities can be made about the residents of all four facilities. They are not young, but they don't want to be called "elderly". "We don't say senior citizens. We don't say inmates either. We say residents." Most are women. Nationally, there are 144 women for every 100 men over 65. In the suburban projects virtually all are white. At Capitol Towers in downtown Washington about 50 per cent of the tenants are black. As a rule, blacks resist special housing for the elderly. "As long as they can function and get help from their families, they will stay in their homes. Only those without families are willing to go," the pastor of a black church in Arlington explained.

Security can mean two things: protection from crime and the assurance of care in an emergency. Crime in the projects I saw is less real than imagined. At Residence 1 the threat is real, and the front door is always locked. At the entrance to Residence 4 there is a gate with a keeper. "We are surrounded on the outside," a resident warned me, "but we don't have much crime here." In the other suburban projects the front doors are unlocked during the day. Traffic is monitored unobtrusively by the manager or his secretary at the front desk and by residents. Upstairs the apartments have a lock and a dead bolt, and in some cases a chain. "The one silly thing they did was put on chains," a resident told me. "If you called for help, how could anybody get past the chain?"

Providing for failing health can be the greatest worry. Residence 3 is the only one of the four projects which can give its residents lifetime care in either their own apartments, a physical assistance wing (for those that need help in performing basic daily tasks) or a specialized care unit. The presence of this unit in the building is apparently not demoralizing. Many residents have not seen the nursing facilities since they moved in. They maintain that—without the nursing facility—it is much more depressing to see ill people in the lobby and dining room. Residence 4 advertises 24-hour nursing service, but this is not long-term care. Residents know that when they can no longer care for themselves, they will have to move on. "There are people living here now who should be in a nursing home," a nurse asserted. "They don't eat properly. They don't take their medicine properly. The families are all too willing to dump them on us." At Residence 2, residents must be "ambulatory", which is defined as being able to get from their rooms to the dining room and through the cafeteria line (a criteria that is a source of desperate feelings in many such institutions). The impracticality of offering only two choices for older people, complete independence or utter dependence, is demonstrated each evening at dinner time. At 4:30 residents line up to go through the cafeteria. Those at the end have to wait half an hour, but many people can't stand that long. Others move laboriously with canes or walkers, slowing the line.

The conveniences which make life easier for older people are standard in the three apartment buildings: grab bars by the bath and toilet, non-skid tubs, night lights and buttons to call for help in case of an emergency. No steps interrupt residents' passage from the front door to their apartments. Handrails have been installed along one side of the residential corridors for those who walk with difficulty. Residents are realistic about aging, and even the most sprightly do not object to living with the hardware of feebleness. They are quick, however, to point out errors of overcompensation: a woman at one facility complained bitterly about the raised toilet seats. They are intended to make it easier to get up and down, "but my feet don't touch the ground."

Companionship, convenience and diversion can be major needs—but they are not always recognized. People "who get out and do" continue to do in their old age, but others are paralyzed by loneliness and depression and must be lured out of their apartments. Communal spaces should be designed to encourage social interaction, but at the same time they should allow residents some privacy.

The entrance lobby is the central meeting place in high-rise projects. At Residence 4, the entrance hall in the clubhouse is used the same way. All of the lobbies have their "regulars". Typically they are among the least well, and though the well elderly complain that "seeing those people slumped in their chairs, sleeping in the front hall makes you feel like you are in a nursing home", lobbysitting is a relatively unobtrusive way for the not-so-well elderly to keep in touch with other people. Sitting together day after day, they monitor each other's health. This is an especially important service in projects without a medical staff.

Even in the best housing for the elderly, most of the apartments are efficiencies. Apartments with bedrooms or at least an alcove to separate the sleeping from the sitting room are better for the morale of people who spend most of their time in their apartments. Though it is claimed that older people hesitate to invite people to their homes if they don't have a proper sitting room, in the projects I saw the amount of entertaining that residents do is determined not by the size of their apartment, but by the atmosphere in the project. The residents in the projects with organized, mandatory activities had more friends.

One type of housing for the elderly is an apartment building full of older people. There is a minimum of communal space and no organized community activity. By one resident's estimate, 60 per cent of the residents of Residence 1 have not left their apartments. They feel warm and comfortable. Their families bring them food, she said. Though the woman has lived in the building since it opened, she knows few of her neighbors. "I knew more people in my previous building. They were all couples and everybody worked on the 'Hill' It was something we could talk about. There isn't much here."

Natural suspiciousness is reinforced in the building's two community spaces, the lobby and the recreation room. The lobby is a square room garnished with two sofas, two tables, four chairs and a school marm's desk where the resident manager sits for eight hours a day. The legs of all the furniture are looped with a heavy chain, which runs around the outside of the room and pins the furniture in place. The effect of chaining the furniture into a waiting room pattern is that people behave as if they were in a doctor's office. The same small group of people sits day after day watching other residents come and go in a silence interrupted only by greetings and sporadic remarks on the weather. Most face the door to avoid staring at each other, and to catch the little snips of action on the street outside.

The recreation room is in the basement. It contains a pool table and a card table and is illuminated by three half windows. To get to it residents have to take the elevator to the basement, climb eight steep steps and walk about 72 feet down a tunnel. A handful of the more agile male tenants use the room in the late afternoon. A female tenant, lamenting "the lack of enthusiasm with the old people in this building", said she once organized an evening bingo game there, "but there were just three of us that went." Perhaps no one else could get to it.

The downtown site may be best for a community of older people. The residents can walk to shops or sit in a park and see young people. They read the news headlines and remark on the changes in their neighborhood. The suburbs are less stimulating and services are less accessible there, but recreation programs and adequate transportation can compensate to a large extent these deficiencies. The great advantage of Residence 1 is its location—downtown. The apartments actu-

ally sit on top of a dry cleaner's shop and a liquor store. "They sell cheese and cold drinks as well."

Shared facilities can be essential to daily life—or useless. At Residence 2, the county runs a recreation program for senior citizens in the basement. The county rents seven rooms, but due to the slope of the site, only the largest room has windows. According to the program director, "seniors don't like rooms without windows and they resist going back into the other rooms." In the large room the elderly people tend to bunch together at the front. The directors say they have tried pulling the tables apart but that people push them back together again. Some residents are resentful of the people who come in from the surrounding community to use the program.

As a result of the activity in the basement, the lobby is both a sitting room for residents and a passageway for outsiders. The view of the traffic between the front door and the elevators is a consolation prize for the residents who have been deprived of direct access to a street. The most popular seating is in the center of the lobby. Sitting there residents are privy to all the activity in the room, at the mailboxes and in the office, the gift shops and the dining room. The chairs are moveable, so that a resident can sit with her friends or, by adjusting the chair slightly, she can be alone without feeling isolated.

Recreation rooms are best used when they are adjacent to the sitting rooms. Only one of the projects I saw has kept the sitting rooms and the recreation rooms together on one floor. Space is a luxury, but if there's too much of it, it's wasted. For example, at Residence 3 the parlor room is often empty since an auditorium was added. Residents don't make the long trek down a handsome but sterile back hall to peek into the arts and crafts room or to visit the activity director. "No one happens by," the director observed.

The fourth project was conceived as a self-sufficient community where all diversions are exluded except those which the homeowners choose to bring in. Though the promised hospital and shopping center have not been built, there is very nearly the realization of the dream of retirement on a well-staffed country estate. All the entertainment is directed out of the "E and R" (education and recreation) office. The daily schedule includes such activities as "slimnastics", ladies' bridge, intermediate Spanish, a practice of the Kiwanis choraliers and a Rotary Club meeting. "It's the clubs and organizations rather than the classes or games which draw people to the clubhouse," according to a resident employed in the "E and R" office. The essential difference between Residence 4 and the other suburban projects is that residents have a choice to participate in the community or not, while in the highrise buildings most residents live in efficiency apartments and share their sitting rooms and the dining room.

In the other residences where residents are required to dine together, the dining rooms and the food are sources of endless conversation. Administrators feel that the communal dinner is essential because it gives them a chance to check on each resident daily, because it guarantees that residents eat at least one balanced meal a day, and because it forces residents to come out of their rooms and meet the community. The residents who have tried both say they prefer meals served in a cafeteria to sit-down dinners because they have more choice about what they eat in a cafeteria. But they move excruciatingly slowly through cafeteria lines.

The furnished sitting rooms on the residential floors are not used in the projects I saw. The residents prefer to sit in their own rooms or in the main lobby; yet they say they like having the upstairs sitting rooms. "It just makes you feel good."

Among the variety of commonly shared rooms that can be fit into a home for older people, the front lobby remains the single most important space. Residents will meet there if it is comfortable and safe and if there is enough activity inside and out to spare them a feeling they have been consigned to a nursing home. (The way that residents dress to come downstairs tells how they feel about the place.) A misunderstanding of the way in which such spaces are actually used may be the most serious problem affecting the architects' roles here.

Elderly housing that exhibits a welcome sense of tradition

When the Home For Aged Men in Portland, Maine, was ready to expand, it could have torn down the fine old residence it was utilizing, and started over. The house was in adequate condition, but it violated many of the more stringent code requirements developed over the last 10 years for this kind of housing, and needed to be completely "modernized." But it was not torn down; it was saved and used as the esthetic keystone for further development of the property, as the photograph at right so nicely shows. Now both the old home and the major new addition that it generated are housing elderly people, and maintaining the architectural continuity of the 18th-century residential neighborhood around them. And the people of Portland, Maine are publicly praising both the sponsor and their architect, as they should.

The old Levi Cutter House, built ca. 1810, with extensions added during the 19th century, was placed in trust by Mr. Cutter when he died to be converted to a home for elderly men. It remained in this use until 1964, housing from six to 24 men in a kind of boarding house arrangement. Then the board of directors of the trust decided they should try to enlarge the effectiveness of the home, and hired the young firm of Bruce Porter Arneill as their architects. Arneill studied the problem, and came up with the solution on these pages. As Arneill puts it: "The basic concept was to have the old and new buildings complement each other, and the space be-

The three plans below show the
major floors of the housing complex,
and the grading, with the previously
existing facilities overlaid
in color. The long neck linking
the two parts allows a clear division
between the two, creates an adequate
space for an entrance vestibule,
and allows the corridor to slope
up or down to meet existing
floor heights. The original house,
it is apparent, had several additions
to it between 1810 and 1900.

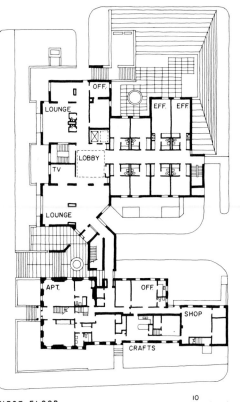

FIRST FLOOR

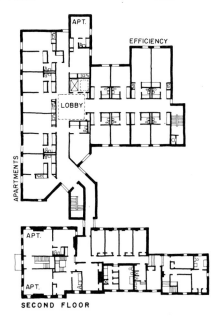

SECOND FLOOR

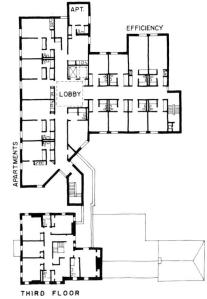

THIRD FLOOR

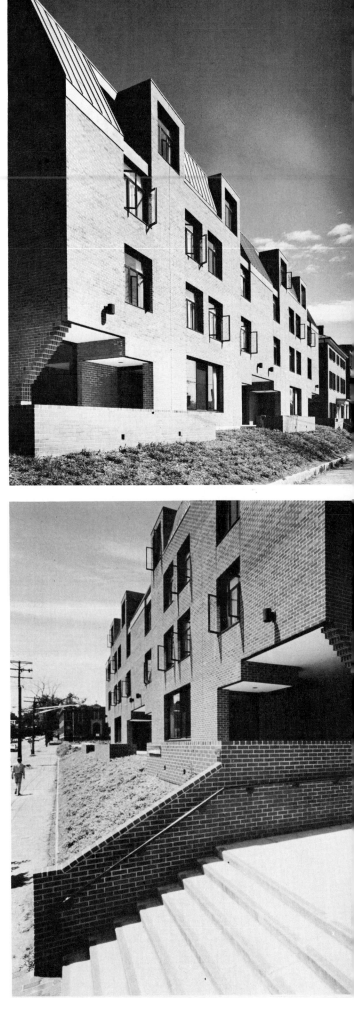

tween invite you in. . . . We studied all the pertinent characteristics of the older building, and these influenced the detail design decisions on our new work."

The first problem of designing a compatible addition was one of scale: the finished new facility was to house 85 people, both men and women, rather than the six people it had housed for the last few years, so it would have been easy to dominate the old house with the new addition. The problem was solved by maintaining the roof line of the house, by making the windows in the new addition about the same size as the old window shapes (including the shutters) and by matching the old brick as closely as possible. The mansard roof of the addition allows a fourth floor to be worked in while still maintaining a three-floor roof line.

Matching the floor elevations in the old house was a problem, because new construction generally requires a greater floor-to-floor height than the nine feet of the original building. The nine foot height was accomplished by using brick bearing wall construction, concrete planking for the floors, and by eliminating dropped and suspended ceilings except in certain corridors. The interior ceiling height is still maintained from eight feet to eight feet six inches throughout. The front facade of the new addition is in exactly the same plane as the facade of the house, and about three times as long, but the undercutting for terraces and porches that occurs at the ground floor of the addition lightens its mass effectively. Because the addition went up four stories, large parts of the site became available for terracing and exterior use (photo, above right) that would not have been available if an earlier two-story concept had been continued.

The old stairway of the original house is intact inside, as well as most of its original moldings. What the architect has added is paint; paint in bright colors and broad stripes to give the interior of the house a fresh new life without permanently harming any of its old forms. The house and its earlier additions now provide sleeping rooms for 22 people, plus activity and storage areas. The new addition houses the kitchen, dining room, administrative offices, lounges, and 15 one-bedroom apartments, eight efficiency apartments, and 27 single rooms.

The main entrance to both the old and the new parts of the complex is now between the two structures, shown in the large photo, opposite. The steps here are fewer than in the old entrance, and because of the grading of the site a person can avoid all steps into the building from the parking area at the rear.

The Park-Danforth Home has room sizes that are substantially larger than the FHA standards for elderly housing. There is no Federal money at all in the project; the original trust itself put up about half the funds and local Portland banks put up the other half. Total cost of the addition and rehabilitation together was $1,-100,000.

PARK-DANFORTH HOME FOR THE ELDERLY, Portland, Maine. Architect: *Bruce Porter Arneill;* structural engineer: *Rudolph Besier;* mechanical engineers: *Francis Associates;* interior design: *Raymond Doernberg;* contractor: *Consolidated Constructors & Builders, Inc.*

CHAPTER FIVE
Child Care Centers

CHILD CARE CENTERS

Child care centers serve many social and community purposes, but their most important job is to be places where young children grow and learn. Child care centers are hard to design. They must be flexible, simulating, scaled for children but comfortable for adults, inviting to the community—and dirt cheap. Despite that last requirement, the buildings we have chosen have been successful in many ways. Child care centers are, by definition, resources available to working parents; but we have included two private nursery schools which are closely involved with their communities and for which most of the architectural problems are the same.

Jonathan Hale

CHILD CARE CENTERS:
THE PROBLEMS AND THE MEANINGS

WHO WANTS CHILD CARE CENTERS?

Child care centers have been going up by the hundred in the last few years. There are two main reasons: the entry, *en masse*, of mothers into the work force, and the still-dawning understanding that a child's earliest experiences are crucial for later ability to learn.

One reason that is missing is any real government support. There is very little Federal money for child care programs, and very little Federal guidance for designing and setting up a child care center. Few states have large-scale care programs and most have no standards for early childhood care away from home. New York City has perhaps the most extensive child care program in the country, but even there, cutbacks in state funds have brought new construction to an end and some existing services are threatened.

Nationwide, one out of three mothers of children under six works. During the time the mothers are away from home, their children are cared for by friends or relatives, by licensed child care centers (about 25 per cent), by unlicensed child care centers where children are often given minimal attention, or the children are left alone. By some estimates, 600,000 small children are left alone each day.

According to education experts, 50 per cent of a person's ability to learn is achieved by the age of four; and a stimulating environment where a child receives considerable attention can affect this ability enormously. Educators have been intuitively aware of this for decades; but during the last ten years, there has been a great increase in the amount of reliable information about how children learn. At the same time, people have been discovering the failure of schools to reach many underprivileged children. The Federal Head Start Program was started under President Johnson to help deprived preschool children attain the patterns of thought necessary for later learning. Head Start was a relatively small program, but it continues to provide the only Federal support for preschool education.

WHO OPPOSES CHILD CARE CENTERS?

In 1971, Congress passed a large-scale program of Federal support for child care centers. President Nixon vetoed the bill, arguing that such a program might weaken family structure, and arguing that the $2 billion program was too expensive. Objections to child care centers have come from some communities because the centers would bring in the children of poorer neighbors. Also, many educators believe that long hours spent away from home are hard on small children. Finally, child care can be extremely expensive. The ratio of teachers to children in the New York City program is about four times that of the city's public schools. What's more, the centers are open from 8 a.m. to 6 p.m.

An alternative to the child care center is the placement of small groups of children in private homes. At least one suburban community claims success with this inexpensive plan; however, in the hands of untrained adults, a great deal is left to chance.

Private child care centers are springing up in large numbers, especially in areas such as Texas, where there is little or no government support for child care. Chains of franchised centers are run for profit at low cost to parents. Many charge as little as $20 per week. The quality of the care varies widely, although some of the franchised centers have achieved a good reputation. Some educators insist decent child care is impossible for less than three times $20 and not a few balk at the whole idea of marketed child care.

THE ROLE OF THE ARCHITECT
... WITH THE COMMUNITY

A good child care center is a real community resource. It frees mothers to work (in this way, freeing many fathers who must hold more than one job) and it gives children a solid foundation which will make it possible for them to survive in school later, often providing a much happier and more stimulating environment than they could get otherwise.

The first group of child care centers on the following pages, by architect Frank E. Williams, in association with architect John Herget, were designed to make the most of their high-density inner city sites, opening out to their neighborhoods. Under the New York City system, the community controls the completed center but does not control its design. That is determined by the Department of Social Services and by the private builder, from whom the building is then rented by the city and given to a community group. Within the set program, there is still room to respond to the community. On one narrow through-block site, Williams terraces his building back and provides two entrance plazas and a through-the-block connection (page 168). On other sites, he provides inviting "front porches" (page 170).

To many in poor communities, monumental or institutional buildings are a threat and an affront by the wealthier society from which they are excluded. It is up to the architect to keep his building from having that image—no mean trick if the building is, in fact, the creation of an outside government agency.

Many architects and administrators of child care centers believe they should provide services for adults as well as children. The center on page 167 contains many community facilities, notably medical and psychiatric counselling. The center at the bottom of page 172 also contains counselling facilities. The center on page 170 includes a drug rehabilitation service. Many centers contain after-school facilities for older children.

While there have been some efforts to make the small children's spaces available to adults at other times of the day, the general feeling appears to favor leaving these small-scale spaces and the children's works-in-progress for the children alone. The furniture is, of course, far too small for adult use, but more important, daily rearrangement makes it very difficult to maintain any sort of continuity.

... WITH THE CHILDREN

If a child care center must appear inviting to the surrounding community, this aspect is even more important to the young children who will use it, many of whom have never been away from home. For example, it's important to avoid large blank walls facing the street, and overscaled—or not clearly visible—entrances. A domestic scale on the outside will make children feel more relaxed.

Easy access to the outdoors is a tremendous asset, and it can be provided in the city by the use of terraces opening directly from the playrooms. Special heaters near the doors can help eliminate drafts. A child care center with little or no play space at ground level can use virtually all of its roof for play (pages 168–172). There are many opportunities for the architect in traditional playground design. However, the non-architectural "adventure playground" is becoming popular among some American educators who have seen its success in Europe. Children are given raw materials and an adviser to help them and they make their own constantly-changing playground. Adventure playgrounds are usually very messy and need to be screened in, but, after all, elegance is not the point in a playground.

Young children are pretty small, but a Lilliputian scale throughout the building has been found not to be a good idea. Most educators favor a combination of small- and large-scale spaces and furniture. Photographs on pages 177–179 show some of the possible alternatives to conventional furniture, which provide, among other things, small spaces to crawl into or climb up to within a larger space. Places which are completely inaccessible to adults give small children a sense of insecurity, but they enjoy having unseen corners to go into. Several preschools use the floor as furniture. As long as the floor is carpeted and warm, children like to sit on it. Floors can include stepped sitting areas (page 177). Windows only at child height (this has been tried in at least one private nursery school) give adults a feeling of insecurity. The most successful buildings we have seen provide standard-sized doors, steps and windows (although it is desirable to keep the window sill at child level).

There is great disagreement among educators about the degree to which environment enters into education. At one end of the scale are the Montessorians, followers of the early-twentieth-century Italian educator, Maria Montessori. In a Montessori school, the facilities are everything. The child moves about freely, but everything in sight has an educational purpose. The architect can have great influence on the way the learning materials are presented, and he can make his building a learning material itself, revealing its construction (page 175) and encouraging awareness of "large" and "small," direction, color, and texture. Other educators prefer a building which provides for everyone's needs but otherwise stays out of the way. One school director told us that given the money, he would not build a more elaborate building, but would put his school on a farm with plenty of animals and plenty of land.

There is also division of opinion on how to arrange the interior spaces. Some educators believe that children between the ages of about 2½ to 5 can get along happily in one space. A large interior space can be divided by temporary or permanent partitions. Such an arrangement has the advantage that no facilities need be duplicated, but it requires sensitive handling to avoid seeming too large. If the children are divided into smaller groups, many facilities, even interior sandboxes, can be made portable enough to be shared. It's a good idea to provide separate areas for wet and messy activities, such as water play, sandbox, and painting.

Most educators agree that the day of the pink and blue nursery with duckies and piggies on the wall is over. Playfulness is fine, sentimentality isn't.

... IN CONSTRUCTION

Building a child care center is an exercise in doing more with less—much less. The A-B-R Partnership, architects, used prefabricated units made by local modular builders to put up three low-cost child care centers in Denver (page 176, top). The Early Learning Center, Stamford, Connecticut (page 175), Egon Ali-Oglu, architect, was built in 1966 for $13 per square foot, using a system of precast concrete elements. In New York City, architect Frank Williams used load-bearing brick to help reduce the cost of his centers to one third the per square foot cost of school construction. The Charlestown Playhouse, north of Philadelphia, Oskar Stonorov, architect (page 173) incorporates the stone bearing walls of an old church. The Henry Street Child Care Center, Welton Becket and Associates, architects (page 172, bottom), uses the roof of an adjoining building for a playing area. Direct remodeling is sometimes more desirable than new construction, although some schools have found it nearly as expensive. The Shady Lane School in Pittsburgh, remodeled by Paul Curtis and Roger Smith (page 177, top) was a Victorian house. The Hilltop Center, Dorchester, Mass., PARD-Team, architects (pages 178, middle, 179, top) is a remodeled supermarket with big plate glass windows that provide a link to the community.

More information

An excellent, highly-detailed book, "Patterns for Designing Children's Centers," by architect Fred Linn Osmon, was recently prepared for the Educational Facilities Laboratories, Inc., a non-profit organization funded by The Ford Foundation. The book is available from EFL, 477 Madison Avenue, New York City, 10022.

The Day Care and Child Development Council of America, Inc., in Washington, D.C., is also a good source of information for the child care architect.

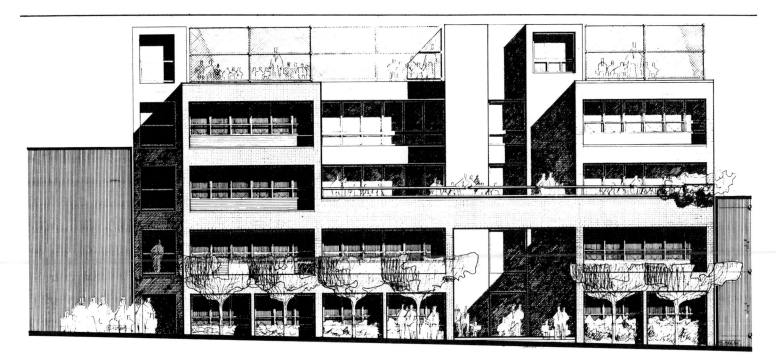

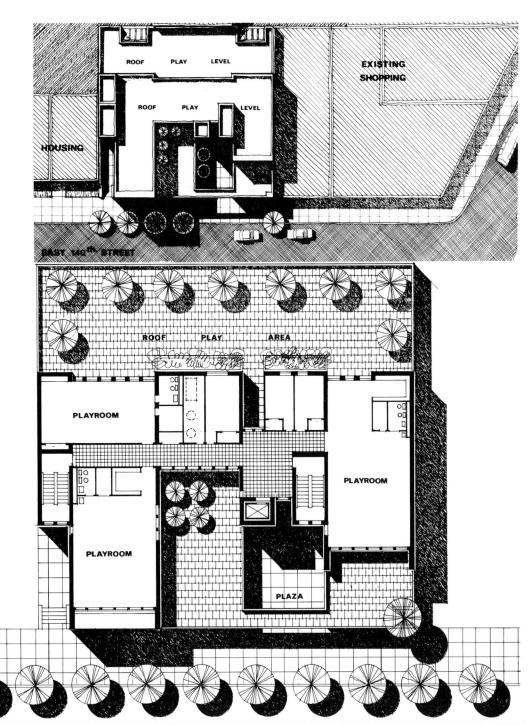

140TH STREET CENTER

The top two levels of this
Bronx, New York center by
architect Frank E. Williams
are a child care center. Lower
floors contain a community
counseling service and an
after-school center. Williams
believes, with many others,
that as many community resources
as possible should be combined
with child care. A small plaza
welcomes passers-by.
Many playrooms open onto a
roof terrace, a second "ground
level" for the child-care
part of the center. A terrace
bridge creates an entrance
portal to the plaza below.

BELMONT DAY CARE CENTER, BRONX, NEW YORK

Given a standard New York City Department of Social Services program and a rock-bottom budget, architect Frank E. Williams opened a narrow site to the neighborhood, providing a through-block connection and two plazas. The site plan (opposite page) shows a proposed mid-block mini-park linked to a shopping street (top). Playrooms for 15 to 20 children each open directly onto terraces for quiet outdoor play. The roof provides a space for active play. The structure is load-bearing brick. The choice of facing materials was up to the builder, not the architect. The configuration of the building, terracing towards the street, with entrances clearly denoted by stair towers, is designed to be inviting to the community. Although the completed building falls below the architect's conception, its basic strengths are not lost.

Jonathan Hale photos

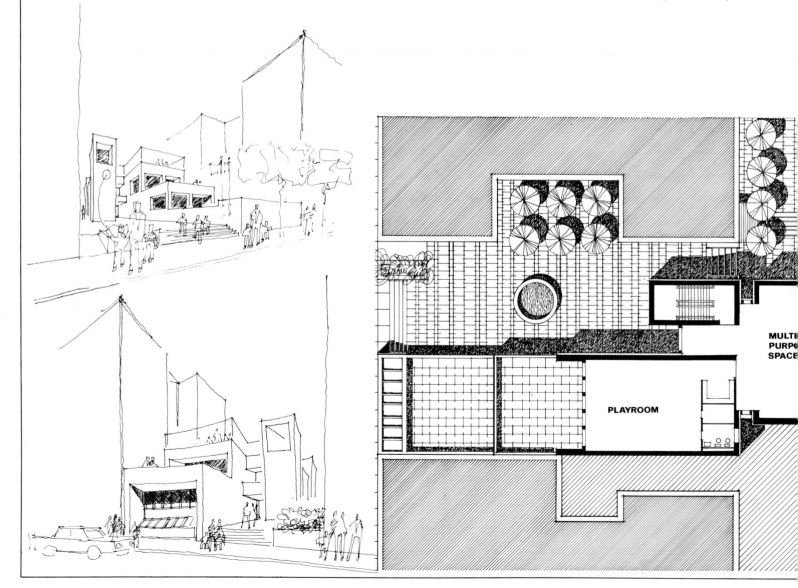

MULTI PURPO SPACE

PLAYROOM

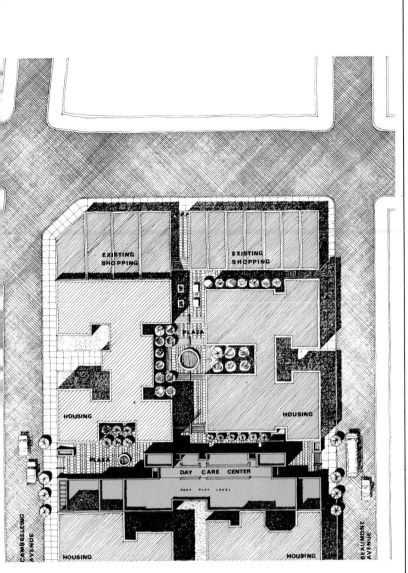

DAUGHTERS OF AFRICAN DESCENT
DAY CARE CENTER, BROOKLYN, NEW YORK

On a more congenial site, and with a very sympathetic builder, this is one of the most successful of architect Frank Williams' centers. The child care section above is an after-school center which has a separate entrance (top left in plan). Classroom arrangement is a direct expression of the New York City program, grouping community and administrative facilities for the child care section around the main entrance (bottom in plan), linked to the playrooms by a sunny gallery. An open "front porch" is an invitation to the neighborhood. This center was started by a women's organization which felt child care was the most immediately effective way they could help their community. Builders were Rentar Development Corporation.

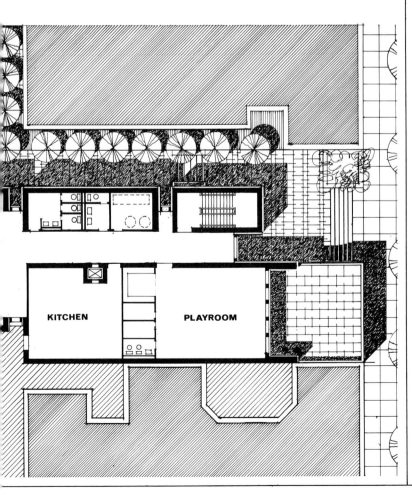

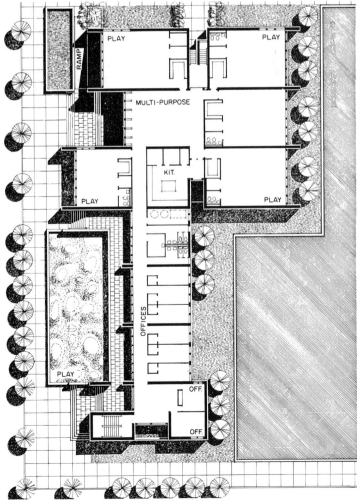

MARCUS GARVEY DAY CARE CENTER, BRONX, NEW YORK

On a tight mid-block site, this center by Frank Williams makes the utmost use of the resources at hand. Keeping to the scale of the surrounding buildings, it provides a "front porch" on which neighborhood kids love to play. Even before it was opened, this building was a part of its community. Two playrooms open onto their own terrace. The rear was designed to make the most of neighboring gardens. Small interior terraces (below) bring light to a central multi-purpose space and also to the adjacent buildings. Typically of New York City child care centers, this is located in a healthy neighborhood which, however, has many underprivileged residents. It combines child care with other community resources, notably in this case, a drug prevention and rehabilitation facility on the lower level.

Jonathan Hale photos

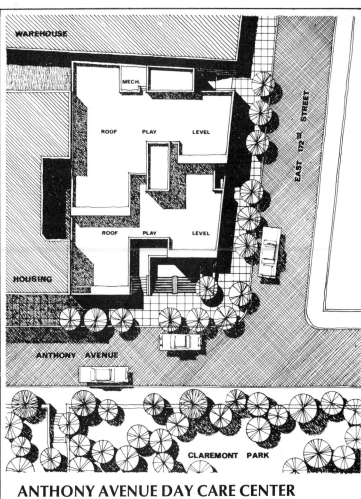

ANTHONY AVENUE DAY CARE CENTER

This Bronx, New York center by
Frank Williams steps down
toward a park across the street
which, in turn slopes sharply
up. Community facilities
on a lower level are reached by
a separate entrance. The
whole corner is given over to
entrances and a "front porch,"
making this one of the most
welcoming of Williams'
buildings. Williams believes
that an open, accessible building
will discourage vandalism,
which is largely a result
of alienation. But the success
of such openness depends also
on the center's administration.
It takes courage
in some neighborhoods.

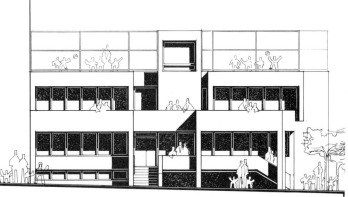

PARK SLOPE NORTH

Child Development Center

This Brooklyn, New York center,
designed by Beyer Blinder Belle,
architects, has a program similar
to those of the preceding centers,
but financing is through the state.
The center is scaled to surrounding
row houses. Back yard play space
supplements a roof play area.
Partner in charge: John H. Beyer,
project architect: Yogesh Sethi,
project design: Joseph Typborowski.

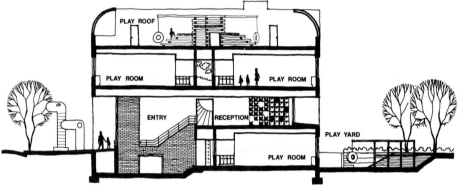

HENRY STREET
CHILD CARE CENTER

Welton Becket and Associates
designed this Manhattan
child care center for the
famous Henry Street Settlement.
The roof of the adjoining
building serves as play area
and supplements a large
ground level play yard
behind the center. Space for
community counseling is also
included. The structure is steel
with brick facing to fit in
with older existing buildings
on either side.

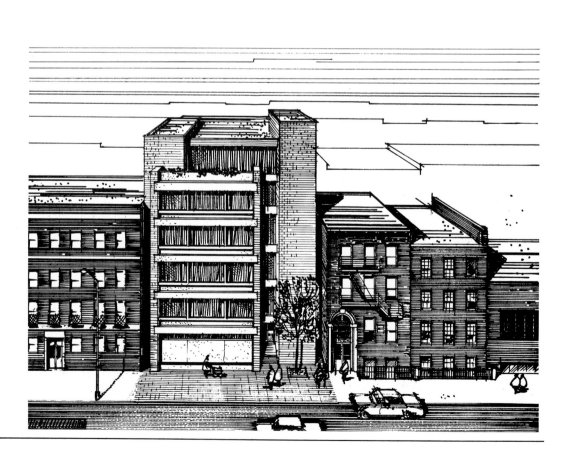

CHARLESTOWN PLAYHOUSE, CHARLESTOWN, PENNSYLVANIA

The late Oskar Stonorov designed the Charlestown Playhouse
in 1937, using the bearing walls of an old church.
Mrs. Stonorov still runs the Playhouse, a private nursery
school which has always had close ties to its community.
The location is a large wooded hillside north of Philadelphia.
Over the years, Mr. Stonorov designed additions—always
clear and simple and full of light. But in 1964,
Mr. Stonorov, writing about the Playhouse, said, "I am sure
that the architectural form of a nursery school has not
yet been developed. . . . Such a building must have the ability
for improvisation to a degree non-existent today. . . . Various
age groups from two to five might be housed in spaces
which have different scales." The Playhouse does contain
a wide variety of spaces, from a two-story glass-walled
central room to small rooms which cantilever out from
the second level (right, above). It is at ease with
its surroundings and informal inside without being dull.

DULWICHWOOD NURSERY SCHOOL, LONDON, ENGLAND

Careful scaling, planning and use of materials reveal a deep
concern for the children in this assured and straightforward
design by architects Stillman and Eastwich-Field, FRIBA.
England and Scandinavia are far ahead of the United States
in child care awareness; however, this facility, which cost about
$70,000 to build in 1966, is more expensive than most
English preschools. The 60 children aged 3 to 5 in each of
two daily sessions are not divided into groups, but move freely
through the building, whose hexagonal spaces provide variety
and reduce the scale. Structure is brick and concrete;
ceilings are wood plank and electrically-heated floors are
covered in resilient tile. Window sills are low, and
large sliding doors provide easy access to the outside play area,
where a popular feature is a hill of earth
excavated during construction.

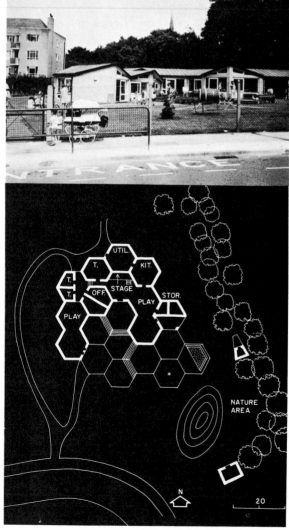

EARLY LEARNING CENTER, STAMFORD, CONNECTICUT

Architect Egon Ali-Oglu designed the Early Learning Center of precast concrete elements, cutting costs to $13 per square foot in 1966. It is a private community-oriented nursery school with a modified Montessori program. Children 2½ to 5 use an undivided space containing a skylighted central area filled with learning materials, which has been compared to a Mexican market place. The carpeted floor is the furniture in this area—dark gray to hide dirt and set off the bright-colored materials. There is also a stepped seating area. Shelves are painted boards on concrete blocks. Children walk directly out to the play area whenever they want. A non-carpeted area (left in plan) is for wet activities. Interesting colors, objects and textures abound. Windows are tinted brown, fixtures are incandescent for warm light. Slightly older children have their own wing (bottom of plan), recently designed by Paul Curtis and Roger Smith into a series of varied multi-level spaces.

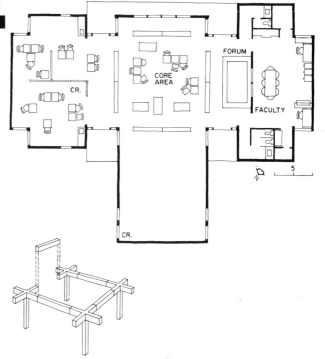

Jonathan Hale photos

THREE DENVER CHILD CARE CENTERS MADE OF MODULAR UNITS

The program called for a temporary facility that could be moved in two to five years, so the A-B-R Partnership, architects, designed a demountable modular building. Denver has at least two modular builders, one in the community to be served, and one nearby, both employing people who would benefit directly from the center. Eventually, the center, funded by Model Cities, expanded into three centers, two in Denver's black ghetto, one in a Chicano neighborhood. As the architects put it, "the design and site development concepts are basic at best"; but this form of construction opens many possibilities.

PROTOTYPE INFANT CENTER FOR CALIFORNIA MIGRANT WORKERS

California migrant workers have a life expectancy of 38 years. A large reason for this average is the very high death rate among children under five. In migrant communities, child care centers can have tremendous importance. The design below, by Sanford Hirshen and Partners, architects, is the result of a highly-detailed study made under a grant from the Rosenberg Foundation. Care is provided for new-born babies to three-year-olds— 32 children in all. Storage units and glass partitions separate groups acoustically but not visually. All playrooms open outside. The center uses prefabricated trusses for the roof spans and a foam core wall panel system made by the Production Technology Corporation, a non-profit organization set up to train migrant workers in factory skills.

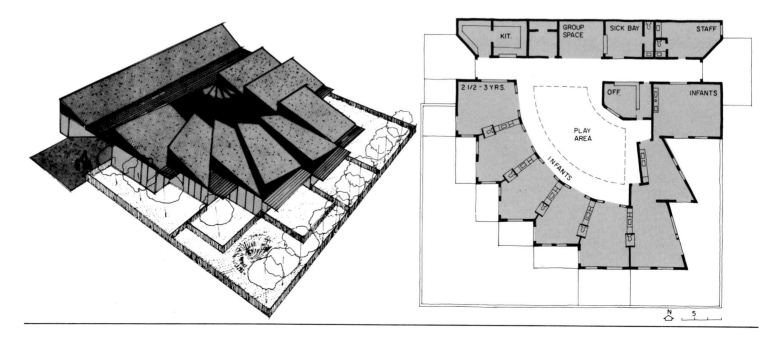

George Zimbel

EIGHT DESIGN IDEAS

The following three pages
show details from several child
care centers—suggestions which
aren't likely to show up
in any program, but which can
add a great deal to the way
a place feels and the way it
is used.

George Zimbel

FLOOR AS FURNITURE

Children and teachers find many ways to use carpeted, stepped areas. In a new building, the steps can be sunken; in a remodeled building the steps can be built on platforms, as in the Shady Lane school (top photo, previous page) in Pittsburgh, designed by Paul Curtis and Roger Smith, and which was originally a large Victorian house.

INDOOR CAVE

Children enjoy special places to crawl into (bottom photo, previous page) but the places need to be open enough that the children can still be in contact with the room outside—and they should have more than one entrance. This is the CLC Good Hope Road Center for Children, Washington, D.C., remodeled from a large store by Paul Curtis and Roger Smith with Margaret Skutch, whose Early Learning Center appears on page 175.

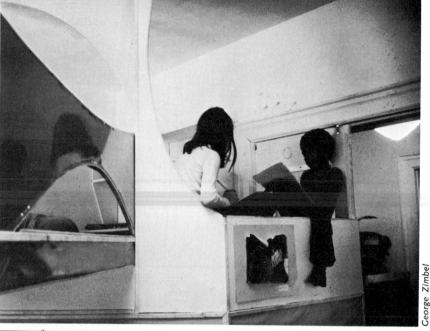

George Zimbel

CONTACT WITH THE STREET

George Zimbel

The big plate glass windows in the Hilltop Center, Dorchester, Massachusetts, give the children a lot to look at and make the community aware of the center. The center was a supermarket, remodeled for child care by PARD-Team, architects, Sam Mintz, architect-in-charge. The atmosphere is relaxed but stimulating. A big red plush Victorian couch sits next to the window (rear, right).

INDOOR TREE HOUSE

By the designers of the indoor cave (photo, left) but for the Shady Lane school in Pittsburgh. Such areas should not be inaccessible, nor completely invisible, to adults.

Robert Utzinger

AWNINGS

A way of taking off the institutional hard edge. All the playrooms in this English child-care center (above) open onto the terrace. Highgate Nursery School, London, England.

PLAY SCULPTURE

Jonathan Hale

This one is at the Charlestown Playhouse, Charlestown, Pennsylvania, a nursery school originally designed by the late Oskar Stonorov in 1937 and expanded by him over the years (see page 173).

George Zimbel

STIMULATION

"You can't have too much in a child care center," say some educators. Others would qualify that, but it's important to note that most of the materials in this room come from or are used by the children. A lot of bright colors or sophisticated supergraphics, by contrast, might or might not be stimulating. The children are playing in an indoor sandbox. Hilltop Center, Dorchester, Massachusetts. PARD-Team, architects, Boston, Massachusetts.

George Zimbel

MAKE YOUR OWN FURNITURE

The seats in this picture are computer reel cans stacked to different heights for users of various sizes—a brainstorm of Margaret Skutch (page 175). The CLC Good Hope Road Center for Children, Washington, D.C. (see also page 177).

FLOORS FOR INFANTS

The floors in the infant area of this Swedish child care center are sheet vinyl with a cushioned backing. Low covered mattresses are used as furniture. Hendriksdalsberget Barnstuga ("child cottage") Stockholm, Sweden.

Robert Utzinger

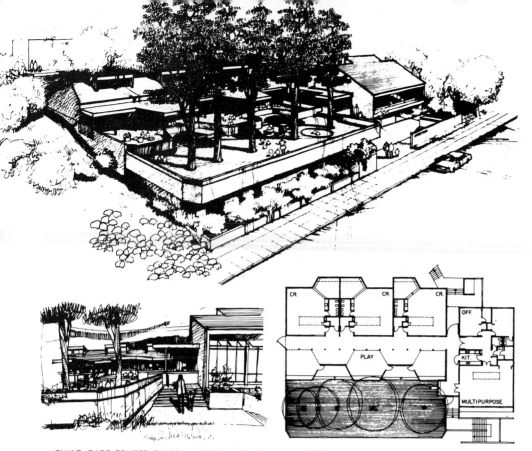

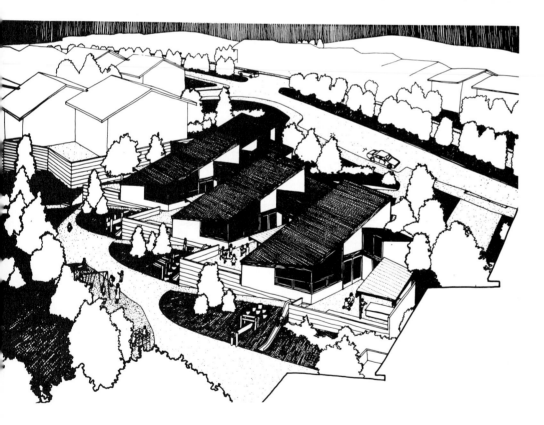

CHILD CARE CENTER #3, Hunter's Point, San Francisco, California.
Architects: *Marquis & Stoller*. Engineers: *Shapiro, Okino, Hom & Associates*, structural; *George Aronovsky*, mechanical; *Tage Hansen*, electrical.

CHILD CARE CENTER #2, Hunter's Point, San Francisco, California. Architects: *Ostwald & Kelly*. Engineers: *Hirsch & Gray*, structural; *Sanford W. Fox*, mechanical; *Beamer-Wilkinson*, electrical.

Child care centers: in the next five years, innovation and design

■ Child care centers, when operated to high standards, are far from mere baby-sitting facilities. Indeed they can be essential to the healthy development of children whose parents must work, and in fact to the general level of health in a community. For a great many of these children, the center is more of a home than their own homes are; they spend more of their waking hours in its environment than in any other.

The child (or day) care center has the opportunity to foster good health, to prevent disease (especially diseases of neglect) and, through its program and its physical environment, to give the child the kind of experiences that contribute to his development and growth. Although the most pressing need is still among poor mothers, the large number of children of working mothers—some 20 million, today—indicates the wide range of income levels where this kind of care is needed. Industries and hospitals, needing to attract employes and keep them, and to cut absenteeism, were the first to provide child care centers. Now municipal and other agencies (as at Hunter's Point near San Francisco) are beginning to assume the responsibility for such centers. Estimates for catching up with the worst of the present backlog indicate, however, that it will be necessary, over the next five years, to provide places for 2 million more than the 800,000 children who now receive care —plus those whose mothers will enter the work force for the first time during that period.

The centers so far built or being built strongly resemble nursery and primary schools—not surprisingly, since keeping a group of children occupied through the long hours of a parent's working day requires some structuring of activity inevitably reminiscent of school programs. Imaginative programs, however, emphasize informality and free activities in as homelike a way as possible.

Usually child care centers are located near the housing (low and moderate income) they are intended to serve. Since transportation from home to center can be a problem for the working mother, this is a real convenience. But it also keeps the child in familiar surroundings. Location near an elementary school is advantageous because the center can then care for school age children during after-school hours. There are obvious advantages when a center can be located near a park, with its opportunities for variety of activity and learning experience.

At left are two centers for the Hunter's Point district of San Francisco, both designed to the same program for the same age levels (2½ years to 5 and, after school hours, up to 12) but for different sites. Controlled play areas adjacent to each classroom were required, as was a multi-purpose room (also used for eating with food trucked from a central kitchen and warmed at the center). Center #3 (top left, Marquis & Stoller, architects) uses the slope of the site to provide additional play space on a deck under existing trees. Center #2 (bottom, Ostwald & Kelly, architects) is similar in facilities but different in design approach. It also provides open play space downhill from the center.

On this page, (top right), is the Crescent Park Children's Center (Hardison & Komatsu, architects) in Richmond, California, located near both a park and the low and moderate income housing whose residents it serves. The center is designed for preschoolers, who attend all day, and for older children (7 to 12 years) from a nearby elementary school who come after school hours. The centrally located office is the daily check-in point for children being left at the center. It is also close to the nurse's office, and from it there is easy supervision of in and out traffic. Behind it is a covered play area for rainy days and for outdoor eating in good weather. There are no corridors: each classroom opens onto the central area, and out to an outdoor play area. Food is prepared at the center and taken by cart to each room.

At the Piedmont Avenue Children's Center (bottom right, Jensen & Langeberg, architects), a project of the Oakland, California Unified School District, the plan is organized as one large space with changing ceiling heights to define areas for different age groups. For younger children, spaces are smaller and more intimate; for older children, they are larger. Movable furniture in each space further modifies its scale. By varying space, volume and quality of light (from skylights as well as sliding glass walls) the environment becomes a means of stimulating interest.

In character, scale, materials and amenities, these centers draw on the child's first base of reference—his home—for precedent. They are scaled to the child's experience but also to the needs of the group. They are non-residential homes, but they are also non-institutional institutions and as such they try to provide the look and feel, as much as is possible, given the number of children served, of a residence.

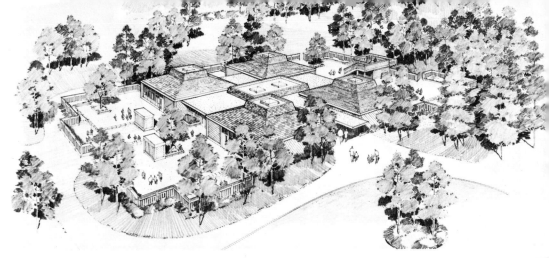

CRESCENT PARK CHILDREN'S CENTER, Richmond, California. Architects: *Hardison & Komatsu, George Ivelich*, partner in charge. Engineers: *Montgomery & Roberts*, mechanical; *Darmstad Parenti & Associates*, electrical. Landscape architects: *Royston, Hanamoto, Beck & Abey.* Contractor: *C. Overaa & Company.*

PIEDMONT AVENUE CHILDREN'S CENTER, Oakland, California. Architects: *Jensen & Langeberg.* Engineers: *McClure & Messinger*, structural; *W. Perry Baker*, mechanical; *Robert Z. Taylor*, electrical. Contractor: *G. M. Labrucherie and Associates.*